RUSSIAN PLURALISM— NOW IRREVERSIBLE?

Also by Uri Ra'anan

Ethnic Resurgence in Modern Democratic States (*editor*)

Gorbachev's USSR (*co-editor*)

Guerrilla Warfare and Counterinsurgency (*editor*)

Hydra of Carnage (*co-editor*)

Inside the *Apparat* (*with Igor Lukes*)

The Soviet Empire and the Challenge of National and
Democratic Movements (*editor*)

State and Nation in Multi-Ethnic Societies (*co-editor*)

The USSR Arms the Third World

The USSR Today and Tomorrow (*editor*)

RUSSIAN PLURALISM—
NOW IRREVERSIBLE?

Edited by
Uri Ra'anan, Keith Armes, and Kate Martin

with a contribution by Yelena Bonner

St. Martin's Press
New York

First published in the United States of America in 1992

Printed in the United States of America

ISBN 0-312-08648-2

Library of Congress Cataloging-in-Publication Data

Russian pluralism, now irreversible? / edited by Uri Ra'anan, Keith Armes,
and Kate Martin ; with a contribution by Yelena Bonner.
    p. cm.
Includes index.
ISBN 0-312-08648-2
1. Political culture—Former Soviet republics. 2. Pluralism
(Social sciences)—Former Soviet republics. 3. Civil rights—Former
Soviet republics. 4. Former Soviet republics—Politics and government.
I. Ra'anan, Uri, 1926- . II. Armes, Keith.
III. Martin, Kate.
JN6581.R87 1992
306.2'0947—dc20   92-28597
                                                                        CIP

This book is dedicated to the memory of

ANDREI SAKHAROV

CONTENTS

Pluralism and Democratization
Uri Ra'anan 1

Part I: Political Pluralism

Toward a Multiparty System?
Vera Tolz 9

The Legislative Process—Institutionalized?
Robert T. Huber 27

Civil Authority and the Security Organs
J. Michael Waller 45

Part II: Law and Society

Toward a Law-Abiding State?
Nina Belyaeva 71

Individual and Group Rights
Yelena Bonner 93

Human Rights: Established or Precarious?
Richard Schifter 103

Part III: Pluralism in the Media

The "Independent Media"
Nicholas Daniloff 127

Press Freedom: New Dangers
Vitaly Korotich 139

The Impact of Foreign Broadcasts
Savik Shuster 147

Part IV: The Role of Religion

The Orthodox Church and a Pluralistic Society
Kent R. Hill 165

Growing Protestant Diversity in the Former Soviet Union
Mark Elliott and Robert Richardson 189

About the Editors and Contributors 215

Index 219

Pluralism and Democratization

Uri Ra'anan

It is not unreasonable to ask why this book focuses on the concept of "pluralism" rather than "democracy." Of course, democracy is the desirable end product, at least as far as the non-"Islamic" republics of the former Soviet Union are concerned. (In the Middle Eastern Islamic environment, for example, in Algeria, experience has demonstrated that democratization may result in a decidedly antidemocratic product, to wit: potential access to power of fundamentalist movements with evident totalitarian tendencies.) In Russia, unfortunately, as in almost all former Soviet republics (with the possible exception of the Baltic states), a free and open political culture resulting from a continuous democratic experience of some duration is simply lacking. The baby steps of the Duma at the beginning of the century and the all-too-brief experience of the provisional government of 1917 could not suffice to serve as a springboard for democratization.

Development of a democratic culture requires an infrastructure of non-arbitrary behavior, respect for law, and the legitimation that such practices confer, as well as the existence of a "civil society," i.e., a sizable segment of the population that, through its spontaneous social, economic, and political interactions and organization, can participate actively in the life and governance of the state.

Above all, such a society requires not only toleration of and respect for pluralism, but the institutionalization of group rights—whether these be of a political, ethnic, socioeconomic, religious, professional, or civic character. Whatever repositories of a civil society had come into existence at the beginning of the current century in Russia were erased during subsequent generations that were products of a totalitarian regime.

The result was fissiparous: the only intermediate entities permitted to exist between an arbitrary regime and the individual were the "transmission belts"—the regimented so-called "mass organizations"—through which the leadership disseminated information and ensured adherence to its directives. Thus, Soviet "society" came to be atomized, consisting of little more than alienated individuals, mutually suspicious and antagonistic—remarkably similar to the Hobbesian universe.

The scholars and practitioners who collaborated in the production of this work attempted to address the sociopolitical organisms that would have to be fully developed and secured in Russia so that genuine democratization could ensue. Without pretending that our survey could encompass all of the elements required to build such an infrastructure, we focused on four that were felt generally to be most significant if pluralism was to become a permanent and irreversible feature of the Russian polity: free, open, and spontaneous political debate and organization; a genuine legal basis to relieve the population from constant exposure to arbitrary action; truly independent electronic and print media; and liberty to choose (and the means to practice) religious observance. Detailed analysis of a fifth element—full cultural and educational facilities as well as political equality for ethnically diverse groups—was omitted since this topic was amply covered in two of the Institute's previous books, *State and Nation in Multi-Ethnic Societies* and *The Soviet Empire and the Challenge of National and Democratic Movements.*

The present work may be viewed as an examination of potentially decisive developments in a transitional stage of post-totalitarian society. Such an analysis can be appropriately evaluated only by comprehending the role of that transition within a broader conceptual framework, as outlined here:

1) During the totalitarian stage, civil society is not only inhibited but is actually destroyed (in as far as it has been able to develop), as are entire classes (e.g., a free peasantry). On the other hand, a "political process" of sorts is set in motion because the leader, in a way, encourages factional strife. Since it is in his interest to keep contenders for succession at odds with one another, he deliberately creates duplicatory or overlapping institutional parameters, thus involving his lieutenants in unending battles for turf. Moreover, by so doing, he prevents any subordinate from attaining potentially dangerous monopolies over vital sectors (security, military forces, etc.). In these power struggles, the contenders need "troops," which are recruited in typically feudal fashion from personal retainers who owe loyalty

and support to their chiefs and receive protection and promotion in return. Such loyalty can be derived only from long-term personal relationships, so that each faction is comprised essentially of members linked by personal rather than ideological ties. Consequently, whereas factions may exploit policy issues to denigrate or delegitimate one another, they have no long-term commitment to any particular platform, unlike political parties. Bureaucratic institutions—while used as "transmission belts" from the leadership to an atomized society—are themselves fragmented, since each faction attempts to gain a foothold in several institutions rather than ensconcing itself in a single agency.

2) The transitional period from a totalitarian to a democratic stage can be divided into two phases:

a) The leadership, constrained by the system and its ideology, finds that an atomized secretive society and a factionalized elite are unable to cope with the demands of a scientific and technological revolution, so that a gradual but steady decline sets in, which manifests itself in the economic, cultural, and social arenas. Consequently, the regime and its ideology fall into disrepute and become objects of ridicule. Deriving its power from the system, the leadership attempts to improve rather than to replace it. The result is incessant "tinkering" with various aspects of the political and economic framework, with chaotic effects—but with little positive impact, in view of the limits imposed by ideological preconceptions and because the population at large (remaining disaffected, suspicious, and cynical at best) is indisposed to cooperate. During this phase, factionalism is intensified because the attempt to "tinker" itself creates opposition within segments of the elite that fear any change, however cosmetic. At this point, not even a consistent effort to move toward the creation of a civil society can be expected.

b) A catalytic event, of one sort or another, produces a different leadership compelled by circumstances to attempt dismantling the system itself and to rid itself of ideological constraints. (In the Soviet case, of course, this event can be dated very precisely to August 19-21, 1991.) Consequently, an opening is created for popular forces to thrust themselves upon the political scene; they seek "self-determination" in two directions—democratic and national. In the beginning, these aspirations are complementary, encouraging popular fronts, and a veritable "springtime of nations" has been known to ensue (*viz.* the early days of Europe's 1848 revolutions). Soon, however, conflicting territorial ambitions lead to ethnic conflict, and initially democratic instincts tend to be superseded by chauvinistic emotions, promoting leaders who exploit this development to amass personal power (e.g., Gamsakhurdia in Georgia or Central Europe's experience of 1849).

Such a trend is reinforced if the "muscle" of the former regime, particularly the military and security element, remains largely unaffected by change. This is likely to be the case because, paradoxically, bureaucratic institutions (especially the armed and secret police forces) generally are strengthened rather than weakened during this phase. Where the totalitarian regime maintained a careful grip on these potentially dangerous entities, a change in the system tends to relax such oversight, particularly since new leaders may have little knowledge of the bureaucracies and operational patterns involved. Moreover, democratic aspirations are not equivalent to the creation of a democratic party system. As pointed out before, democracy requires the existence of a civil society, resting upon a law-based state (*Rechtsstaat*), and pluralism (e.g., spontaneously and freely organized political, religious, and social institutions, as well as media that are legally protected rather than constrained). Such a society requires at least a full generation to develop. In addition, factional habits and the frequent co-option of new movements by survivors of the old regime delay the creation of genuinely democratic political organizations based upon a commonality of aims. Thus, the post-totalitarian stage is littered with splinter groups that merge and break apart kaleidoscopically because of the personal predilections of their would-be leaders. (Some, moreover, are former dissidents who, forced to live in "internal emigration"—spiritual isolation—under the previous system, adopted the "émigré mentality" with its penchant for minuscule political associations engaged in endless polemics.)

3) The eventual emergence of a fully democratic system is not inevitable. It requires a period free of ethnic and other internecine bloodshed as well as uninterrupted development of civic institutions. For the reasons mentioned, such an idyll cannot be anticipated in the short term (unlike the German case, in which defeat and foreign occupation, after a relatively brief totalitarian interlude, compressed revolutionary transformation into a few short years). Indeed, the second phase of the transitional period is as full of peril as of opportunity and frequently presents tempting openings for a reversal to an authoritarian regime, particularly a military (or secret police) dictatorship. Consequently, painstaking analysis of the plethora of relevant data is essential if meaningful conclusions are to be reached at each stage concerning the direction of developments in the post-totalitarian period.

Clearly, the questions posed in this book pertain to the initial stages of the second phase of the transitional period leading *potentially* from totalitarianism toward authentic democratization. The question mark in the title represents genuine doubts and reservations which had to be voiced precisely because one wished the post-coup leadership well.

The analytical work that led to this volume (including the symposium in which most of the contributors interacted creatively) and the documentary resources contained in the Institute's database (that provides the infrastructure for most of its endeavors) were made possible by the generosity and support of Boston University's central leadership, the Sarah Scaife and Carthage foundations, the Arthur Vining Davis Foundations, and the Earhart Foundation, as well as the U.S. Air Force, which has given invaluable assistance through the annual appointment of a senior officer as National Defense Fellow at the Institute. We wish to express our deep appreciation and gratitude for the support given by all of these institutions and personalities. In addition, we are happy to acknowledge the excellent contributions made by the graduate fellows of the Institute's database research team—Susan Cavan, Joseph Gibbs, Lisa Godek, Gordon Hahn, Ann Kassler, William Mahoney, J. Michael Waller, and Bernard Way—and the assistance provided by our support staff—Nancy Clusen, David Junius, and Christopher Makuc.

Part I: Political Pluralism

Toward a Multiparty System?

Vera Tolz

Today, the political landscape in every former union republic is marked by the existence of different political parties. In Russia, and in the majority (but not all) of the republics, the Communist Party of the Soviet Union (CPSU) seems to be defeated; its central organs (the Politburo and the Central Committee) have been dissolved. However, the members of the *nomenklatura* still maintain a grip over many parts of the former Soviet Union, albeit under different guises.

If one looks back at the developments since 1985, one sees that the creation of political groups independent of the government and the CPSU was not so difficult to achieve. In fact, this was completed already by 1988. In October 1990, the USSR law on public associations legalized this achievement.[1] It was much more difficult, however, to defeat the CPSU, although the article on its leading role was dropped from the USSR Constitution in early 1990.[2] Indeed, until the events in August 1991, the CPSU remained the largest, best organized, and richest political force on the all-union level and in many republics—despite the fact that it had been under strong criticism for some time, had suffered considerable defeats in the 1989 and 1990 elections, and had become discredited in the eyes of large segments of the population. Had it not been for the attempted coup, the CPSU's influence on the country's politics would have remained very significant today and for an indefinite time in the future.

Even before the attempted coup, it was becoming clear that the creation of noncommunist or anticommunist political parties could not be equated with the introduction of democracy. In those areas of the former Soviet Union where the communists were defeated prior to the coup and their influence on politics became insignificant, democracy was not established overnight. Thus, in the Baltic states, and above all in Lithuania, where the communist parties ceased to be the main political force by late 1989 or early 1990,[3] there are still many obstacles on the way to the building of viable democratic structures. Setbacks on the way to democracy in these areas are largely due to the influence of nationalism (which is hardly compatible with democracy) on politics. Even worse is the situation in Georgia, where in November 1990 the communist party lost in parliamentary elections to nationalistic forces. The brief presidency of Zviad Gamsakhurdia was no less repressive towards the opposition and the media than the communists had been before 1985 and was clearly more repressive than the communists were during the years of *perestroika*.[4]

Similarly, in Russia, the defeat of communist forces in the attempted coup did not mean the victory of democracy. The new Russian government, the Moscow and St. Petersburg city governments, and the democratically oriented political parties are torn by internal strife and are consequently ineffective. Boris Yel'tsin has put before the Russian Federation Supreme Soviet a plan of economic reforms, but it is not clear how successful the implementation of the plan will be or what impact the proposed drastic economic reforms will have on the situation in Russia.

Why has this situation arisen? Why have expectations that democracy would result from the abolition of the Soviet Constitution's Article 6—which concerns the CPSU's monopoly of power and the legalization of party pluralism—proven futile?

GORBACHEV'S POSITION

Sharp debates have been going on over the question whether, upon coming to power in 1985, Mikhail Gorbachev had already realized that the drastic decline in the USSR's economic growth rate was a symptom of a general crisis of the Soviet system that could be overcome only by the complete transformation of the country's political structure, ideology, and traditional values. Some observers argue that a real *perestroika* began only in 1987 and that earlier, during his first two years of power, Gorbachev had no program of his own but responded spontaneously to economic problems.[5] In contrast, in a stimulating article in *Soviet Studies,* John Gooding argues that Gorbachev assumed power with the aim of drastically changing the Soviet Union's political system and revising some of its main ideological dogmas.[6]

The author of this chapter tends to agree with the latter view, while considering that over time Gorbachev's position naturally became more radical under the influence of the situation in the country and pressure from below from the forces that his policies had unleashed. One can also argue that neither Gorbachev nor anyone else, inside or outside the USSR, could have predicted the results today of the process initiated in 1985.

The initial steps that Gorbachev undertook in 1985 and 1986 were cautious, but they already entailed great innovations compared to the policies of his predecessors. In many ways, Gorbachev took concepts that his predecessors had employed merely as propaganda tools (*glasnost'*, socialist democracy, mass participation of the population in the life of society) and attempted to fill them with real meaning. The need to stimulate independent activities among Soviet citizens occupied a prominent place in the new leadership's concept almost from the beginning. For instance, speaking in Khabarovsk in July 1986, Gorbachev told local party officials that they would have to learn to work under the "new conditions of expanding democracy," show respect for the people and their opinions, and encourage the growth of grass-root political activities.[7]

In contrast to Yuri Andropov's reforms, which attempted to improve the economic situation by tightening discipline, fighting corruption, and using other means of coercion, the Gorbachev leadership, upon assuming power, demonstrated a deeper understanding of the position. Statements by Gorbachev's associates revealed an early awareness on the part of the leadership of a connection between economic problems and the suppression of public initiative. One of the architects of Gorbachev's reforms, then-Politburo member Aleksandr Yakovlev, succinctly summed up the pre-*perestroika* situation by saying that the "administrative command system created under Stalin in the 1930s and 1940s allowed the state to swallow up civil society. The result was economic stagnation."[8]

It is clear, however, that during the first years of *perestroika,* up until 1989, the new Soviet leadership, including Gorbachev himself, had in mind only a limited relaxation of state power vis-à-vis society. Describing what he called a "civil socialist society," political commentator Fedor Burlatsky, who at the time was reflecting the official point of view, defined the division of responsibility between the state and society in the following way:

> The state can provide for domestic order and national security. It can protect those below the poverty line and the small nationalities, it can ensure basic human rights, save society from excessive differentiation in income, and provide for a basic standard of living. But the state cannot directly control the economy,

the development of culture, or public and private morality. These are the responsibility of a civil society.[9]

As late as 1988, at the 19th Party Conference, Gorbachev himself stressed that the task of various newly emerging political and social forces would be to achieve what was possible within the framework of a single-party system.[10]

Such statements did not allow for independent political activities on the part of unofficial groups and encouraged their activities only in the social sphere. Events have not, however, unfolded as the leadership evidently envisaged that they would.

THE RESPONSE OF SOCIETY

The response of society to the new challenges posed by Gorbachev's policies demonstrated that Soviet society was far more ready for reforms than outside observers and even Soviet intellectuals had dared to believe. Indeed, on the eve of the reforms the Soviet intelligentsia, which had lived through Andropov's campaign for tightening up discipline and Yuri Chernenko's stagnation period, seemed pessimistic and disillusioned about prospects for the future. In their turn, some Western observers speculated that reforms were unlikely given the deep-rooted conservatism of Soviet society and the preference on the part of the man in the street for order at the expense of individual freedom.[11]

These predictions proved to be shortsighted. The increasingly independent social and, later, political activities of the population, leading in 1989-90 to the appearance of organizations that attempted to behave as political parties, are the best illustration of this point. Moreover, on reconsidering Soviet history, one realizes that Soviet society has never been so passive and monolithic as Soviet propaganda tried to portray it.

Although soon after the October Revolution the Bolsheviks banned all political opposition in the country, some nonpolitical, unofficial associations (e.g., cultural and scientific organizations) created in Russia after the reforms of the 1860s remained in being throughout the 1920s, and new ones continued to appear. These associations were only abolished as late as the end of the 1920s and the beginning of the 1930s.[12] But even in the worst period of Stalin's rule, according to the recollections of witnesses, some people (mostly young) organized groups to discuss issues of common interest and even to criticize Stalin's policies. Of course, these gatherings often ended with the arrest of the group's participants. Thanks to the activities of the

"Memorial" society, which collects information on victims of Stalin's repressions, we are gaining more and more information about the existence of such groups.[13]

During the 1960s, which many publications in the Soviet press have mistakenly considered to be the period when the first unofficial groups arose, it simply became easier and less dangerous to conduct activities outside government control than it had been under Stalin. Indeed, ever since the de-Stalinization campaign of the 1950s, Soviet society had been slowly asserting its independence. During the three pre-*perestroika* decades, the USSR as a whole became more urban, better educated, and more open. The post-Stalin years witnessed a resurgence of independent culture, the appearance of political *samizdat,* and the establishment of human rights movements. Voices in the non-Russian republics started clamoring for the preservation of their national languages and heritage. In other words, when Gorbachev announced in June 1986 that "Soviet society is ripe for change," he was merely acknowledging the obvious.

DEVELOPMENT OF INDEPENDENT POLITICAL GROUPS UNDER GORBACHEV

From 1986 to August 21, 1991

In 1986, the official Soviet press acknowledged the existence of groups set up by Soviet citizens without official permission. These groups were called in the press *neformal' nye gruppy* (informal organizations). The Soviet press concentrated its attention on apolitical groups. In 1987, however, groups for the preservation of historical monuments and ecological groups emerged as the first sociopolitical organizations to participate openly in the country's public life.

Early in that year, groups such as *"Spasenie"* (Salvation), *"Mir"* (Peace) and *"Sovet ekologii kul' tury"* (Council of Cultural Ecology) staged a demonstration in Leningrad protesting the decision of the local authorities to demolish the Hotel Angleterre, where Esenin had committed suicide in 1925.[14] Members of the group were given an audience with officials of the Leningrad City Council and the *Oblast'* Party Committee. *Izvestia* and *Literaturnaya gazeta* warned officials in Leningrad not to take repressive actions against members of liberally oriented groups for the preservation of monuments.[15] At this stage, political developments proceeded much more rapidly in the center, especially in Moscow and Leningrad. The new political waves did not reach the Russian provinces and the non-Russian republics until later. Indeed, it was only in 1988, a year later than in the center, that ecological and cultural groups in the non-Russian republics expanded their activities.[16]

The year 1987 was also marked by the first officially sanctioned conference of informal groups, held in Moscow in August. It was revealing, however, that even reform-minded journals such as *Ogonek* and *Moscow News* failed to report the political initiatives discussed at the gathering and covered only the social aspects of the debate.[17] Although it was clear that the authorities wanted to bring the activities of unofficial groups out of the "underground," calls in *Ogonek* for the groups to place more trust in the authorities and in official organizations and to combine their activities with those of the latter indicated that the authorities wished to discourage unofficial groups from acting too independently. The fact that the press concealed most of the politically colored proposals made at the conference suggested that the authorities still hoped to channel the activities of informal groups away from politics and confine them to cultural, ecological, and social issues.

The first conference of publishers of unofficial journals was held in the same year. These journals, many of which continued the tradition of *samizdat,* had been instrumental in challenging the CPSU and government monopoly over the Soviet media. Together with representatives of reformist official journals, the unofficial journals brought about the adoption of the Soviet law on the mass media that gave the right to independent organizations and even individuals to set up their own media organs.[18]

In October 1987, historian Roy Medvedev commented that unofficial sociopolitical associations were actually "political parties."[19] Because at the time these groups were principally preoccupied with internal matters such as recruiting members and establishing links with one another, this judgment was somewhat of an exaggeration; by 1988, however, it no longer was. Indeed, in 1988, unofficial associations throughout the Soviet Union entered the sociopolitical arena in earnest. These movements became especially strong in the Baltic republics, which at the time stood at the forefront of political reforms.

The year 1988 was marked by the creation (with the approval of the top authorities) of popular fronts—umbrella organizations for unofficial sociopolitical groups. Again, it was in the Baltic republics that these fronts first arose. Many observers have speculated that the Soviet government played a direct part in the creation of "popular fronts" in the spring of 1988 to back Gorbachev's reform programs.[20] This seemed to be Gorbachev's purpose in allowing sociologist Tat'yana Zaslavskaya and lawyer Boris Kurashvili to put out the call to set up such groups. If so, there was a serious miscalculation on the part of the authorities. Within months, large sectors of the public had moved well ahead of the central leadership and were demanding reforms far more radical than those advocated by Gorbachev and the communist party. The initial programs of the Baltic popular fronts emphasized their intention to cooperate with the communist party and the local governments in implementing *perestroika* and denied that they had any plans to function as unofficial opposition groups. Within a few months, however, the logic of events and pressure from below made such a stance infeasible. The movements gradually adopted more radical positions and began to set the tone for public life in the republics. During 1989, the Baltic popular fronts went even further and changed their goal from sovereignty to complete independence.[21]

The year 1989 saw a strong politicization of informal movements. Popular fronts imitating the Baltic models were established in other union republics. In the same year, Lithuania legalized political parties other than the communist party. In 1988, the groups had already posed a challenge to the *Komsomol,* whose prestige among Soviet youth was waning in any case, but in 1989 some informal groups were able to challenge the CPSU itself. Indeed, their rise coincided with growing public dissatisfaction with the communist party, which had been blamed by the reformist press for virtually all the USSR's misfortunes.

Elections: The CPSU Suffers a Major Setback

The elections to the USSR Congress of People's Deputies in 1989 and to the republican parliaments and local governments in 1990 constituted a major test of the role of the unofficial organizations in the politics of the USSR. Not surprisingly, in these elections—particularly the 1989 elections—the most successful performance was demonstrated by the groups in the Baltic republics. Indeed, in these elections, the Lithuanian restructuring movement *Sajudis* won 31 of the 42 seats assigned to the republic.[22]

Outside the Baltic area, representatives of unofficial movements were cautious in their attempts to put forward candidates during the 1989 elections. Although some activists belonging to unofficial political movements were successful in being elected to the Congress, in the majority of cases their victory was the result of their fame acquired outside the framework of unofficial organizations.[23] In turn, the unofficial movements themselves tended to support not their own leaders but well-known public figures, even if they had not been involved in the activities of any of the unofficial movements. For instance, Kharkov's Anarcho-Syndicalists campaigned for the election of the poet Yevgeni Yevtushenko and the editor-in-chief of *Ogonek,* Vitali Korotich.[24]

In the 1990 elections, the situation was different. Many political movements put forward their own members as candidates and also produced their own electoral platforms. The Leningrad Popular Front, for example, managed to nominate its members and supporters as candidates in the majority of Leningrad's electoral districts.[25]

By the beginning of 1990, it was obvious that a de facto multiparty system had emerged in the Soviet Union. In view of this, the CPSU agreed to abolish Article 6 of the Soviet Constitution, which guaranteed the CPSU's monopoly on power.[26] The party itself appeared to be on the verge of a split with the creation, in January 1990, of the so-called Democratic Platform in the CPSU. (However, this split did not occur. The majority of the Democratic Platform members left the CPSU at the 28th CPSU Congress in order to set up their own party, although as a result they lost the right to claim part of the CPSU's property.)[27]

In October 1990, a law on public associations was adopted that legalized many organizations that had already been created. The law also permitted the creation of many new groups that started to define themselves as political parties.[28]

Differing Situations: the RSFSR vs. the Non-Russian Republics

In the non-Russian republics, ideas of national sovereignty and later of independence, as well as the preservation of the local culture and language, became the main unifying forces behind new political movements, just as they had formed the main basis on which popular fronts were created. In contrast, in the RSFSR it was much more difficult for unofficial groups to unite, and consequently the Russian Popular Front turned out to be a very feeble organization.[29] The main reason for this situation seems to be that the idea of a Russian national revival had been identified with chauvinism and therefore was finding it difficult to make any headway. Indeed, until early 1990, it was only extreme groups such as *Pamyat'* that had attempted to present themselves as the sole advocates of specific Russian interests. Leaders of unofficial groups of democratic orientation tended to ignore Russian issues, discussing democratic reforms on the all-union level. The democrats decided to turn to the discussion of Russian issues only in 1990 in connection with the electoral campaign for the RSFSR parliament and local governments.[30] In the meantime, no other platform was formed on which various political groups in Russia could have united.

As a result of the 1990 elections, representatives of new democratically oriented as well as anticommunist, nationalist political forces won a majority in some republican parliaments, i.e., in Armenia, Georgia, the Baltic republics, and Moldavia, as well as in local governments, including such major cities as Moscow and Leningrad.

It was nonetheless obvious that no viable democratic opposition had been created. The reason was that until August 1991, at the all-union level, the communist party continued to parallel governmental structures, control the Army and the KGB, and interfere in the economy and other spheres of life. It also still exercised a strong influence on the central media, especially television.

Another reason lay in the weakness of the democratic movements themselves. It was relatively easy to announce the creation of new political groups with very broad and vague programs, like the introduction of democratic institutions and a market economy. It was much more difficult, however, to move from words to deeds, from criticizing obvious shortcomings of the existing system to elaborating action programs aimed at solving the problems of the country as a whole or of individual republics. Perhaps, however, the weakness of the new political movements should not have come as a surprise in a country where no real independent political activities outside the framework of the CPSU had been possible until the beginning of *perestroika*.

Other problems faced by the democrats are related to the lack of a consistent democratic tradition in prerevolutionary Russia. Many leaders of the democratic opposition still do not understand that Western democracy is founded on the principle of the separation of powers between major state institutions and a system of checks and balances that ensures that no one branch of government can dominate the others. Instead, these leaders are influenced by the idea, deeply rooted in nineteenth-century Russian philosophical thought, that a good political system can be created simply by appointing competent and honest people to leading positions. The absence of a democratic tradition is also an obstacle to democratic developments in the non-Russian republics, with the result that nationalistic rather than democratic ideas emerge victorious.

The Attitudes of the Authorities

Although in 1986 and 1987 the Soviet leadership began to revise its traditional policies for dealing with unofficial groups, i.e., either to ignore them or to criticize them and harass their members, in practice many officials, especially outside Moscow, continued to follow old stereotypes.

By 1988, the position of the top leadership toward supporting these unofficial groups, including sociopolitical organizations that did not go beyond the perceived tolerable limits, paved the way for the groups' members to act relatively freely in Moscow. In the Russian provinces and in some union republics, however, the authorities often continued to suppress even those movements that had received approval from Moscow. The use of police and tear gas against participants in a meeting held in the Belorussian capital of Minsk in November 1988 to commemorate Stalin's victims is a case in point.[31] At the same time, the Memorial society, set up with the same purpose in the Soviet capital in August 1988, was able to demonstrate freely in Moscow. In 1988, however, even the authorities in Moscow were not prepared to tolerate groups which openly challenged the dominant role of the communist party, advocated the separation of union republics from the Soviet Union, or rejected the socialist system. (The Democratic Union, the first self-proclaimed opposition party, created in Moscow in May 1988, is an example.)[32]

By 1989, the control of the Soviet leadership and local authorities over unofficial movements had weakened drastically. This process was taken as a worrisome sign not only by the conservatives in the party, but also by Mikhail Gorbachev personally. At the July 1989 meeting of the CPSU CC, Gorbachev called for increased cooperation with informal groups, saying that the party had no alternative, whereas Yegor Ligachev attacked unofficial groups, maintaining that they created a situation of "dual power" in some areas of the USSR.[33]

A few months later, however, with the economic situation deteriorating and the Soviet leadership feeling increasing anxiety about the possibility of the defeat of party representatives in elections to republican parliaments and local governments, Gorbachev started to speak very differently. At a meeting with journalists and other media representatives in October 1989, the Soviet leader attacked the reformist Interregional Group of Deputies as a "gangster clique striving for power."[34] By this time, however, there was little that the leadership could do to control unofficial movements.

In 1989, the Soviet press openly admitted that political pluralism already existed in many parts of the Soviet Union and that in some places, for instance the Baltic area, it was not the party organs but independent political organizations that held the initiative. Under these circumstances, the CPSU seemed to abandon the ambitious task of manipulating and controlling the groups, and limited its activities to infiltrating party officials into influential emerging organizations in order to manipulate their activities from within. Special departments were set up in regional party committees and in the CPSU CC for analyzing the activities of unofficial groups and establishing relations with them.[35]

In 1990, when many new groups calling themselves political parties were created, the CPSU, the central Soviet government, and state bodies tended to support weak groups that posed no challenge to the CPSU. The groups whose representatives won in the 1990 parliamentary elections and topped opinion polls showing the relative popularity of new political organizations were ignored by the central authorities, while at the same time often being criticized on central television and in the communist party press. The following incidents are good examples of this situation. In October 1990, the deputy chairman of the USSR Supreme Soviet Council of Nationalities, Boris Oleinik, met with representatives of 16 political groups to discuss the drafting of a new Union Treaty.[36] The invited participants represented a broad range of groups, from the liberal Constitutional Democratic Party to Unity for Leninism and Communist Ideals, led by the notorious Leningrad Stalinist Nina Andreyeva. Other participants included the Liberal Democratic Party of the USSR (LDPSS), the Anarcho-Syndicalists, and the ultranationalist, anti-Semitic *Pamyat'* society.

On October 29, leaders of the LDPSS and several other insignificant groups were again invited to a meeting with a top representative of the central leadership. This time it was the chairman of the USSR Council of Ministers, Nikolai Ryzhkov, who discussed with his guests the formation of a coalition government. On November 1, the Chairman of the USSR Supreme Soviet, Anatoli Luk'yanov, also met with representatives of various political parties and movements. Apart from the LDPSS, this meeting was attended by representatives of various national and religious groups, i.e., the Anarcho-Syndicalists, the Greens, the Russian People's Front, the Marxist Platform of the CPSU, the Russian Orthodox Monarchists, and the Committee for the Salvation of the Volga River.

There is one similarity among all these groups that the central Soviet leadership at the time was patronizing and inviting for consultations. Representatives of these parties either did not participate in the 1990 elections or, if they did, lost heavily. Their popularity with the public was low and their influence on politics was insignificant. Those groups that had been far more influential and whose representatives won seats either in the Russian parliament or in local governments, such as the Democratic Russian Movement or the Democratic Party of Russia, were ignored. In sum, in the second half of 1990, the central authorities adopted tactics aimed at establishing a fake multiparty system. This policy continued until August 1991. It was apparently decided that, if it was not feasible to avoid the emergence of new

political groups altogether, hardliners in the CPSU and the central government and state structures should do everything possible to block the creation
of a viable union of democratic forces.

After the Attempted Coup: Prospects for the Future

By August 1991, party pluralism had been achieved. Most of the parties
either had been created by representatives of the old structures who tried to
reform these structures, or were, in the Soviet context, entirely new under-
takings.[37] The latter groups put forward abstract ideas, such as the general
democratization of the country and the introduction of a market economy.
The most influential organizations were successful in blocking some anti-
reformist moves undertaken by the central government and in arranging mass
meetings in support of reforms. They have not, however, been very effective
when it comes to proposing their own detailed anticrisis programs.

The anticipated split in the CPSU and the division of its property between
the reformist and reactionary wings of the party did not occur. Instead, the
majority of reform-minded communists either were expelled from the CPSU
or left it of their own free will. Thus, the conservatives remained the owners
of the CPSU's immense property, to a considerable extent even after its
dissolution.

In the RSFSR, the Democratic Russia movement emerged as the strongest
force. It united in its ranks the best-known political figures on the Russian
republican arena and it secured the election on June 12, 1991 of Boris
Yel'tsin as Russian president. And yet on the eve of the coup even this
movement began to be torn by internal strife.[38]

The coup drastically changed the situation, sweeping away major obstacles in the path of the country's democratization and of economic reform.
From being in opposition to the central authorities, Russian political leaders
began to dominate not only the republican but, to a large extent, the political
scene of the entire country. What are the prospects for the maturing of a
multiparty system under the new conditions?

It is likely that many feeble parties created after the abolition of Article 6
of the Soviet Constitution will disappear. Even the Democratic Russia
movement, which has united in its ranks many reform activists, seems to
have fulfilled its main purpose of securing Yel'tsin's election and has since
failed to find a new identity.

With the gradual move toward a market economy, only those parties that
represent definite social or interest groups seem to have a chance of success.
If this assumption is correct, one can predict the emergence of the following

political parties. The first tendency which appears to have a promising future is represented by new entrepreneurs who will most probably enter the political arena in order to lobby for their interests. Signs of this process were visible even prior to the coup. On December 9, 1990, Soviet private businessmen met in Moscow to found their own political party, to be called the Free Labor Party.[39] On November 6, 1991, the RSFSR Ministry of Justice officially registered another organization of businessmen called the Bourgeois-Democratic Party.[40] The activities of these parties will need to be carefully monitored in the future.

It looks as if there will be a place for liberal parties in Russia, i.e., parties representing views that in the West would be termed moderate conservative. These parties, however, must unite in order to put forward their ideas more forcefully. There have been attempts to set up a so-called Liberal Union of different political parties. Thus, in October 1991, St. Petersburg Mayor Anatoli Sobchak—one of the most prominent politicians in Russia—called for a liberal union of various democratic parties. He called on the Soviet and Western media to advocate the idea of such a union. So far, however, there have been no real results.[41]

In addition to the above-mentioned groups, parties with nationalistic platforms will be very influential in the non-Russian republics, as is already the case in many areas of the former USSR.

On the Russian Federation level, a force that was created prior to the attempted coup and has a chance of survival, although it is not clear exactly in what form, is the Movement for Democratic Reform. It was set up in July 1991 by pro-reform leaders from the old structures, i.e., the CPSU, local governments, and the military-industrial complex, notably Aleksandr Yakovlev, Eduard Shevardnadze, Gavriil Popov, Anatoli Sobchak, and Arkadi Vol'sky.[42] The strength of this movement lies mainly in the fact that it includes the most experienced politicians in the country. Its future political program will probably be social democratic in orientation, since its leading member, Aleksandr Yakovlev, who has emerged as a major postcommunist ideologist in Russia, is a social democrat.

Organizations further to the political left are being created to defend the rights of those who will lose as a result of a transition to a market economy. Although the ideals of communism and even socialism are now to a large extent discredited in the country, more than seventy years of communist propaganda in conjunction with traditional Russian views on social justice undoubtedly exercise an influence. Thus, soon after the coup, the chairman of the Moscow City Soviet, Nikolai Gonchar, a leader of the Socialist Party,

Boris Kagarlitsky, and a leader of the Moscow anarchists, Andrei Isaev, proposed to set up a labor party (*partiya truda*) to defend workers' rights.[43] Communists are also likely to remain active in political life in some form. In several republics, especially in Central Asia, they have retained considerable power. In the Russian Federation, there have been clear attempts to replace the disbanded CP structures with some new hardline organizations. While the top leadership of the CPSU and the Russian Communist Party (CPR) have obeyed the orders by Gorbachev and Yel'tsin to dissolve themselves, on a lower level attempts are being made to create new communist groups. In September 1991, *Komsomol'skaya pravda* referred to the plan by Nina Andreyeva to re-establish the All-Russian Bolshevik Communist Party and the call by the Initiative Congress of the CPR to hold a meeting in Sverdlovsk in November 1991 to recreate the Russian Communist Party. The newspaper also wrote that a group of members of the Marxist Platform in the CPSU intended to set up their own communist organization.[44] On October 26, TASS reported the creation of the Socialist Party of Working People, which sees itself as "virtually the legal successor to the CPSU."

CONCLUSION

The initial optimism over the emergence of a multiparty system in the USSR—visible in 1989 and early 1990, both in the USSR and among outside observers—was replaced in the second half of 1990 by the sober realization that most of the newly emerging political groups were not viable. Even the most successful organizations that lead in opinion polls regarding attitudes toward political organizations lack concrete programs for getting the country out of its political and economic crises and are unable to develop a strategy for carrying out reforms.

This situation should not be surprising given the former political system in which, until the death of Stalin, civil society had little if any chance of taking root, and any meaningful political activity outside the CPSU was impossible until the late 1980s. As a result, many active political figures belonging to movements called democratic do not know what real democracy means. Instead of building viable democratic structures, representatives of democratic movements are involved in fights over important government positions. In the meantime, parliaments with an anticommunist majority are not workable since deputies spend an excessive amount of time discussing technical details and settling personal quarrels.

In the non-Russian republics, the majority of movements that call themselves democratic have adopted political platforms characterized by strong nationalism. Virtually every republic has problems with national minorities that opposed a breakup of the Soviet Union, while the Russian Federation does not know how to cope with the separatist tendencies of the autonomous republics within it.[45] None of the new political movements knows how to deal with this kind of problem.

The changes that occurred in the USSR after the coup, i.e., the suspension of the activities of the CPSU and the disintegration of the USSR, took place too rapidly and long before the new political forces could become experienced enough to exercise rule in republics that are torn by political and economic crises.[46]

In sum, the current situation in every part of the former Soviet Union is chaotic and the paths of the individual republics to democracy and economic prosperity seem likely to be long and thorny. The situation is such that strong individual political figures, rather than political movements, are shaping politics at the present stage.

NOTES

1. For the text of the law, see *Izvestia*, October 16, 1990.
2. At the February 1990 plenum, the CPSU CC expressed readiness to relinquish the party's guaranteed monopoly on power. This recommendation was then enacted into law by the USSR Congress of People's Deputies in March 1990.
3. See Saulius Girnius, "Lithuania," Dzintra Bungs, "Latvia," Riina Kionka, "Estonia," *Report on the USSR*, no. 52, December 29, 1989, pp. 23-30.
4. Elizabeth Fuller, "Spotlights on Georgia," *Report on the USSR*, no. 7 (1991), pp. 17-22; Fuller, "Gamsakhurdia's First 100 Days," *Report on the USSR*, no. 10 (1991), pp. 10-12.
5. Seweryn Bialer, "The Changing Soviet Political System: The Nineteenth Party Conference and After," in Seweryn Bialer, ed., *Politics, Society and Nationality Inside Gorbachev's Russia*, (Boulder, 1989), p. 193.
6. John Gooding, "Gorbachev and Democracy," *Soviet Studies* 42, no. 2 (April 1990), pp. 195-231.
7. M. S. Gorbachev, *Izbrannye Rechi i Stat' i* 4 (Moscow, 1988), pp. 49-50.
8. Stephen F. Cohen and Katerina van den Huevel, *Voices of Glasnost': Interviews with Gorbachev's Reformers* (New York: W. W. Norton, 1989), p. 39.
9. Fedor Burlatsky, "Pervy, no vazhny shag," *Literaturnaya gazeta*, June 14, 1989.
10. Pravda, June 29, 1988.
11. See Richard Pipes, *Time*, February 25, 1982.

12. *Pamyat'*: *Istoricheski Sbornik* 4 (Moscow, 1979-Paris, 1981), pp. 128-29; N. Okhotin and A. Roginsky, eds., *Zven'ya*, (Moscow: Progress, Feniks, Atheneum, 1991), p. 166.
13. *Ibid.*, vol. 1 (Moscow, 1976-New York, 1978), pp. 232-68; vol. 3 (Moscow, 1978-1980), pp. 539-57; vol. 5 (Moscow, 1981-Paris, 1982), pp. 226-27; N. Okhotin and A. Roginsky, eds., *Zven'ya*, pp. 528-34.
14. *Stroitel' naya gazeta*, April 24, 1987.
15. *Izvestia*, March 27, 1987; *Literaturnaya gazeta*, March 25, 1987.
16. Bohdan Nahaylo, "Informal Ukrainian Culturological Club Helps to Break New Ground for Glasnost," Radio Liberty Research Bulletin (RL) 57/88, February 8, 1988; Kathleen Mihalisko, "A Profile of Informal Patriotic Youth Groups in Belorussia," RL 318/88, July 14, 1988. See also *Russkaya mysl'*, September 9, 1988 on the "Ukrainian Association of Independent Creative Intelligentsia."
17. *Ogonek*, no. 36 (1987); *Moscow News*, no. 37 (1987).
18. A report on the conference appeared in the first issue of the *samizdat* periodical, *Zhurnal zhurnalov*, published in Leningrad in December, 1987. See *Bulletin of Radio Liberty Samizdat Department*, AS 6127 and 6132.
19. *La Repubblica*, October 11-12, 1987, p.11.
20. See Vera Tolz, *The USSR's Emerging Multiparty System* (New York and London: Praeger Publishers, 1990), pp. 16-17.
21. *Ibid.*, pp. 18-20.
22. Saulius Girnius, "Sajudis Candidates Sweep Elections in Lithuania," *Report of the USSR*, no. 15 (1989), pp. 29-30.
23. Tolz, *The USSR's Emerging Multiparty System*, p. 37.
24. *Russkaya mysl'*, February 2, 1990.
25. *Express khronika*, no. 4, 1990; *Leningradsky literator*, no. 2 (1990), p. 2.
26. See note 2.
27. Igor' Chubais, "The Democratic Opposition: An Insider's View," *Report on the USSR*, no. 18 (1991), pp. 12-15.
28. Tolz, "The Law on Public Associations: Legalization of the Multiparty System," *Report on the USSR*, no. 46 (1990), pp. 1-3.
29. Geoffrey Hosking, "The Russian National Revival," *Report on the USSR*, no. 44 (1991), pp. 5-8.
30. Tolz, *The USSR's Emerging Multiparty System*, pp. 68-72.
31. Reuters report, November 1, 1988.
32. Tolz, *The USSR's Emerging Multiparty System*, pp. 56-60.
33. *Pravda*, July 21, 1989.
34. The text of Gorbachev's speech was not published in the USSR. See Michael Dobbs, "Gorbachev Criticizes Irresponsible Editors," *Washington Post*, October 17, 1989; Bill Keller, "Gorbachev Waffles on Glasnost," *The New York Times*, October 19, 1989; and David Remnick, "Gorbachev Seen to Take a Sharp Conservative Turn," *Washington Post*, October 19, 1989.
35. See *Partiinaya zhizn'*, no. 2 (1990), pp. 31-36; no. 3 (1990), pp. 29-33.

36. For details on these meetings, see Julia Wishnevsky, "Multiparty System, Soviet Style," *Report on the USSR*, no. 47 (1990).

37. Igor' Klyamkin, "Trends in the Political Parties," *Report on the USSR*, no. 42 (1991), pp. 5-6.

38. The Democratic Russia Movement was formally set up as an umbrella organization of democratically oriented parties in October 1990. The movement also allows individual membership. At the second congress of the movement held in November 1991, a split occurred within its ranks. The Democratic Party of Russia, headed by Nikolai Travkin, the Christian Democratic Movement of Russia, and the Party of People's Freedom left Democratic Russia to set up their own coalition. The leaders of these three parties disagreed with the leadership of Democratic Russia (Yuri Afanas'ev, Galina Starovoitova, Arkadi Murashev) over the issue of independence for the RSFSR's autonomies. While the leaders of the three parties thought that independence should not be granted to the autonomies under any circumstances, Afanas'ev and Starovoitova held that complete independence should be granted to any autonomy within the RSFSR if it wanted it. (See TASS, November 10, 1990.)

39. *Radio Moscow 1*, December 9, 1990.

40. *Vesti* program, November 6, 1991.

41. On one attempt by representatives of Democratic Russia and other democratic parties in the RSFSR to set up a Liberal Union, see *Svobodnoe slovo* (newspaper of the Democratic Union), no. 26 (1991).

42. Elizabeth Teague and Vera Tolz, "Prominent Reformers Create Opposition Movement," *Report on the USSR*, no. 28 (1991), pp. 1-4.

43. *Komsomol'skaya pravda*, September 21, 1991.

44. *Ibid.*

45. On October 23, 1991, the RSFSR Procuracy announced that all political parties and public associations on the territory of the republic which call for the violation of the territorial integrity of the RSFSR had been banned. The Procuracy was referring primarily to organizations in Tatarstan and Chechen-Ingushetia, where anti-Russian feelings run very high. (TASS, October 23, 1991). The weakness of such measures becomes clear when one recalls that the USSR law on public associations, adopted in 1990, had a similar provision. This provision, however, was rarely implemented, and the law naturally did nothing to prevent the increased influence of separatist movements in the union republics and failed to save the USSR from disintegration.

46. See Peter Reddaway, "The End of the Empire," *The New York Review of Books*, November 7, 1991.

—

The Legislative
Process—Institutionalized?

Robert T. Huber[1]

INTRODUCTION

The success of pluralism in Russia and the other successor states rests on the ability of emerging political elites to become stable institutional influences in the emerging political systems. Nowhere is this more clear than with respect to the institutionalization of national legislatures.

The development of stable legislatures is a critical element in the process of political pluralism for several reasons. Legislatures are a recruiting ground for emerging political elites. Legislators may represent the public in dealing with unelected elites in the executive bureaucracy. The legislature also can serve as an institution through which societal groups form coalitions and political parties to promote or frustrate social action and change, channel, or harness dissent, and challenge or reinforce regime legitimation.

MEASURES OF THE
INSTITUTIONALIZATION OF LEGISLATURES

If one accepts the argument that stable legislatures are a key measure for the success of political institutionalization and pluralism, just how is such a measure evaluated? The literature of political science[2] does provide us with several possible indicators, including:

- the age of the institution
- the complexity of goals, units, and subunits
- institutional independence from other institutions identified by defined norms and methods of behavior
- the regulation of resources between units and subunits
- institutional coherence, defined by the degree of consensus about the functional boundaries of the institution and expectations of performance
- openness of elite positions within institutions and interchangeability of tasks
- receptiveness of existing elites to newly mobilized subgroups
- established criteria for the conduct of internal business and professional relations between legislators
- the nature and intrusiveness of legislative oversight of executive agencies and the legislature's ability by a variety of means to bring about changes in the operations of policy
- the amount of time devoted to legislative work (full-time versus part-time legislators)
- the influence of legislative committees versus the influence of the legislative leadership (e.g., on agenda-setting, consideration of legislation on the floor of the parliament, the degree of preservation of committee positions on legislation after floor consideration)
- the intensity of legislative involvement in budgetary matters, the creation, amendment, and enforcement of legislation and laws, and the presence or absence of informal influences on policy-making (i.e., whether legislative units and subunits influence policy outcomes without recourse to formal powers of budgetary approval and law-making)
- the role of partisanship in making decisions (e.g., the significance of party identification in explaining and predicting legislative outcomes)
- the degree of perceived accountability of legislators to their constituencies
- the self-image of legislators as policy makers

THE SOVIET LEGISLATURE TRACK RECORD 1989-1991

During the period from the election of the transformed and revitalized Soviet legislature in 1989 to the August 1991 *coup d'état,* the institutionalization of the Soviet national legislature made impressive, albeit uncertain, strides. In both domestic and foreign policy, as well as in matters of internal organization and executive relations, a close examination of legislative activity gives cause for both optimism and pessimism concerning the future of political pluralism in Russia.

With regard to domestic policy, the Supreme Soviet in particular, as well as the Congress of People's Deputies, did adopt a number of important measures and demonstrated institutional autonomy on a number of issues. For example, a far-reaching law on the press and media was enacted in spite of bureaucratic interference. This law helped set in motion a framework for independent publications which proved crucial in providing alternative sources of information during the August *coup d' état.*[3]

Prior to the creation of a new national legislature, the press law had been a very conservative document which established more obligations than rights for journalists. Over the course of a year of legislative consideration, the law was amended into a measure which gave independent groups and individuals the right to establish media organizations, dramatically relaxed censorship, and led to major changes in the editorial and financial management of a number of established publications. This type of intensive legislative involvement in the creation, amendment, and enforcement of legislation was one of the stronger pieces of evidence supporting the institutionalization of pluralistic organizations.

Domestic policy issues also provided the background for other signs of emerging institutions, most notably the nature and intrusiveness of legislative oversight of executive agencies. The new parliament passed a series of laws dealing with domestic issues which made major inroads in the executive bureaucracy's ability to control everyday life in the Soviet Union through thousands of decrees, both published and unpublished.[4] Decrees numbering in the thousands were annulled, representing a serious challenge to *proizvol,* the Brezhnevite tradition of socialist legality and simultaneous arbitrariness. Remaining decrees were required by law to be published and statutory laws were given legal precedence over regulations.

In a number of instances, the Soviet parliament also exercised its newly found powers to reject executive nominees or critically question others before finally approving them. Nominations and debates were frequently accompanied by requests for more information from the Gorbachev government, which were complied with unevenly. The original nominee for the State Committee on Prices was rejected, as were those for the Minister of Roads, the Minister of the Timber Industry, the head of the Foreign Economic Commission, and several internal security nominations. Most notably, Mikhail Gorbachev's choice for Vice President, Gennadi Yanaev, was rejected by the parliament only to be resuscitated and eventually approved at Gorbachev's insistence, a move he would later seriously regret. Moreover, the parliament also insisted on using the nomination process in the manner of a well-institutionalized legislature which sees the process as an opportunity to elicit the nominee's views on critical issues within his or her own purview and occasionally to reject nominees as a sign of dissatisfaction with the president's conduct of policy in a particular area.

Unfortunately, the domestic policy arena also showed evidence of poor institutional development within the parliament. The effort to attack the bureaucratic practice of issuing regulations *without reference* to statutory law was often frustrated by new bureaucratic obfuscation by means of implementing regulations after enactment of the relevant legislation. Key elements of economic reform packages, such as the Law on the State Enterprise, suffered from waves of new ministerial regulations undermining their effects.

It is also clear that, with respect to the consideration of critical issues of economic reform, the Soviet national legislature did not shower itself with glory. Laws on product quality and consumer rights, intellectual property, taxes, allocation of economic powers (among the union, the republics, and local governments), and labor management and worker rights were continually debated without effective resolution. A number of economic reform blueprints (the Ryzhkov, Shatalin, Shmelev, and Abalkin projects) all went down to defeat or were shelved as issues of price deregulation, monetary projection, credit control and management, and ruble convertibility led to disagreement and inconclusive, long-winded debates.

In the area of defense and foreign policy, increasing transparency of the decision-making process was achieved during the 1989-91 period. The relevant committees scrutinized executive nominations and testimony from executive officials and sought formal contacts with a number of foreign parliaments. Reports to the parliament were not the same desultory affairs that they had been in the pre-1989, rubber-stamp Supreme Soviet. On a number of occasions, Foreign Ministers Eduard Shevardnadze and Aleksandr Bessmertnykh, who served under Gorbachev, as well as other foreign policy-makers were criticized, particularly by the right-wing Soyuz faction in the parliament, for one-sided concessions in U.S.-Soviet arms-control negotiations. Soviet cooperation with the United States during the Persian Gulf crisis as well as Soviet acquiescence in the reunification of Germany came under intense right-wing criticism, the latter for its negative security implications and the profoundly dislocating effects of the demobilization of Soviet troops in the former German Democratic Republic.

The parliament was also a key forum for debate between liberals and conservatives about the appropriate missions and funding levels of the

Ministry of Defense, the issue of conscription as opposed to an all-volunteer military force, arms procurement reforms, and the reorganization of the intelligence agencies.

In fact, legislative involvement in defense and foreign policy matters was intense. Liberal legislators succeeded, albeit marginally, in reducing defense spending levels. Conservative legislators forced the reluctant Gorbachev and Shevardnadze to agree to postpone consideration of the German reunification and normalization treaties, resulting in the subsequent German agreement to increase financial assistance for the demobilization and relocation of Soviet troops. With several International Affairs Committee members serving as intermediaries—"parliament men," as in established parliaments around the world—the Gorbachev government finally agreed to seek the formal approval of the Supreme Soviet for any sending of Soviet troops into military action in the Persian Gulf.

In defense, as in domestic policy, the 1989-91 Soviet legislative landscape was strewn with failures. On critical issues of military reform, the parliament split into several factions and ultimately failed to act. An organic law governing the operation of the Ministry of Defense, similar to the laws that for decades have governed defense establishments in liberal political systems, did not materialize. Defense conversion proposals from the Gorbachev government were vague and halfhearted. The Defense and State Security Committee, dominated by military officers and defense industry officials, was reluctant to challenge the Ministry of Defense.

Military reform groups led by Major Vladimir Lopatin sought a number of changes in the operation of defense policy. Among the more notable were the prosecution of abuses by officers, an all-volunteer army, the development of national formations responsible to the central government but stationed in the constituent republics, and the elimination of communist party political units from the armed forces. Unfortunately, the Lopatin proposals were shelved in the fall of 1990 as Gorbachev's efforts to appease conservative political forces stalemated any serious effort to overhaul the Ministry of Defense's organization, doctrine, procurement, manpower, and spending levels.

Institutionalization also proceeded in an uncertain direction when one examines matters of the internal organization of the legislature as well as the parliament's institutional relations with the executive bureaucracy. The rules governing membership during the 1989-91 period called for rotation of one-fifth of the membership of both the Congress of People's Deputies and the Supreme Soviet. Taken in conjunction with an additional requirement that standing committees be composed of equal numbers of members from both bodies, the development of full-time legislators was stymied since the Congress of People's Deputies was a part-time legislature and its members were often not in Moscow. Consequently, committees were prevented from having stable membership.

On the positive side, the 1989-91 Soviet national legislature did contain a number of notable political figures whose reputations from careers established outside the parliament were a major asset to the legislative bodies in obtaining information from the executive bureaucracy and in drafting legislation. In the case of legislation like the press law, or the provision for prior legislative approval regarding the sending of troops into combat that was attached to a resolution supporting Gorbachev's Persian Gulf policy, legislative elites emerged who played key roles in formally and informally shaping policy outcomes.[5]

Nonetheless, the parliament did suffer from chronic problems of internal organization. Committees were frequently understaffed. Control of committee budgets was exercised not by the committees themselves, but—curiously—by the Presidium of the Supreme Soviet and the ministries that the committees were to oversee. This budgetary dependence badly crippled the institutional autonomy of committees and undermined their ability to control resources critical to the initiation of legislation and supervision of compliance with already enacted laws. Reliance on outside experts who were not on the committee payroll often proved to be an ineffective substitute for an adequate committee budget.

The result was that the Presidium of the Supreme Soviet often constituted the legislative center of gravity during the 1989-91 period. With a personnel strength of over 700, the Presidium did provide staffing to committees, but its staff was dedicated to serving the Presidium. The staff was managed by Anatoli Luk'yanov after he became chairman of the Presidium in 1990 in connection with the constitutional revision introducing a USSR executive presidency.

Luk'yanov served in the Supreme Soviet as a combination of legislative speaker in the American sense and (probably) the second most powerful figure in the executive arm of the Soviet government. Luk'yanov's Presidium was the rule-making body for the parliament and the source of delegate appointments to committees. In addition, it was a key player in selecting committee chairmen and the focus for agenda setting.

Unlike the practice in a number of other parliaments, at the beginning of each Supreme Soviet session the Presidium introduced a lengthy resolution stating the priorities of each of the parliamentary committees, as well as an agenda of issues to be considered during the entire session. Not surprisingly, the agenda reflected the priorities not so much of the parliament as of President Gorbachev. Perhaps in response to both the substance and the arbitrariness of such an agenda, the Supreme Soviet rejected Luk'yanov's proposed organizational resolution in the fall of 1990. Yet while the parliament rejected that agenda, it was unable to propose one of its own.

Luk'yanov often showed little tolerance for amendments to legislation during floor debate and frequently sought approval to ram through legislative adoption of Gorbachev's domestic and foreign policy programs. The arbitrary calling upon speakers, the shelving of legislation ready for floor action after due committee consideration, and the commissioning and sudden decommissioning of committee working groups were all evident characteristics of Luk'yanov's iron-handed control of the legislative process. When three legislative committees produced a liberal draft for a press law, Luk'yanov's concerns led him to ignore the draft and appoint a new grouping to reconcile disagreements between parliamentary liberals and conservatives in the executive ministries.[6] The Lopatin military reform group, which Luk'yanov had constituted as a sitting subcommittee of the Defense and State Security Committee, was later abruptly decommissioned when conservatives on the committee and in the Ministry of Defense vigorously opposed Lopatin's reform proposals.[7]

In addition to arbitrariness emanating from the Presidium, executive ministers often showed a minimal regard for legislative oversight functions. Attendance by executive officials at committee hearings was spotty, and requests for information were not fully satisfied. While a law on the rights of deputies provided increased rights for deputies to demand information and receive satisfactory answers to questions formally submitted to ministers, direct interventions by Gorbachev and Luk'yanov were frequently necessary to obtain the information requested.

For example, at various times during the consideration of a new emigration law, International Affairs Committee deputies complained that draft provisions were sent to them only days or hours before committee consideration. Efforts to question ministry officials about implementation issues and provisions of the law were ineffective. Moreover, efforts to elicit information about various aspects of foreign policy (e.g., hard currency derived from arms sales, details of arms control negotiating positions, details of Ministry of Defense and KGB budgets, the number and types of economic and security agreements with foreign countries) did not receive a satisfactory response.

To be sure, deficiencies of legislative behavior and decorum often gave Luk'yanov justification for exercising his own kind of legislative *proizvol*. During the 1989-91 period, the deputies themselves showed rather uneven respect for regularized rules and procedures. The parliament often lacked a quorum for consideration of legislation, while low roll-call numbers resulted in a corresponding lack of political accountability. The absence of quora in some instances also delayed consideration of legislation.

The conduct of legislative business also frequently degenerated into shouting matches, with catcalls drowning out speakers and frustrating efforts to develop a procedural and substantive consensus. Luk'yanov and Gorbachev too often resorted to violations of norms in recognizing speakers, while deputies in turn engaged in dilatory tactics, seeking explanations about provisions already considered in detail, engaging in debate on non-germane subject matter, and asking for repeated votes on issues which already had been decided. The impulse to delay and filibuster, while by no means confined to Soviet legislative experience, often served as a substitute for credible action amidst a growing economic and political crisis in the country. Instead of engaging in artful compromises in order to move ahead with law-based approaches to these crises, the Gorbachev leadership and the Soviet parliament resorted to the proliferation of committees and task forces to study alternative policy prescriptions.

Dissatisfaction with the legislative process also affected legislators' perceptions of the value of their oversight and constituency work. Many laws passed by parliament were not of high technical quality, but hastily drawn up and correspondingly subject to continual revision. Compounding this problem were deliberate efforts by ministers to sabotage the implementation of laws through regulations that frequently countermanded the purposes of the original statute.

As living standards continued to decline between 1989 and 1991, deputies tolerated, and in some instances even encouraged, the provision by the state of various perquisites of legislative office (apartments, telephones, foreign travel, transportation, and so on). Needless to say, such a compromise of professional standards rendered resolute action for dealing with the systemic crises of society more difficult.[8]

As a consequence, many legislators began to feel increasingly inadequate about their own effectiveness as well as the effectiveness of the institution itself. Many became convinced that the legislature could not deal with the "seriousness of their country's needs, the high expectations and presumably growing impatience of the public, and the importance of the work they have undertaken."[9] Problems of dealing with a rapidly deteriorating economy, widespread defiance of legal statutes and executive decrees by union republican leaderships, and the dislocations caused by

Soviet troop demobilizations in Eastern Europe raised public demands upon a fledgling democratic institution which was ill-equipped to meet them. The chronic inability of the Soviet parliament to organize itself also demonstrated itself with regard to party formations. While the liberal Interregional Group displayed some voting cohesion on domestic issues and the right-wing Soyuz faction exercised some policy-making muscle on foreign policy issues, nothing resembling floor leaders, party whips, or caucus chairmen emerged. The closest cohesion often occurred among local legislators regardless of party faction, although even this was not often a reliable indicator of legislators' real policy preferences. Gorbachev and Luk'yanov, to be sure, did nothing to encourage stable party formation, often ignoring factional leaders and even committee chairmen in order to work with political figures outside the legislature to produce Presidium-dominated legislative approaches.

All the indicators of low levels of institutionalization discussed above helped produce continuing frustration with the results of Supreme Soviet deliberations in both domestic and foreign policy. However, Gorbachev's own response to this problem was not to seek ways of invigorating legislative power and effectiveness. The promotion of an independent legislature had been part of his overall political strategy in 1988, when legislative reform was seen as a means of challenging the executive bureaucracy to implement economic reform, as well as increasing public accountability regarding the bureaucracy.

Gorbachev then sought to work around both the legislature and the bureaucracy, eventually persuading a reluctant legislature in September 1990 to grant him authority to issue decrees having the force of law without parliamentary approval. This action was perhaps one of Gorbachev's most critical political mistakes. While doing nothing to reverse the growing defiance of union republics to policy emanating from the center, the new presidential decree power badly demoralized the legislature. Its authority was reduced, thus making it less able to resist effectively the increasing right-wing challenge to Gorbachev's authority that the Soviet president had inadvertently encouraged.

THE AUGUST COUP AND THE DEVELOPMENT OF THE RUSSIAN LEGISLATURE

The August *coup d'état* had an enormous disintegrating impact on all of the central institutions, be they authoritative or ostensibly democratic. The Congress of People's Deputies and the Supreme Soviet were obviously no exceptions; by the end of 1991, the Soviet parliament had collapsed, and the focus of legislative power had shifted to the new successor states.

This shift of focus was ushered in by extraordinary sessions of both the Supreme Soviet and the Congress of People's Deputies in late August and early September. The euphoria over the coup was accompanied by an often frenzied dismantling of central institutions. In an extraordinary nine-day period from August 26 to September 5, the national legislature disbanded the Communist Party of the Soviet Union, dismissed the Council of the Union, and removed nearly all of the Supreme Soviet's legislative authority. While two new state executive bodies (the State Council and the Interrepublic Economic Committee) were set up, they possessed only weak power during their brief existence. The Congress of People's Deputies was voted out of existence, and the USSR Supreme Soviet emerged from this dizzying process an emasculated body, eventually collapsing as well by the end of 1991.

While the August coup dramatically accelerated the shift of executive and legislative power from the center to the republics and even to the local level, this process had actually been underway for several years. Since the coup, republican parliaments have proceeded with breakneck speed to exercise their new legal muscle. The long festering "war of laws" has turned into a republic-level offensive after an initial period of bloodletting over who did or did not cooperate with the August 19 putschists. In rapid fire, one republic after another has sought to enact far-reaching legislation on such issues as privatization, ownership and bankruptcy of enterprises, the creation of territorial defenses, the significance of borders and relations between the new successor states, the renaming of cities and towns, the regulation of labor-management relations, housing and insurance program establishment, the transfer of assets of union ministries to republican control, the establishment of new rules for the operation of local government, and the passage of measures on judicial reform, income indexation, and labor-management relations.

Furthermore, the Russian parliament provides a particularly acute example of a new legislature encountering enormous difficulties in exercising its newfound authority. A number of major problems have developed. Political parties have proliferated and split repeatedly, with dissolution and reformation a continuous process. Parties have sometimes formed blocs only to have individual parties defect from one bloc to another.

The proliferation of parties has also produced coalitions with somewhat fluid membership. On domestic issues, Democratic Russia has been able to count on the support of at least considerable elements of the Social

Democratic Party, the Democratic Reform movement, the Democratic Party, the People's Party, and the liberal Kadets. The communist parties seem to have the strongest voting cohesion while other elements of the noncommunist parties, the Liberal Democratic Party, and the statist Kadets have joined the communists on some issues, particularly in efforts to ameliorate the social effects of liberal economic reforms and to support strong nationalist positions with respect to relations with the successor states.

In addition to party formation, other indicators of legislative activity suggest a rather incomplete institutionalization. During the fifth session of the Congress of People's Deputies in the fall of 1991, a series of extraordinary powers was granted to Yel'tsin, including the right to issue legal decrees and appoint government ministers without parliamentary approval. The granting of these extraordinary powers has obviously limited the parliament's freedom of action. Widespread dissatisfaction with the government's liberalization program at the Congress of People's Deputies meeting in April 1991 had led to initial passage (over government objections) of a sharply critical resolution on government performance. The resolution sought, among other things, to index incomes to the rate of inflation, to modify price increases, to strengthen state regulation of prices (particularly for staples, fuel, and power), and to rescind after three months the extraordinary presidential powers granted to Yel'tsin, forcing him to submit to parliament the candidates for the prime ministership and the cabinet.

While this resolution was ultimately watered down, the session was raucous, punctuated by calls for the resignation of Yel'tsin and several government ministers, the threatened resignation of the government after the initial passage of the resolution, and the erratic performance of the speaker of the Supreme Soviet (Ruslan Khasbulatov, who presided over the Congress of People's Deputies), who first chastised the government for its overreaction to the passage of the resolution and then retreated to a pro-Yel'tsin position after Democratic Russia legislators pressed for Khasbulatov's resignation. Yel'tsin's compromise resolution, ultimately supported by the Congress, delayed until the fall of 1991 the submission of ministers and a prime minister for parliamentary approval. The parliament also received an official endorsement of strengthened oversight powers and the right to remove government ministers. Contrary to Western media reporting, Yel'tsin did not emerge from those parliamentary debates with a strengthened political position, and at this point the future direction of the Russian political system towards either presidential or parliamentary government is very much an open question. The Russian legislature as a body is showing ability to bring changes in policy-making through its legislative process of formal action and private persuasion.

The nature and intrusiveness of legislative oversight of executive agencies and the influence of the Russian Federation Supreme Soviet's legislative committees are less impressive, as is the intensity of legislative involvement in budgetary matters and statutory authorities. The legislature's agenda is set by the body's Presidium and particularly by its chairman, Khasbulatov. The Presidium, like its predecessor in the USSR Supreme Soviet, is a very powerful organization controlling resources, staff, and floor scheduling for deputies and their committees. Khasbulatov, an unpredictable and imperious supporter of the basic policy direction of the Yel'tsin government, has often been regarded as highhanded in his scheduling of legislation, recognition of speakers, and consideration of amendments. Khasbulatov has been highly sensitive to media criticism, which he regards as malicious and equivalent to "war on the state."[10]

For their part, deputies also have not always distinguished themselves for decorum when it comes to parliamentary procedure and the seriousness with which work is taken. Deputies from communist factions have tried often to shout down or interrupt speakers or to seek repeated votes on sections of bills or amendments already considered. This has led to surreal kinds of parliamentary voting, as was the case during a recent session of the RSFSR Congress of People's Deputies, when communist deputies were able to prevent the two-thirds majority necessary to amend the Russian Constitution in order to remove references to the Soviet Union and the name of Leningrad.

Deputies themselves have been critical of the performance of the parliament, particularly on domestic issues. Attendance has been spotty, and a frequent lack of quora has frustrated the consideration of legislation. Despite complaints about Yel'tsin's decree power, a number of draft laws submitted to the Supreme Soviet have bogged down in disagreement. Frequent complaints were voiced about the quality of budgetary documents and foreign policy programs, but the budget was ultimately approved with few changes.

In general, many deputies have expressed the view that legislative debate on domestic and foreign policy has been a waste of time, since members have been unable to produce credible modifications or alternatives to the Yel'tsin liberalization program, and have been susceptible to public posturing on issues of wage indexation and the removal of state price controls. Many have advocated the abolition of the Congress of People's Deputies, the direct election of the Supreme Soviet, and the abolition of this body's Presidium as measures that would enhance the ability of the legislature to be a key institutional focus for debate and the direction of economic and political reforms.[11]

The accountability of legislators to their constituencies is also seriously questionable. Both executive and legislative centers of authority suffer from the widespread defiance of statutes by local government authorities, who are scrambling themselves for control of resources and consumer goods in the wake of the collapse of the command economy supply structures, delays in privatization, and unregulated marketization in the consumer sector. Renewing the problem of the "war of laws" that existed between the republics and the central government in the *perestroika* era, new political struggles between federal and local authorities in Russia have sprung up, leaving legislators with a sense of alienation and doubts about the effectiveness of their work.[12] As if the problem of unclear jurisdictional authority were not enough, ministerial regulations (including a longstanding practice of basing such regulations on unpublished or even unwritten implementing decrees) and poor craftsmanship in the preparation of legislation further threaten the viability of statutes enacted by the Supreme Soviet.

The role of partisanship in shaping legislative decisions is also unclear. While a semblance of a whip system can be identified in the Democratic Russia and communist factions, other party-affiliated deputies appear to cross over in a pattern difficult to discern. Many parties support the government, then defect, and subsequently rejoin, or reorganize themselves with frequency. As one legislator has noted, partisan affiliation in the Russian legislature is "more of a political game, a desire to occupy a more comfortable place in the upcoming events, and an opportunity to distance oneself from a government which has discredited itself and to attempt once more to survive by dint of political opportunism."[13] In the case of Democratic Russia, many of its most notable parliamentarians have left to join the Yel'tsin government, depleting the ranks of the government's parliamentary supporters. The communist deputies, while more cohesive in their voting patterns than the members of other parliamentary parties, were elected prior to the collapse of the Soviet Union, and lack the necessary popular support or alternative programs to be anything more than an—often effective—obstacle to government proposals.

CONCLUSION

While the failure of the August 19 *coup d'état* clearly prevented earlier *perestroika* reforms and progress in political pluralism from atrophying, gains achieved in the institutionalization of new representative forms of government, particularly by the elected legislatures during the 1989-91 period, now face a new form of challenge in the post-Gorbachev period. Many of the indices of institutionalization discussed in this chapter were observed in the revitalized USSR Supreme Soviet, although they were slow and uneven. But if current Russian politics are any indication, even these gains are now threatened by the lack of respect for rules, undefined procedures, hastily drawn laws, and a deadlock between presidents and parliaments on essential issues of government operations, separation of powers, relations with the successor states, and government policy on the economy. Legislators' perceptions of the value of their work also remain low. The apparent inability of the legislature as well as the executive to deal with the growing defiance of laws by local governments is a clear indication that the systematic breakdown at the center has not as yet been replaced by functional alternatives. This vacuum of institutional power increases the temptation for strong-willed republican presidents to concentrate authority in their own hands and vault over legislative and bureaucratic disagreements. However, such a strategy, which Gorbachev pursued in 1990-91 and which Yel'tsin has also pursued in the main, seems doomed to failure in the long term.

What, then, of the future direction of political pluralism in Russia? If we accept the premise that representative legislatures perform vital functions in the promotion of political pluralism, then progress or lack thereof in the institutionalization of legislatures (as evaluated by various indices such as those considered earlier) is a key measure of the degree of political pluralism in future political systems.

From the literature on the comparative study of national legislatures, a useful typology has been proposed that can help us understand the extent of political pluralism. Michael Mezey has listed five categories:[14]

1. active legislatures (capacity to modify policy; fundamental legitimacy unchallenged by the executive; strong support by mass and elite publics)

2. vulnerable legislatures (tradition of formerly extensive powers, including modification of policy, which have been suspended or replaced by executive action; legitimacy among executive, elite, and mass publics uneven and sporadic)

3. reactive legislatures (informal influences on parameters of suitable policy-making, but only rare exercises of formal power in opposition to the executive; legitimacy widely accepted by executive, elite, and mass publics)

4. marginal legislatures (extensive formal limits on budgetary and law-making powers; remaining powers exercised with informal regulation by the executive, periodic suspensions of legislative power by the executive; low or falling legitimacy among executive, elite, and mass publics)

5. minimal legislatures (nominal powers to modify budgets or propose laws; symbolic ratification of decisions made by other institutions; legitimacy conferred by executive, accepted by elite and mass publics).

To be sure, the rich experience of political systems should not be reified by such a typology. Wide variations could well exist within categories and certain functions can be fulfilled by a given legislature across a number of categories. In the extreme example, an active legislature can perform functions ascribed to a minimalist one by acting favorably on non-binding resolutions in support of an existing policy direction initiated by the executive, or by passing without amendment legislation submitted by the executive.

Nonetheless, this typology does serve a useful purpose in outlining the possible future of political pluralism on a legislative continuum. While there is some evidence supporting a characterization of the Russian national legislature as moving toward reactive legislatures, the preponderance of evidence suggests that they are marginal legislatures. Mezey has elaborated on the nature of a marginal legislature as follows:

> Marginal legislatures are characterized by a lack of congruence between the behavior of legislators and the expectations of both mass publics and executive-centered elites. In addition, role consensus among the legislators seems to be absent . . . these legislatures are the objects of a very heavy demand volume despite their limited capacities because they are the most accessible institutions in their countries. But their members do not deal very effectively with this demand level because many of them do not perceive their role in these terms and those who do, although they devote a great deal of effort to the task, are stymied both by the sheer volume of requests and by the attitudes of uncooperative executive elites without whose assistance these demands cannot be met. Given these "failures" there is no reason for executive-centered elites to support the legislature. Thus, coups or other extraconstitutional action directed against marginal legislatures are quite common and these institutions disappear once again on a more or less regular basis.[15]

No offense should be taken, in a normative sense, by this characterization of the Russian parliament as marginal. After over 70 years of Soviet history in which legislative power was clearly minimal, the revitalization of the USSR Supreme Soviet during the 1989-91 period and the emergence of the Russian legislature since the August coup, as the major sources of legislative authority, represent a remarkable transformation in such a short space of time. The rough-and-tumble legislative politics described in this chapter should not be unexpected with parliaments emerging so quickly from a minimalist status. New, awesome responsibilities are bound to bring institutional uncertainties, unstable rules and procedures, unsettled roles, and an unclear sense of legitimacy.

In view of all this, legislative institutionalization and the cementing of political pluralism will depend on mass and elite perceptions that republican governments, including their legislatures, will act effectively in dealing with the complex relationship between the individual and the state. The course of political pluralism will unfold in the "value-rich environment of entwined, supporting sociolegal networks encompassing concepts of property, risk, liability, service, quality control and even bankruptcy."[16] Centralized power in the Soviet state, including a federal legislature, is gone. But there is no agreement about functioning alternatives. If political pluralism is to be further advanced, a new consensus will need to be forged from the bottom up through elections and legislative delegation, not by executive *diktat* or abstract notions of a center whose practical meaning has ceased to exist.

NOTES

1. The author is grateful to Sarah Tarrow of the Social Science Research Council, New York, for her assistance in preparing this paper.

2. For further discussion of measures of legislative institutionalism see Robert T. Huber, "Soviet Defense and Foreign Policy and the Supreme Soviet," in Robert T. Huber and Donald R. Kelley, eds., *Perestroika-Era Politics: The New Soviet Legislature and Gorbachev's Political Reforms* (Armonk, N.Y.: M. E. Sharpe, 1991), p. 206.

3. For an excellent analysis of the Supreme Soviet debate about and influence on the media law see Thomas F. Remington, "Parliamentary Government in the USSR," in Robert T. Huber and Donald R. Kelley, eds., *Perestroika-Era Politics,* pp. 186-94.

4. For more on the evolution and operation of the Soviet regulatory process within the ministerial bureaucracy see Eugene Huskey, "Legislative-Executive Relations," in Robert T. Huber and Donald R. Kelley, eds., *Perestroika-Era Politics,* pp. 160-66.

5. For further discussion, see Remington, "Parliamentary Government," pp. 186-194, and Huber, "Soviet Defense," pp. 207-16.

6. Despite the fact that a working group, led by Deputy Mikhail Fedorov, whose members were drawn from three legislative committees—Legislation, Legality, and Law and Order, *Glasnost'* and Citizens Rights and Appeals, and International Affairs—prepared a draft acceptable to the Supreme Soviet, Luk'yanov, influenced by conservatives in the communist party and the executive bureaucracy, persuaded the Presidium to appoint a new special

commission to dissolve the Fedorov working group (see Remington, "Parliamentary Government," pp. 186-193).

7. Lopatin's group on military reform was forced to reconstitute itself as a working group attached to the Committee on Science, Public Education and Culture after Luk'yanov had dissolved the group within the Committee on Defense and State and State Security (Huber, "Soviet Defense," pp. 216-19).

8. Further information on legislative "perks" and Gorbachev's use of them to advance his policy agenda is to be found in Huskey, "Legislative-Executive Relations," pp. 165-166.

9. United States, House Committee on Armed Services, 101st Congress, 2nd Session, Mark Lowenthal, *The New Soviet Legislature: Committee on Defense and State Security*, Congressional Research Service, Library of Congress (Washington, D.C.: Government Printing Office, 1990), p. 12.

10. Sergei Chugaev, "Ruslan Khasbulatov Puts the Government and the Press on the Right Track," *Izvestia*, January 22, 1992.

11. See for example Otto Latsis, "The Congress as a Source of Danger," *Izvestia*, April 14, 1992, pp. 1-2; also see "Khasbulatov Report on Constitution," *Foreign Broadcast Information Service*, April 21, 1992, pp. 27-33.

12. Valeri Kucher, "On the Knife Edge of Reform," *Rossiiskie vesti*, p. 1.

13. V. Isakov, "The Kind of Opposition That is Needed," *Pravda*, January 29, 1992, pp. 1-2.

14. See Michael J. Mezey, *Comparative Legislatures* (Durham, N.C.: Duke University Press, 1979), pp. 6-44.

15. *Ibid.*, pp. 280-81.

16. Robert Sharlet, "Constitutional Reform, " in Robert T. Huber and Donald R. Kelley, eds., *Perestroika-Era Politics*, p. 22.

—

Civil Authority and the Security Organs

J. Michael Waller

INTRODUCTION

Six years of *perestroika* failed to provide a legal mandate for, or civilian control of, the security organs of the Soviet Union. The first six months following the USSR's collapse left little room for optimism that true reform would come soon. Throughout that period, however, intensive efforts were made to project the illusion that the state security bodies, the Interior Ministry, and the military were under direct democratic control of a partially elected parliament. The Committee for State Security (KGB) and its successor bodies, and to a lesser extent the Ministry of Internal Affairs, attempted to mask their far-reaching powers by unprecedented public relations campaigns, selective and fragmentary opening of archives, live interviews with top security officers, and public interaction with the citizenry.

From the time he entered office as Communist Party General Secretary in March 1985 until his brief overthrow in August 1991, Mikhail Gorbachev made no substantive attempt to bring *perestroika* to the security organs. The changes that did take place served only to make the organs more efficient in serving the party and the central government. KGB Analytical Directorate Chief Vladimir Rubanov observed shortly after the August putsch that since Gorbachev had taken power, "essentially nothing was done to restructure the organs of law enforcement and repression. Despite the semblance of democratic changes, the strong-arm, punitive approach has survived in all spheres."[1]

The collapse of the Soviet Union which followed the putsch made possible a turning point away from a society dominated by a secret police. A window of opportunity was opened for democratic forces to bring the security organs under civil control. Yet the greatest opportunities that arose in the autumn of 1991 were squandered. Democratic reformers were divided and indecisive. Little existed in Russian tradition to build a true law-governed state in which the branches of government check one another to safeguard against abuse of power. Precious time was lost—time that gave the Chekists the ability to regroup and reassert their power.

THE FICTION OF CIVIL CONTROL BEFORE THE PUTSCH

The security organs, especially the KGB, took pains to create an image that they were under the strict control of parliament and operated legally, consistent with Gorbachev's theme of a "law-governed state." The active measures campaign was designed for both domestic and foreign audiences. KGB Chairman Vladimir Kryuchkov described to a western newspaper the constraints under which he supposedly worked in mid-1989:

> Today the principal control is exercised by the highest organs of state power: the Congress of People's Deputies and the Supreme Soviet of the USSR, both directly and through the Committee on Questions of Defense and State Security, the Constitutional Control Committee, . . . the USSR Council of Ministers. Control functions are also carried out by the Procurator's Office, in the realm of its functions, by the Ministry of Finance and other departments. Control of the state security organs, at least in the last two decades, developed in many directions: financial activity is controlled rigorously by the Ministry of Finance, the Council of Ministers monitors us in individual questions, organizes commissions and summons us to meetings. There is a very strict party control . . . I do not think there is any state institution as strict as the KGB towards its employees. I will tell you that at one of the first meetings of the committee of the Supreme Soviet we very soon took up the problem of control.[2]

First Deputy Chairman Viktor Grushko gave a similar account for domestic consumption. He said that the KGB was:

> Subordinate only to the Congress of People's Deputies, the president, the Supreme Soviet, and the Council of Ministers of the USSR. We continuously send information to these organs on all questions that fall within the jurisdiction of the KGB, and we report regularly to the USSR Supreme Soviet Committee on Defense and State Security Organs.[3]

Formed ostensibly to assume the party's oversight of the KGB and to draft laws governing the military and security organs,[4] the Defense and National Security Committee in practice performed no oversight functions. Its members tried but were unable to gain access to the most basic information, even in nonsecret areas such as the Border Troops.[5] Nor was the committee able to inspect or question the KGB's budget.[6] The same was true of the military budget.[7]

Not that the committee tried seriously to challenge the center. Prior to the putsch, the CPSU Central Committee ensured control over all Supreme Soviet committee chairmanships, effectively denying important posts to opponents. The system of committee appointments was run by the top leadership, with no input from the parliamentary rank and file. Supreme Soviet Chairman Anatoli Luk'yanov, in consultation with party technocrats and Central Committee leaders who chaired the parliament's two chambers, formally chose each committee chairman and, after the fact, presented a single candidate for approval by the full Supreme Soviet membership without prior screening. The complicated and secretive process of selection of committee members was unclear, even to people's deputies themselves.[8] Of the oversight committee's 43 members prior to the putsch, according to Mikhail Tsypkin, 32 were "defense ministry executives, military officers, party functionaries, and government officials, including three high-ranking KGB officers."[9] There would be no challenge to the center. In short, the USSR parliamentary oversight committee had no oversight capacity at all.

The 1991 Law on State Security Organs

Nevertheless, the KGB and the parliament continued the charade of civil control over the security organs as part of the "law-governed state" game. With Gorbachev's approval, the KGB drew up a "Draft Law on State Security Organs" to be enacted by both houses of parliament. Though ready for submission to the Congress of People's Deputies on December 3, 1990, the draft law was not actually presented until February 28, 1991. This lag coincided with Gorbachev's removal of reformist MVD Minister Vadim Bakatin and the subsequent decrees that led to the crackdowns in the Baltic states and the Caucasus.

According to *Moscow News,* the law was rammed through the Congress of People's Deputies without being subject to committee review, leaving lawmakers little chance to study or debate the document. Many deputies expressed dissatisfaction with the manner in which the law was presented and voting took place. *Moscow News* commented, "the legislators who voted 'for' did not fully understand the nature of the vote since the draft circulated among them, as announced in the conference hall, did not contain the latest changes and addenda, i.e., it was simply incomplete."[10]

Reformist deputies were dismayed to learn that, unknown to them when they had voted, the law contained a series of secret amendments granting the KGB extraordinary powers. The amendments had been ruled unconstitutional by the USSR Constitutional Oversight Committee the previous November, even before the draft law was completed.[11] The law permitted the KGB to continue operating as it always had and left the state security structure intact. It granted the KGB secret powers through 1992, including: total control over files; the ability to continue widespread use of secret informants without allowing the accused to face his accuser; and warrantless searches, telephone taps, and mail interception. It made no provision for effective parliamentary oversight.[12] Reformist people's deputies who drew up an alternative civil control law were denounced by the KGB and by USSR Supreme Soviet Chairman Anatoli Luk'yanov as "subversive."[13]

The Security Organs Were Accountable to No One

Not even the Soviet leader himself had sufficient checks against the security organs. Following the 26th Party Congress in July 1990, at which KGB Chairman Kryuchkov made a militant speech in favor of communist orthodoxy, Gorbachev visibly acquiesced time and again to the state security and other repressive organs.

As Gorbachev's reformist advisers fell away or were removed in 1990, they were replaced by more hardline communists, many of whom either worked for or were dependent on Kryuchkov and the KGB. Major General Oleg Kalugin, a former top KGB counterintelligence officer who had been cashiered months before for criticizing the politicization of the intelligence services, publicly warned at the time of the Party Congress that the Presidential Council included "KGB people, not identified as such but KGB all the same, not KGB officers but people who have cooperated with the KGB their entire careers, who grew up with the KGB and are dependent on the KGB." He added, "Gorbachev may not know who they are . . . he probably does not."[14]

The KGB also regularly disinformed Gorbachev, causing him to make decisions he would not otherwise have made, according to some of his apologists in the state security committee.[15] According to these Gorbachev supporters, the heavily centralized analysis and dissemination process gave Kryuchkov a near monopoly on the information Gorbachev received.

Compounding the matter was the KGB's domination of counterintelligence and of internal state security. While the KGB customarily monitored few members of the nation's *nomenklatura,* it apparently wiretapped the conversations of those its leaders deemed were damaging to the communist party, including the general secretary himself. News emerged after the putsch that Gorbachev thought that his phones had been tapped on Kryuchkov's orders. The KGB revealed, after a new State Commission to Investigate the Activities of the Security Organs learned of the activity, that it had tapped conversations of parliament members and state and public figures.[16]

Gorbachev's Rule by Decree Gave Security Forces Free Rein

With no checks and balances against their activities, the leaders of the security organs drafted decrees for Gorbachev to sign that effectively caused him to turn his back on his old colleagues and to cast his lot with Kryuchkov. By the time he fired his moderate Interior Minister, Vadim Bakatin, on December 3, 1990, and replaced him with hard-core Latvian KGB Chief Boris Pugo, it became clear that Gorbachev had indeed allowed himself to become co-opted by the security organs. Thereafter, Gorbachev meekly followed the lead of the security troika of KGB Chairman Kryuchkov, Interior Minister Pugo, and Defense Minister Dmitri Yazov.

Kryuchkov made an unscheduled, live television appearance on December 11, pledging in the name of the president to smash the "anticommunist tide" sweeping the Soviet Union.[17] Gorbachev made no attempt to distance himself from Kryuchkov's remarks. Foreign Minister Eduard Shevardnadze's dramatic resignation speech, in which he warned of impending dictatorship, should have prepared the world for what was to follow. For the next six months, Gorbachev responded with shameless obedience to the security troika's every whim.

With the KGB-authored Draft Law on State Security Organs withheld from parliament, the security forces operated by decree. Gorbachev agreed to naming Army General Boris Gromov, a former commander of Soviet occupation forces in Afghanistan, as Pugo's first deputy in the MVD in charge of internal troops. With the appointments of Pugo and Gromov, Gorbachev helped turn the country's nominal law-enforcement ministry back into a repressive, political police apparatus. Within days of assuming his post in the MVD, Gromov oversaw the secret and apparently illegal transfer of three crack army divisions into the MVD Internal Troops.[18]

By January 1991, the army joined MVD and KGB troops in repressing not a foreign foe, but a domestic enemy. During a public relations campaign, Kryuchkov commented on how the security services were being run:

> We have prepared decrees—draft decrees of the president—these follow the line of the Procuracy, MVD, KGB; they have been coordinated with the services of the Ministry of Justice and we hope that these decrees will be issued in the very near future. Indeed, if there are no decrees, then we shall not have the necessary legal steps to enable us to act more boldly.[19]

In Vilnius, army and KGB units attacked the television tower, killing 14; in Riga, MVD forces stormed the Latvian Interior Ministry building and killed five. Over the next six months, MVD OMON commando units ("Black Berets") continued to terrorize the three Baltic states by means of attacks on customs posts and other soft targets. There was no civil control over these actions. The attacks—including beatings, robberies, and execution-style murders—continued despite a ruling by the USSR Procurator that they were illegal.[20]

While Gorbachev arguably was ultimately responsible for these attacks, it became clear that the security forces were beyond his control when the attacks were timed to embarrass him politically. The following incidents which occurred in 1991 are illustrative:

- June 4: During Gorbachev's historic visit to Sweden, just prior to his trip to Norway to deliver his Nobel Peace Prize acceptance speech, army units moved threateningly around Lithuania while the USSR Procurator General issued an inflammatory report absolving the military from any wrongdoing during the January repressions in Vilnius.[21]
- June 27: On the eve of the London Group of Seven summit, at which Gorbachev was to have been a special guest, the OMON raided the Vilnius telephone exchange and claimed to have found a cache of weapons and explosives. In the process, they briefly cut Lithuania's communication with the outside world. A frustrated Gorbachev disclaimed responsibility, marking the first time he publicly criticized the OMON attacks.[22]
- Late July: The night before President Bush's appearance in Kiev during the July 1991 summit, unidentified gunmen burst into a Lithuanian customs post near the Belorussian border, rounded up the eight officers inside, and shot each of them, execution-style, in the back of the head. One officer survived. Again, Gorbachev showed impotence. Although he pledged a full investigation, Lithuanian officials said that

the central authorities would not cooperate. The culprits were identified as belonging to the military and the KGB, according to members of the military reform group *Shchit* (Shield).[23]

- July 30: During President Bush's visit to Kiev, KGB personnel flown in from Moscow harassed, manhandled, and assaulted members of his personal entourage, including White House spokesman Marlin Fitzwater, according to administration sources.[24]

REFORM OF THE SECURITY ORGANS AFTER THE AUGUST 1991 PUTSCH

The failed putsch of August 19, 1991, unleashed several forces which brought about the rapid reorganization—but not the undoing—of the security organs. Quickly filling the power vacuum was Russian Federation President Boris Yel'tsin, the former Politburo member who had renounced the communist party and included in his circle many of Gorbachev's former reformist allies. With Gorbachev temporarily incommunicado, Yel'tsin issued sweeping decrees in the name of the Russian Federation, including acts bringing USSR KGB and MVD personnel on Russian soil under his control. Upon Gorbachev's rapid return, decrees were issued by both leaders, with varying degrees of cooperation, which began the dismemberment of the KGB. The decrees illustrate the extraordinary powers the presidencies of the union and the Russian Federation enjoyed, and mark the first time a democratically elected leader—Yel'tsin—exercised any authority over the security organs.

All members of the KGB Collegium resigned or were dismissed, and the body was abolished.[25] President Yel'tsin brought the Eighth Directorate, responsible for codes and ciphers, under direct RSFSR control, an action which was followed by a move by Gorbachev that shifted the directorate and all its resources and personnel back to the union under a new USSR State Committee for Special Communications.[26] Gorbachev decreed that the Ninth Directorate of guards would become an independent department under direct presidential control.[27]

The KGB's crack antiterrorist Alpha Group, which saw action in Vilnius the previous January and was to have led the attack on the Russian Supreme Soviet building during the coup, was placed under direct USSR presidential control as an independent guard force.[28] Three divisions and a brigade of KGB Special Troops were transferred to the army.[29] It is important to note that all these actions were by decree in a crisis environment, and the elected civilian authorities, i.e., those in the Supreme Soviet, played no role whatsoever. However, both Gorbachev and Yel'tsin addressed and conferred with the union and Russian parliaments frequently, and received enthusiastic support for their actions. It was an emergency; there was no time for parliamentary meddling.

To complicate matters further, the official status of the parliaments themselves was open to question. Numerous delegates had been elected from communist party mass organizations whose activities were suspended or that were abolished altogether following the putsch. The 2,250-member Congress of People's Deputies dissolved itself, and the USSR Supreme Soviet was in a shambles, while committee memberships changed with no one in control. The whole atmosphere was one of chaos; yet most parliamentary votes were close to unanimous in support of the reforms. For the first time ever, the elected representatives of the people had been asked for, and had given, their consent on substantive matters related to state security issues.

Further dismemberment of the KGB, involving its Border Guard Troops—which vastly exceed the number of other armed KGB elements—and the transfer of large sub-bureaucracies to other state entities (or their establishment as independent services of their own), would have taken longer than these initial reorganizations. Moreover, one would have expected that they would have involved the active advice and consent of the parliament. Professionals inside the intelligence services harshly criticized the "spur-of-the-moment" decision to transfer responsibility for ciphers and communications from the KGB, an action which reportedly damaged operational work abroad.[30] It could be expected that subsequent reorganizations would be well-planned. Gorbachev, Yel'tsin, and KGB professionals seemed eager to press forward with reorganization as rapidly but prudently as possible.

By late October, what remained of the KGB was split into three separate services. The Border Troops Directorate became the Committee for Protection of the USSR State Borders. The First Chief Directorate (the foreign intelligence bureaucracy) became the Central Intelligence Service (*Tsentralnaya Sluzhba Razvedki, TsSR*). The KGB's counterintelligence and internal security bodies were spun into a central Inter-Republican Security Service (*Mezhrespublikanskaya Sluzhba Besopasnosti,* MSB), headed by the Committee for State Security's final chairman, Vadim Bakatin.[31] In most republics, the USSR KGB organs had been brought under the control of the republican governments, often by unilateral local decrees or laws. Rather than challenge these moves, the center accommodated them. The new MSB reflected this accommodation, officially having the function of coordinating operations between each republic and the center. With the collapse of the USSR in December, the MSB lost its utility and, together with the USSR KGB Second Chief Directorate, was merged into the small but growing

Russian KGB, called the Federal Security Agency (*Agentstvo Federal' noi Bezopasnosti*, AFB).

Embryonic Oversight Provisions

The breakup of the KGB, though accomplished by decree, was designed in part by what appears to be an embryonic democratic civilian intelligence oversight body. Created by President Yel'tsin in the wake of the putsch, the State Commission to Investigate the Activities of the State Security Organs was given three tasks: to investigate independently the role of the organs in preparing and executing the coup; to propose a thorough restructuring of the security and intelligence organs; and to draw up a new law on state security, new state regulations for the USSR and RSFSR, and amendments to the union and Russian constitutions.[32]

The State Commission was not a parliamentary body. Its moderately reformist chairman, Sergei Stepashin, was a career MVD officer. Members included high officials from the union and RSFSR KGBs. Although not a rubber-stamp body, neither was it an aggressive challenge to the state security organs. It remained committed to a strong state security system, but saw as its objective the creation of a security regime truly subordinate to democratic civilian leaders. At least, the commission appeared to be headed in that direction before the USSR's disintegration.

The manner of Bakatin's appointment as KGB chairman also marked a distinct break with the past. Several versions of his selection circulate, but Bakatin has said that he was summoned without prior consultation to a meeting with the "nine presidents": Gorbachev, Yel'tsin, and the presidents of seven non-Russian republics that had not yet seceded from the USSR. They jointly told him that they wanted him to head the KGB. He responded, "You are sending me to the department which I have said on more than one occasion should be eliminated. So it turns out that I have come to destroy the Committee for State Security."[33]

Bakatin's dramatic story shows how severely the center's power of appointment had eroded. It was perhaps as democratic a selection as possible, considering the emergency. Yet when given the opportunity, the USSR Supreme Soviet did not seriously question Bakatin's appointment, and confirmed him with virtually no scrutiny. His "confirmation hearing" consisted of a 22-minute exchange with the deputies, who voted 366 to 9, with 12 abstentions, in support of his appointment.[34] This stands in marked contrast to the ordeal of his American counterpart Robert Gates, whose first appointment as CIA director in 1987 was withdrawn because of unsubstantiated and subsequently disproven allegations related to his possible role in the Iran-Contra affair, while hearings on his second appointment in 1991 dragged on for months.

Yet there were serious questions about Bakatin that were neither asked nor answered. Did he resign from the communist party, and if not, why not? Why, when he was Interior Minister, did he follow Politburo orders to dispatch MVD troops to smash protests and commit atrocities against unarmed demonstrators in Tblisi and elsewhere? Finally, a question that has become a staple in the American hearing process: what did he know, and when did he know it?

Nevertheless, it appears that Bakatin made good-faith efforts to dismantle the KGB and make a serious break with the past, going as far as asking U.S. Secretary of State James A. Baker for CIA help in writing legislation to create a functioning security and intelligence charter and oversight laws.[35]

Inexperienced Parliament

Among reformist members of the Soviet and Russian parliaments, the author found the desire, but not the knowledge or self-confidence, to challenge the center. With no democratic tradition or practical experience with the separation of powers—and marginalized within a parliamentary system that is strongly controlled from the top by the old guard Khasbulatov faction—reformist Russian lawmakers lack both the legislative machinery and the know-how to be an effective force. The concept of power exercised from below by the people through their elected representatives is still too new to be effective in practice. The power of the purse is an elusive concept. Initiative is scarce. "Loyal opposition" is a term yet to be appreciated, authoritarian traditions remain strong, and consequently so does the security apparatus.

Even among politicians with a thorough understanding of the principles, there is often a lack of knowledge of what to do. How should they proceed? Many have openly sought the assistance of American experts. Some have taken the initiative and gone directly to the FBI and the CIA for advice.[36] Others, lacking even the questions to ask, request American political and legal experts from private foundations, universities, and the U.S. Congress to provide them with these questions. In this respect, as parliament-to-Congress ties are strengthened with the help of private American organizations, one can be somewhat optimistic about the long-term prospect.

CONTINUING PROBLEM AREAS IN POST-SOVIET RUSSIA

Parliamentary Checks and Balances Remain Elusive

Enormous problems have yet to be resolved in the post-Soviet republics. The parliament of Russia, led by the old guard communists, has not proven a viable check and balance to presidential power. President Yel'tsin himself got off to a poor start during the final Soviet collapse in December 1991. Rather than decentralize the security forces further, he attempted to centralize them to a degree not seen since the Stalin era, apparently believing that his political survival depended on a strong power base of the state security apparatus under the control of MVD professionals. On December 19, he signed a decree merging the Federal Security Agency (formerly the KGB Second Chief Directorate) with the Ministry of Internal Affairs into a behemoth called the Ministry of Security and Internal Affairs (*Ministerstvo Bezopasnosti i Vnutrennikh Del,* MBVD). Parliament was alarmed; reformers saw it as a reincarnation of Stalin's NKVD, while hardliners objected to the fact that it was *Yel'tsin's* NKVD. An *Izvestia* commentator reflected the popular mood, noting, "It seems to me that they are today trying to hide the old KGB from the eyes of the public."[37] The legislature voted almost unanimously to ask the president to repeal the decree. However, Yel'tsin held his ground, despite the counsel of his democratic allies and of professional *Chekists,* the last being reportedly loath to have to report to an MVD man, MBVD Minister Viktor Barannikov.[38]

Bright Ray of Hope: The Constitutional Court

Judicial restraint may be emerging in Russia by way of the new Constitutional Court, although, overall, Russia's judicial system is hardly different from the old Soviet one. In its first decision, the court ruled less than a month after the MBVD was created that it was an illegal organization. Instead of accepting the court decision, Yel'tsin's legal deputy Sergei Shakhrai initially criticized the finding as being "not a decision of law, but a political decision."[39] Nevertheless, President Yel'tsin respected the court's decision and withdrew his decree on January 18, 1992. It was a major development, for the court was regarded even by reformers as little more than a paper organization, and no one knew if its decisions would be respected. A precedent was thus set for judicial balance against executive abuse of power and legislative inaction.

Russia's Internal Security System: Re-Formed, but Not Reformed

Despite a number of reshufflings, the pervasive internal security system in Russia has not been dissolved. Had a reformer such as Bakatin, armed with presidential directives to carry out large-scale personnel changes, been named to lead the internal security service, the Russian government would have provided a reassurance that progress would soon be underway. However, no such signal was given. Although the government agreed with the letter of the Constitutional Court's decision that state security and the MVD must be split, it did not abide by the intent. In creating a new Ministry of Security (*Ministerstvo Bezopasnosti*, MB) which replaced the USSR KGB Second Chief Directorate and the Russian Federal Security Agency, Yel'tsin authorized the transfer of top MVD officers to direct internal operations in the Lubyanka, in effect merging the two services at the top under the direction of Barannikov, who had masterminded the December KGB-MVD merger decree that Yel'tsin had signed.

Communists Hold Top Posts in Security Organs

A related problem is the dearth of democrats in top security posts. After the Soviet breakup, Bakatin was denied a position in the Russian services and dismissed in January 1992. "Old guard" officers took his place, with Barannikov as Security Minister and KGB Lieutenant General Anatoli Oleinikov as First Deputy Minister. Yel'tsin retained foreign intelligence chief Yevgeni Primakov, a lifelong communist and 35-year KGB associate, to head this service, renamed *Sluzhba Vneshnei Razvedki* (SVR).[40] Primakov is a Brezhnev holdover who was one of the prime movers in Moscow's campaign of support for international terrorism in the 1970s and 1980s.[41] According to former CPSU International Department officer Yevgeni Novikov, Primakov merged this department with foreign intelligence.[42] Similarly, the MVD, now staffed by Barannikov's former deputies, has not undergone any significant structural changes.

Tainted Personnel Remain Throughout the Security Services

The officers and personnel who ordered, collaborated, and carried out mass violations of human rights, including murder, are apparently to go unpunished, unless they were among the few who played a role in the putsch.[43] The expected housecleaning in the KGB and MVD never took place. Entire units whose only function is repression—such as the MVD OMON troops—remain intact. Even the putschists, with the exception of Kryuchkov and a few co-conspirators, received better treatment from Gorbachev than did dissident KGB Major General Oleg Kalugin. That distinguished intelligence officer was stripped of his rank, decorations, and pension by presidential decree in March 1990 for having criticized the KGB's subservience to the party, and was not rehabilitated until after the putsch, when he became an adviser to Bakatin. Other critics of Kryuchkov received similar treatment. In contrast, some top KGB leaders involved in the August 1991 coup were fired, but kept their rank and pensions, while several others were merely retired from the service.[44] A much larger number of security personnel guilty of abuses or corruption remain in their positions.

The "hundreds or thousands" of KGB dismissals that were promised following the putsch never occurred.[45] As a leading RSFSR parliamentary investigator observed early in a probe, the top coup plotters "are not even the tip of the iceberg. The conspiracy has roots. They lie in the structures of the party and state apparatus of the very highest rank. They go down both into the army and into the KGB and MVD structures. Very specific categories of troops displayed the greatest activeness."[46]

Security Personnel Lack a Legal Mindset

A major problem to be surmounted is the mentality of the people who staff the security organs. Virtually none of these officials has demonstrated respect for the rule of law. The appointment in September 1991 of a young, legal-minded, democratic, anticommunist geophysicist-turned-politician, Yevgeni Savost'yanov, as Moscow KGB chief generated heated controversy within the security apparatus.[47] Even USSR KGB Chairman Bakatin complained of a pervasive absence of legal consciousness among KGB personnel, adding, "So far I am dissatisfied. I thought that the level was considerably higher here."[48] The training of security and intelligence officers continues as if it were in a time warp. The statue of the founder of the secret police, Felix Dzerzhinsky, may be gone from its pedestal in Lubyanka Square, but his image is enshrined inside. The training center is still adorned with the symbols of communist power: "The very name of this worthy educational institution perpetuates Dzerzhinsky's name, there are still busts of Lenin on its landings and communist emblems on display." According to Ponomarev, "The system of professional education and retraining for top [Ministry of Security] cadres has remained totally unchanged ... coursework is conducted on the basis of manuals dating from the 1970s and 1980s."[49]

The sole shining star in the entire MVD leadership is Arkadi Murashev, a 34-year-old physicist who was executive secretary of the Interregional

Group of Deputies in the USSR Supreme Soviet.[50] Like his radical colleague Savast'yanov in state security, Murashev was appointed by former Moscow Mayor Gavriil Popov after the putsch. Aside from Murashev, Savast'yanov, and a handful of others, the security organs remain a fraternity of communists politically distant from the civil authorities.

Apparatchiki Who Tried to Subvert Russian Independence Remain in Power

Certain civil authorities themselves are part of the problem. Russian government personnel with dubious motivations worked to undermine the Russian Federation's security to the center's advantage following the coup attempt. The USSR state communications structure apparently placed RSFSR communications, including codes, under union control. This measure was reportedly engineered by Yel'tsin's *apparatchiki,* almost all of whom were former communists. According to *Argumenty i fakty,* these officials acted with "suspicious thoroughness and diligence" in pushing the draft legislation. The newspaper commented, "Judging by its contents, it envisages, among other things, the Union agency's control over information of state significance to Russia. According to the draft, all code keys and other elements of protecting Russia's state secrets are to stay in the same department rather than in its Russian equivalent."[51] Although Russia soon absorbed the USSR services, this class of *apparatchiki* remained.

Archives Can Still be Used for Blackmail

Important accomplishments have been made as far as the transfer of archives to the control of republican governments is concerned. While the process remains uncompleted, a mechanism seems to have been developed which would give each republic control of pertinent KGB archives, while protecting the identities of KGB personnel and informants. Bakatin and his successors were adamant that the identities never be made public and that the archives never be destroyed.[52] Bakatin stated that to release the identities of KGB collaborators and informants would be to tear society apart by unleashing acts of revenge. It is noteworthy that former dissident Vladimir Bukovsky wholeheartedly supported Bakatin's policy.[53]

While the argument has merit, such a policy preserves the ability of the security organs to blackmail everyone who, for whatever reason, had collaborated with the KGB in the past, even if they originally had been blackmailed into cooperating. Furthermore, the policy protects the identities of politicians and other civic leaders who were KGB collaborators. The security organs thus will retain the ability to blackmail future political and civic leaders, thereby potentially subverting the democratic process for decades to come. By keeping control of the operational archives, Russia also has exploitable information on current and future leaders of the 14 other former Soviet republics, as well as on citizens of the former Warsaw Pact countries.

The Fate of Most Repressive Organs Remains Uncertain

Ominously, the fate of the former Fifth or "Ideological" Directorate that repressed opponents of the communist party is unclear. Supposedly, it had been abolished under Kryuchkov, but in reality had been merely renamed the Directorate for the Defense of the Constitutional System.[54] Hopes that the dreaded unit would be abolished following the putsch were short-lived. KGB Chairman Bakatin hesitated when given the opportunity to disclose the fate of the Fifth Directorate at an August 29, 1991, news conference.[55] However, it was revealed nearly a month later that the Fifth Directorate still existed, under the name "Directorate Z."[56] A top KGB official announced that the directorate was abolished in mid-October 1991.[57] Reliable reports stated that the unit was dissolved by early 1992. However, Fifth Directorate personnel remained on the payroll.[58] There were persistent indications that the Fifth Directorate networks were still operational. A Russian television newscast reported in February 1992, "The political council of the coalition of Moscow's democratic forces has demanded that KGB agents be immediately recalled from political parties and movements. Representatives of the former KGB confirmed recently that KGB agents have currently merely mothballed their activity."[59]

Unchecked, Aggressive Espionage Abroad Continues

Russian espionage operations against the industrialized democracies continue almost unabated. In April 1992, Russia initiated a Commonwealth of Independent States (CIS) intelligence treaty, whereby eight CIS members signed a cooperation agreement pledging to coordinate foreign intelligence operations and not to spy on one another.[60] In early and mid-1992, several Western democracies recognized Moscow's continued espionage activities, but were lenient in dealing with them while continuing to provide large amounts of aid to Russia and the CIS. In late March, the United States instructed a military intelligence (GRU) officer operating out of the Russian Embassy in Washington to leave the country discreetly. The expulsion was kept secret so as not to endanger the multibillion-dollar G-7 aid package whose provisions were just being announced, and to avoid embarrassing President Yel'tsin prior to a difficult Congress of People's Deputies session.[61]

This issue, however, hampered U.S.-Russian security cooperation in countering terrorism and organized crime, areas in which Moscow has requested assistance. Washington was reluctant to help, at least in the near term. FBI counterintelligence official Patrick Watson commented, "You can't expect to be invited to dinner if you want to steal the silverware."[62]

The United States was not the only country to deport Russian spies in early 1992. Belgium quickly—but publicly—followed, expelling four Russian agents involved in a large technology theft ring.[63] Soon afterward, the Dutch government acknowledged that earlier, in an unrelated case, it had ordered four Russians suspected of spying to leave. One was under cover as a trade attaché.[64] The others had posed as journalists, thus proving that Russian Foreign Intelligence Service Director Yevgeni Primakov failed to live up to his word that he would instruct espionage agents to stop using journalistic cover.

Denmark complained in May that Russian espionage operations against the country were continuing. Police Intelligence deputy commissioner Henning Thisen said, "Spies from Russia and the other states of the CIS are still operational in the country . . . involved in military and industrial spying."[65] In the same week, Finland expelled two Russian agents who had entered the country with forged British passports.[66]

These espionage activities were not rogue operations or bureaucratic inertia, but appear to be consistent with the policies of President Yel'tsin. According to sources connected to Russia's intelligence and security services, Yel'tsin did not give a political directive that espionage agencies call a halt to their work. Indeed, he seems to have directed the opposite. In early June 1992, the Russian journal *Postfactum* reported that President Yel'tsin was setting up a new secret service, separate from the SVR Foreign Intelligence Service that formerly had been the KGB First Chief Directorate. According to one Russian security source, this special agency, which reports directly to Yel'tsin, is to engage in economic espionage against other countries.[67] This decision was taken at a time when Russia seeks Western business and aid.

Civil Control over Former KGB Lacking

Virtually nothing of substance has changed since the KGB was formally dismembered in the autumn of 1991 into separate foreign intelligence, internal security, and other services. The parliamentary committee in charge of overseeing security and intelligence reforms, whose membership is dominated by current and former officers of the security services, has done little to promote meaningful reform. A special, non-co-opted parliamentary commission to probe KGB abuses was shut down early in 1992, when its revelations threw too much light on the apparatus. The commission's former chairman, Lev Ponomarev, notes: "The successor organization to the KGB is still able to undertake technical measures directed against its opponents, with virtually no risk that legal action will be taken against it."[68] Ponomarev observes, "No radical, significant changes whatever have occurred within the Ministry of Security," which is the old KGB Second Chief Directorate with a new name and expanded mission.

Neither President Yel'tsin nor the Russian parliament has yet offered much hope of reform. Indeed, the country's 1992 basic law on security, though full of language about individual rights, contains so many *caveats* that it grants the former KGB what Russian lawyer Sergei Zamoshkin calls "sweeping powers that are invasive of privacy and endanger personal freedoms." He wrote in *Moscow News,* "The law grants the same powers to agencies that combat crime, security services, border guards, the external intelligence service and the main security department. . . . The law provides for an entire arsenal of clandestine methods to be used on any of us."[69]

Could the result of the extensive security reorganization simply be the same old wine in new bottles? The KGB, while dismembered, was not dissolved. The *apparat* has been partitioned, but its bureaucracies have been preserved; its communist personnel remains largely in place—still very much a club of old colleagues. The new security organs are not being created from scratch, as in Czechoslovakia, but are being recast, in the words of one Muscovite critic, from the "same old KGB, endowed with totalitarian power."[70]

Parliamentary Oversight Co-opted by the Security *Apparat*

Just as the USSR Supreme Soviet Committee on Defense and Security was co-opted by the security and military apparatus, the same has happened to its Russian Federation counterpart. More reformist than its union predecessor, the Russian parliamentary Committee on Defense and Security nevertheless is structured and staffed to ensure that the system based in the

Lubyanka remains unscathed by parliamentary action. Its chairman, Sergei Stepashin, advocated radical reform of the KGB when Bakatin was chairman in late 1991, but after Barannikov was named security minister in January 1992, Stepashin's enthusiasm for comprehensive reform cooled.

Stepashin was originally elected to parliament as an active-duty MVD lieutenant colonel. Yel'tsin appointed him state security chief for St. Petersburg city and region in late 1991, with promotion to major general. However reformist Stepashin may be, he is torn inevitably by divided loyalties between his permanent position in the apparat and his part-time, nonpermanent job in parliament. Because much of his time is spent away from Moscow, Stepashin must leave day-to-day committee work to the deputy chairman, Boris Bol'shakov. A career KGB colonel, Bol'shakov is far from reformist, according to other people's deputies who were interviewed. The chairman of the committee's Subcommittee on Security, Nikolai Kuznetsov, is another career KGB officer; he is somewhat more reformist, however, than Bol'shakov.[71] In summary, the Russian parliamentary oversight committee leadership is comprised of state security officers who suffer from severe conflict of interest owing to their holding dual posts. The question arises: who is overseeing whom?

An answer may be gleaned from the actions of the Russian parliament speaker Ruslan Khasbulatov, who in early 1992 shut down a parliamentary investigative commission chaired by Lev Ponomarev. This Commission to Investigate the Causes and Circumstances of the *Coup d'Etat* of August 1991 carried out a mandate to probe the security apparatus. However, when Ponomarev and his colleagues began to uncover apparently illegal KGB operations abroad, foreign intelligence chief Yevgeni Primakov and others— including Orthodox Church Patriarch Aleksi II, reliably reported to have been a KGB agent—called on Khasbulatov to stop Ponomarev's work. The parliament leader permanently closed down the commission.[72]

Grounds for Optimism

Despite solid reasons for pessimism, there are nevertheless positive signs that, over the long term, reform will indeed be carried out. The process promises to be extended and painful. Information is in great demand. Although still under constraints, the media in Russia are comparatively free, and independent journalism flourishes. More and more information is being pried from the security *apparat* archives and from disgruntled or conscience-stricken security officers. The lure of hard currency elicits an increasing number of secrets and widens the cracks in the old KGB's armor. Foreign news and publishing firms, as well as academic institutes and intelligence services, are paying significant sums for information sometimes supplied selectively, but in other cases made available in quantity. The remains of the corrupt Soviet system are rotten to the core—and that core consists of the KGB. Compared with the benefits its members drew from corruption in the Soviet years, the security *apparat* now suffers from a worsened material situation. As a result, there is little that money cannot buy in Russia today.

More congenial factors also provide reason for hope. Growing person-to-person exchanges are providing knowledge, confidence, and support for reformers in Russian media, academia, and politics. Ties between Russian members of parliament and American members of Congress are growing in number and strength. Official governmental delegations and staff exchanges are increasing in substance and frequency. The introduction of electronic news databases and privately funded information exchange centers and the proliferation of fax machines, personal computers, photocopiers, video cameras, and other communication devices are increasingly frustrating any attempt at guarding secrecy. Scholarships provided by private foundations, universities, and governments are helping to train new cadres of young professional businessmen, journalists, administrators, and civil experts. These people will run Russia in the next decades. Their numbers may be few compared to the country's huge population. But that was also true of the Bolsheviks.

CONCLUSION

The system of decrees that governed the security *apparats* led by Kryuchkov and Pugo still governs the reformed security organs of post-Soviet Russia. A daunting challenge lies ahead for democrats in Russia and other republics striving to bring the security organs under true civil authority. The old KGB remains almost completely unimpaired; it has only been divided into more efficient components. The security organs continue to operate without legal mandate. They remain almost completely staffed by communists, since relatively few officials have been removed. The vast archives on informants remain intact, even if shared by republican governments, and are apparently safe from disclosure or destruction. In short, the informant networks are still potentially operational.

Democratic forces have an historic opportunity to consolidate their gains and begin dismantling the Soviet police state. Armed with a new sense of purpose, enhanced prestige, and the realization that people power really works, the federation and republican parliaments are in a position to exploit the humiliating political defeat of the KGB, MVD, and military and to take concrete steps to ensure that such abuses of power can never happen again. Yet their progress promises to be difficult. After a few short bursts of decisive decrees, the first steps taken by democratic forces have been tentative. The current parliamentary leadership is part of the problem, and is preventing a solution. The reformers are traveling uncharted territory. Transitions of the kind facing democrats in Moscow have been carried out successfully in a few small countries, although in larger nations like post-Nazi Germany the transitions occurred only under military occupation.

Remarkable, if still modest, progress has been made in the short time since real reforms began. Democrats have seen the potential power within their grasp and are unlikely to sacrifice it in the long term. Russian journalists and academics are staking their careers on unearthing the excesses of the past and present, and are drawing blueprints for future civil control. A wealth of expertise and goodwill is available in Europe and North America to assist the democratic reformers in bringing the security forces under strict parliamentary oversight. Formal and informal nongovernmental networks are flourishing. There may be setbacks, perhaps even a future putsch. But history is no longer on the side of the *Chekists*.

NOTES

1. *Izvestia,* September 18, 1991, FBIS-SOV-91-183, September 20, 1991, p. 16.
2. Kryuchkov, *L' Unità,* August 19, 1989, pp. 6-7, FBIS-SOV-89-201, October 19, 1989, p. 50.
3. *Argumenty i fakty,* No. 48, December 1990, pp. 6-7, FBIS-SOV-90-235, December 6, 1990, pp. 47-48.
4. *The Economist Foreign Report,* April 5, 1990, pp. 4-5.
5. *Ibid.*; author's interviews with members of the Defense and Security Committee, Moscow, December 1991.
6. Maj. Gen. Oleg Kalugin, in *Komsomol'skoye znamya* (Kiev), September 16, 1990, pp. 8-9, FBIS-SOV-90-193, October 4, 1990, p. 56.
7. Françoise Thom, "The Red Army: A New Role?" *Perspective* (Boston University Institute for the Study of Conflict, Ideology and Policy) vol. 1, no. 3, February 1991, p. 6; Jennifer Scheck Lee, *The Supreme Soviet Defense and Security Committee: Limited Oversight Capabilities* (Palo Alto, Calif.: Global Outlook, 1991).
8. See, for example, the confusion and questions from the floor to Supreme Soviet Council of Soviets Chairman Yevgeni Primakov during the election of chairmen of joint committees of the USSR Supreme Soviet, *Izvestia,* June 1, 1989,

pp. 2-3, *Current Digest of the Soviet Press*, Vol. XLI, No. 33, September 13, 1989, p. 20.

9. "Commentary by Mikhail Tsypkin," *RFE/RL Report on the USSR*, December 1989, p. 30.

10. *Moscow News* (English edition), no. 11, March 17-24, 1991, p. 6, FBIS-SOV-91-068-S, pp. 10-11.

11. Ernst Orlovsky, *Novoe vremya*, no. 23, June 1991, pp. 34-35, FBIS-SOV-91-115, June 14, 1991, pp. 25-27.

12. *Moscow News*, no. 11; and Orlovsky, *ibid.*

13. Author's interviews with four post-putsch members of the Committee on Defense and Security, Moscow, December 1991.

14. Oleg Kalugin, interview with Michael Parks, "Ex-Agent Leads Fight Against Powerful KGB," *Los Angeles Times*, July 23, 1990.

15. Kalugin, Central Television First Program Network (Moscow), 1800 GMT, September 14, 1991, FBIS-SOV-91-179, September 16, 1991, p. 27; KGB Analytical Directorate Chief Col. Vladimir Rubanov, *Komsomol'skaya pravda*, September 20, 1991, p. 2, FBIS-SOV-91-187, September 26, 1991, p. 23; and KGB Chairman Vadim Bakatin, Russian Television Network (Moscow), 2108 GMT, September 19, 1991, FBIS-SOV-91-184, September 23, 1991, p. 27.

16. Rubanov, *Komsomol'skaya pravda*, October 1, 1991, p. 1, FBIS-SOV-91-191, October 2, 1991, p. 35.

17. Speech on Soviet television, December 11, 1990, Official Kremlin International News Broadcast, Federal News Service, December 11, 1990.

18. Intelligence leak to Rowland Evans and Robert Novak, "Gorbachev's Iron Fist," *Washington Post*, January 4, 1991, p. A17.

19. Kryuchkov on live call-in television show (Moscow), *BBC Summary of World Broadcasts*, January 21, 1991.

20. USSR Procurator General Nikolai Trubin, "Vremya" television program, cited by TASS in English, June 1, 1991.

21. Russian Television Network (Moscow), 1700 GMT, June 4, 1991, FBIS-SOV-91-108, June 5, 1991; procuracy report, *Sovetskaya Rossiya*, June 4, 1991, p. 4, excerpted in *Current Digest of the Soviet Press* 43, no. 22, July 3, 1991, p. 11.

22. Associated Press, June 29, 1991.

23. *Nezavisimaya gazeta*, August 10, 1991, p. 2; *Soviet Press Digest*, August 10, 1991.

24. Paul Bedard, "KGB Abuses U.S. Officials," *Washington Times*, August 5, 1991.

25. Rubanov, in *Komsomol'skaya pravda*, September 20, 1991, p. 2, FBIS-SOV-91-187, September 26, 1991, p. 22.

26. *Komsomol'skaya pravda*, October 2, 1991, pp. 2-3, FBIS-SOV-91-193, October 4, 1991, p. 22; TASS international service in Russian, 1426 GMT, August 29, 1991, FBIS-SOV-91-169, August 30, 1991, pp. 53-54; Bakatin, All-Union Radio Mayak Network, Moscow, 1200 GMT, August 30, 1991, FBIS-SOV-91-170, September 3, 1991, p. 35.

27. TASS in English, 1703 GMT, September 4, 1991, FBIS-SOV-91-172, September 5, 1991, pp. 53-54. The new guards would serve the USSR and RSFSR presidents equally, according to KGB Chairman Bakatin, in All-Union Radio Mayak Network, 1200 GMT, August 30, 1991, FBIS-SOV-91-170, September 3, 1991, pp. 40-41.

28. *Komsomol'skaya pravda,* August 24, 1991, p. 1, FBIS-SOV-91-166, August 27, 1991, pp. 14-15.

29. *Moskovskie novosti,* no. 36, September 8, 1991, p. 6, FBIS-SOV-91-182, September 19, 1991, p. 22.

30. Former KGB First Chief Directorate Chairman Leonid Shebarshin, in *Komsomol'skaya pravda,* October 2, 1991, pp. 2-3, FBIS-SOV-91-193, October 4, 1991, p. 22.

31. Radio Free Europe/Radio Liberty *Daily Report,* no. 213, November 8, 1991, p. 1.

32. All-Union Radio Mayak Network coverage of commission's first news conference, Moscow, 1900 GMT, August 29, 1991, FBIS-SOV-91-170, September 3, 1991, p. 50.

33. Russian Television Network (Moscow), 2000 GMT, August 28, 1991, FBIS-SOV-91-168, August 29, 1991, p. 42.

34. FBIS editorial report on live coverage of extraordinary session of USSR Supreme Soviet, Moscow Central Television First Program Network, 1408 GMT, August 29, 1991, FBIS-SOV-91-169, August 30, 1991, p. 29.

35. George Lardner, Jr., and Gary Lee, "Russian Security Group Meets with U.S. Intelligence to Seek Cooperation," *Washington Post,* October 14, 1991, p. A4.

36. The delegation to Washington in October 1991 was led by Sergei Stepashin, chairman of the Russian parliamentary Committee on Defense and Security and of the USSR State Commission to Investigate the Activities of the Security Bodies. Lardner and Lee, "Russian Security Group Meets with U.S. Intelligence to Seek Cooperation." Stepashin was named by Yel'tsin to head the Russian state security apparatus in St. Petersburg in December 1991, while retaining his position in the Russian parliament.

37. Valeri Rudnev, "Viktor Barannikov, You Have to Possess Courage In Order to Preserve Democracy," *Izvestia,* December 31, 1991, BBC *Summary of World Broadcasts,* January 1, 1992.

38. Barannikov, a career *militsia* officer, was RSFSR MVD Minister, and briefly held the same position in the USSR following the putsch. KGB Major General Viktor Ivanenko, appointed leader of the RSFSR KGB by USSR KGB Chairman Vladimir Kryuchkov, and named by Yel'tsin as first chief of the Federal Security Agency (AFB), was one of those in opposition. Ivanenko was removed in January 1992 when the Ministry of Security was created in place of the AFB and Barannikov was named as his replacement.

39. *RFE/RL Daily Report,* no. 9, January 15, 1992, p. 1.

40. Yevgeniya Albats, "KGB-MSB-MBVD: Substantive Changes?" *Moscow News,* no. 2, January 13, 1992, p. 5.

41. J. Michael Waller, "New KGB Spymaster, Same Nasty Tricks," *The Wall Street Journal Europe,* October 10, 1991.

42. Radio Free Europe/Radio Liberty *Daily Report,* no. 211, November 6, 1991, p. 2, citing *The Wall Street Journal Europe,* November 5, 1991.

43. At least one exception has emerged to date: the arrest of the former Riga OMON commander, who was detained by Russian authorities in October at the request of the Latvian government.

44. Lt. Gen. Leonov, who headed the KGB Information Analysis Directorate, was reportedly retired on pension after the coup. As many as sixty KGB generals were dismissed, but far fewer were actually arrested, according to RSFSR Procurator Valentin Stepankov (Radio Free Europe/Radio Liberty *Daily Report,* no. 209, November 4, 1991, p. 3).

45. Bakatin had stated, "There will be quite a few more dismissals. We may be talking about hundreds or thousands across the country." (*Moskovskie novosti,* no. 36, September 8, 1991, p. 6; FBIS-SOV-91-182, September 19, 1991, pp. 22-23.)

46. Sergey Shakhrai, chairman of the RSFSR Parliamentary Committee on Legislation, *Rossiyskaya gazeta,* August 23, 1991, p. 1; FBIS-SOV-91-167, August 28, 1991, p. 44. In a strange twist, it was Shakhrai who, as a minister in Yel'tsin's government, had defended the president's decree to merge the former KGB with the MVD in an argument before the Constitutional Court in January 1992. Shakhrai resigned from the government in May 1992, protesting the resurgence of hard-line policies.

47. *Moskovskie novosti,* no. 38, September 22, 1991, p. 11; FBIS-SOV-91-197, October 10, 1991, p. 27.

48. Russian Television Network (Moscow), 2108 GMT, September 19, 1991; FBIS-SOV-91-184, September 23, 1991, p. 27.

49. L. A. Ponomarev, "Has Reform Hit Security Organs?" *Perspective* (Institute for the Study of Conflict, Ideology & Policy, Boston University), May-June 1992.

50. For a profile of Murashev, see Jonas Bernstein, "Offbeat Russian Heat," *Insight,* June 14, 1992, pp. 6-11, 26-27.

51. *Argumenty i fakty,* no. 39, October 1991, p. 1; FBIS-SOV-91-197, October 10, 1991, p. 28.

52. *Moskovskie novosti,* no. 36, September 8, 1991, p. 6; FBIS-SOV-91-182, September 19, 1991, p. 22.

53. Vladimir Bukovsky, on Central Television First Program Network (Moscow), 1846 GMT, September 9, 1991; FBIS-SOV-91-175, September 10, 1991, pp. 19-21.

54. Victor Yasmann, "KGB: The 'Patriot' Connection," *RFE/RL Soviet/East European Report* 8, no. 27, April 10, 1991, p. 2.

55. KGB Chairman Bakatin, in Russian Television Network, Moscow, 1731 GMT, August 29, 1991; FBIS-SOV-91-170, September 3, 1991, pp. 47-48.

56. Col. Vladimir Rubanov, Chief, KGB Analytical Directorate, *Komsomol'skaya pravda,* September 20, 1991, p. 2; FBIS-SOV-91-187, September 26, 1991, p. 23.

57. KGB First Deputy Chairman Anatoli Oleinikov, *Izvestia,* October 15, 1991, p. 2; FBIS-SOV-91-202, October 18, 1991, p. 22.

58. Yevgenia Albats, "KGB-MSB-MBVD: Substantive Changes?" *Moscow News*, no. 2, January 13, 1992, p. 5; People's Deputies Lev Ponomarev and Fr. Gleb Yakunin, statement at news conference sponsored by the Jamestown Foundation and the Ethics & Public Policy Center, Washington, D.C., March 20, 1992.

59. Russian Television Network, 2000 GMT, February 6, 1992; FBIS-SOV-92-026, February 7, 1992, p. 57.

60. "Agreement on Joint CIS Foreign Intelligence Signed," *RFE/RL Research Report* 1, no. 16, April 17, 1992, pp. 67-68. Armenia, Azerbaijan, and Ukraine declined to sign, according to ITAR-TASS.

61. Source not for attribution.

62. R. Patrick Watson, Deputy Assistant Director, FBI Foreign Counterintelligence Division, SecurTech '92 Conference, Arlington, Virginia, April 7, 1992.

63. The French broke up a related network at about the same time. Therry Oberle, "The French Spies Who Were Still Working for Moscow," *Le Figaro* (Paris), April 23, 1992, p. 10; FBIS-WEU-92-088, May 6, 1992, pp. 6-7.

64. Alexander Rahr, "Russia Continues Spying on the West," *RFE/RL Daily Report,* no. 80, April 27, 1992, p. 3.

65. "Soviet Spies Continue to Operate in Denmark," Agence France Presse, citing *Det Fri Aktuelt* (Copenhagen), May 26, 1992.

66. Arkady Prisyazhny, "Russian Citizens Travelling on Forged Documents Detained," ITAR-TASS, May 21, 1992; and "Russian Spies Used British Passports—Police," Reuter Library Report, May 22, 1992.

67. Alexander Rahr, "Commercial Espionage Service Created," *RFE/RL Daily Report,* no. 106, June 4, 1992, p. 2.

68. L. A. Ponomarev, "Has Reform Hit Security Organs?" *Perspective* (Institute for the Study of Conflict, Ideology and Policy, Boston University), May-June 1992.

69. Sergei Zamoshkin, "Special Services Get More Powers Than Is Good for Citizens," *Moscow News,* no. 22, May 27, 1992. The text of this law (No. 2646-1) was published in *Rossiiskaya gazeta,* May 6, 1992, p. 5; FBIS-SOV-92-088, May 6, 1992, pp. 34-38.

70. *Moskovskie novosti,* no. 38, September 22, 1991, p. 11, FBIS-SOV-91-197, October 10, 1991, p. 27.

71. Author's confidential interviews of Russian people's deputies.

72. Ponomarev and Yakunin, press conference, March 20, 1992.

Part II: Law and Society

—

Toward a Law-Abiding State?

Nina Belyaeva

Now that the country's economic disaster and the newly born political movements have utterly discredited the idea of socialism and, indeed, the very word itself, it may have been forgotten that, originally, the concept of the rule-of-law state was presented to the public as a means of strengthening the existing socialist framework.

At that time, the goals were proclaimed to be the expansion of the boundaries of social and spiritual life and the establishment of complete freedom of thought and self-expression, with the result that the values originally attributed to socialism would be manifested in real life. Advocating the creation of a rule-of-law state in April 1989, the General Secretary of the Communist Party of the Soviet Union, Mikhail Gorbachev, proclaimed the following ultimate aims of *perestroika* that were to be achieved using legal mechanisms: "We are creating a society that is open, democratic, and free, that has learned the lessons of the past, (a society) resting on Law and on citizens who are informed and responsible, on their initiative and entrepreneurial activity, on Soviet socialist patriotism and faithfulness to humanist socialism, the principal function of which is to elevate the condition of human beings."

In articles and speeches, Gorbachev made it clear that the rule-of-law state and law in general were viewed as a means rather than a goal. The law was used as an instrument of *perestroika* to achieve the political aim of rescuing the system by reshaping it from above. This approach to law goes back to Lenin, who as early as 1919 stated openly that Soviet power required definite rules in order to become legitimized and gain the support of the people; without such rules, the foes of socialism would be victorious: "[T]he slightest infringement of Soviet laws, the slightest laxity or negligence at once serve to strengthen the landowners and capitalists and make for their victory."[1] This exemplifies the way in which the Soviet leadership very clearly understood the need for legality, so long as the regime itself created the laws used to strengthen its position.

Gorbachev planned to establish a rule-of-law state to constitute a new form of governance for the transitional period until *perestroika* was completed. Thus, legal means were to be used to support and strengthen the communist system of rule that was on the point of collapse. The existing organs of Soviet power that had been controlled by personal orders from the leadership were now to be given properly defined functions in accordance with the international norms that were then beginning to be recognized in the Soviet Union.

The new approach was to be implemented by Soviet lawyers who had been working in official state institutions under the guidance of the CPSU and consequently were very obedient to appeals from above. They were all the more willing to cooperate because the strengthening of the authority of law naturally tended to raise the status of the lawyers themselves. Thus, the idea of the creation of a law-based state was wholeheartedly supported by lawyers as a group. Many were able to find publishers for books, articles, and reports on the new legal issues. Indeed, a large number of books appeared on all conceivable aspects of the "rule-of-law state." However, all these publications had one common factor—they were not devoted to a rule-of-law state as such, but to a socialist rule-of-law regime. As the editors of the collection *The Socialist Legal State: Problems and Opinions* stated, "In designing the concept of the rule-of-law state and describing its democratic principles, we must not fail to point out the decisive meaning of the features that organically link the model of socialism and the rule-of-law state."[2]

During 1985-1990, the population's legal consciousness was influenced by official legal commentators who tried to convince the public that the concept of a rule-of-law state mainly meant obedience to existing laws. Now, however, public opinion, as well as the lawyers' professional point of view, have changed radically. It was only after the Law on the Press was adopted in 1990 that not merely "distinguished lawyers," but anyone with experience in the field or ideas on legal matters, began to express views in the democratic press. Consequently, there is constant criticism of the stumbling progress of legal reform and discussion of the controversial issues of normative acts, the "war of laws" between different republics, and the "war of decrees" between different vertical levels of power.

When the first normative acts were issued on political rights, especially with regard to the law on demonstrations, a heated debate ensued in the press and at public meetings. Although the 1977 Soviet Constitution proclaimed a number of political rights and freedoms, including the right of free speech and the right to hold demonstrations, these principles were never secured by specific legislation laying down procedures for their implementation. As a result, it was essentially impossible to make use of such rights. Soviet authorities argued that in a rule-of-law state laws were needed to cover the areas of social life that had never before been legally regulated. In fact, by means of new legislation they wanted to establish control over new forms of activity on the part of citizens, since individuals were no longer afraid to take part in demonstrations, organize public meetings, or go on strike.

According to the official point of view, the concept of the rule of law principally meant ensuring a societal order in accordance with which the regime would govern the population. Thus, the first law on demonstrations that was adopted contained a number of restrictive provisions, including the requirement that the organizers obtain the authorization of the local authorities where a demonstration was to be held. It was passed long before the democratic movement brought to power new leaders in municipalities and rural areas, and consequently there was very little prospect that the existing authorities would welcome demonstrations organized by the emerging alternative political movements.

Under Soviet rule, legal norms had always served as a means of restriction and punishment at the hands of the government, but most individuals had become accustomed to this situation as an unavoidable evil, resisting it with various degrees of courage—from just ignoring the law, as did the general population, to practicing open disobedience, as was the case with political dissidents.

Under *perestroika,* however, the situation became essentially different, since the enforcement of state restrictions was legitimized by legislation imposed under the new "rule-of-law" concept as a means of restructuring society in accordance with democratic forms. Official legal doctrine played an invidious role in the fight for civil liberties, since the introduction of a socialist rule-of-law state meant the defense of socialism with its social order and all its structures, including decisions of the Supreme Soviet (the membership of which consisted of *apparatchiki*), the militia, and the procuracy— institutions which served the interests of the state, not of the individual.

Since they formed part of the socialist "rule-of-law state," government ministries and local authorities, which were principally concerned with preserving their status and privileges, were also protected by this doctrine. In fact, the sole entity to lack protection was the individual citizen, although there was a great deal of talk about securing individual rights and freedoms. It was much easier to proclaim human rights and the protection of the individual as basic goals of the rule-of-law state than to establish an independent court system capable of becoming an effective mechanism for ensuring the legal protection of the citizen. Thus, during the first few years of *perestroika,* legal reforms were carried out mostly in the interests of the existing state organs, which secured their own positions by means of new normative acts, while proclaiming these measures to be the beginning of the development of the "rule-of-law state."

However, the new legal doctrine did not remain the only motor of legal reform for long. New forms of public activity began to reshape the political and legal surface of the country, beginning with the 1989 miners' strikes in the Kuzbass and the Donbass. These strikes showed that legal norms as reflected in labor regulations applying to the Soviet industrial complex had become completely irrelevant to the situation that had developed. The USSR Supreme Soviet was forced to pass a law on strikes, and although there were still provisions requiring official authorization for work stoppages, in practice strike committees followed these rules only very rarely. The same could be said of public meetings and demonstrations: although they were prohibited in many cases by local authorities, waves of huge rallies and protests swept across the entire area of the former USSR, from Estonia to Uzbekistan.

Legal reform, whether doctrinal or legislative, could not keep up with the explosive force of public activity that had been unleashed and that was driving political developments. During the period of the "parade of sovereignties" that created independent states out of the former union republics, many witnessed the hopelessness of attempts to impose legal restrictions on the political process. Thus, although Gorbachev issued decrees and the USSR Supreme Soviet passed resolutions annulling the declarations of independence by the Baltic states, these legal measures did not begin to resolve the problem, but instead only brought about confrontation and deadlock, as well as the outbreak of a "war of words." Here was yet another example of the way in which the law could become a very dangerous instrument if not used wisely.

Nevertheless, it would be wrong to limit oneself to criticism of developments in legal doctrine. The so-called "public demand" for legal studies and the support of publications in the field stimulated research into new approaches to the separation and distribution of powers, to the independence of the courts, and to defining the roles of the procuracy and the militia. Most importantly, there were new approaches to legal support for private entrepreneurs, guaranteeing the rights of participants in economic activity and developing mutual agreement as the major legal form for restructuring relations in industry, giving both partners an interest in the results of economic activity.

The massive production of legal analysis after the beginning of legal reform allowed many useful ideas to be extracted from this pile of publications. It provided the necessary basis for the rapid development of new legislation that occurred after the election of the RSFSR parliament and the "legal competition" that sprang up between union and Russian republican legislators as to who would adopt the more progressive and democratic legal norms. Here was evidence that the proclamation of the "rule-of-law state" idea had performed a valuable function in awakening professional lawyers, making them think about the fate of the country, and encouraging them to take an active role in designing new approaches to legal regulation after truly democratic development became possible.

As a result of this process, whereby lawyers wrote on professional legal issues for public consumption, many jurists were given the opportunity to build themselves up as politicians. Eventually they participated as advisers or experts in government commissions at various levels, or were themselves elected as People's Deputies. Aleksandr Yakovlev, a professor of criminal law, is a case in point. Yakovlev wrote an article in 1988 in *Ogonek* advancing the idea that there could be no freedom or equality without individual property and that political and social rights essentially are secured by economic rights. At that time, the fact that this rather commonplace idea was expressed by a law professor aroused a sensation and brought him a lot of publicity. As a result, Yakovlev was elected to the USSR Supreme Soviet.

Another example is Leonid Mamut, also a law professor, who specialized in the area of legal philosophy and theory. In a report to the Democratic Club of the Moscow Intelligentsia, Mamut expressed the view that law did not represent the will of the ruling class, but reflected an objective relationship between persons or groups that is established by consensus and gradually develops into a general rule. Like Yakovlev, Mamut had been courageous enough to give public utterance to a commonplace thought. Moreover, he had never tried to please the authorities with his professional publications; the result was that he became one of the key consultants on the new draft Russian republican constitution.

A further significant development in the field of legal doctrine is the appearance of a completely new concept, "civilism," elaborated by Vladik Nersisiantz, which establishes relationships between law, freedom, and property. His theory states that, in a global historical perspective, post-socialism is only possible in the form of civilism—a new order based on the recognition of the free and inalienable right of every citizen ("civis," hence "civilism") to civil property, i.e., a share in all desocialized and individualized socialist property. Socialism and law are incompatible, since socialism is the negation of all private property and hence of "formal-legal" equality. There is no reverse route from socialism to capitalism.

According to "civilism," only the preliminary recognition of civil property can open the way leading from anticapitalist, anti-private-property, and anti-law socialism to individual property, individual legal rights and freedoms, market economic relations, a civil society, and a law-based state. These instances of valuable developments in legal doctrine show what has been achieved despite the burdens of the past.

THE "WAR OF LAWS" DURING THE PUTSCH OF AUGUST 1991 AND ITS LEGISLATIVE CONSEQUENCES

It must not be forgotten that the organizers of the coup had plenty of time to draw up their decrees, while the RSFSR president was compelled to make decisions under tremendous time pressure. Yel'tsin had no choice but to enter the legislative battle, because the basic thrust of the State Emergency Committee's legal policy, i.e., to ensure the execution of USSR laws throughout Soviet territory, was directly aimed against the RSFSR's Declaration of Sovereignty, against Russian statehood, and, to a very significant degree, against the RSFSR president personally.

Above all, Yel'tsin was forced to spell out his attitude toward the self-proclaimed committee. In his first decree, adopted at 10:10 A.M. on August 19, the RSFSR president ruled the proclamation of the committee to be unconstitutional and described the actions of its organizers as a "coup d'état, which is an obvious crime of high treason." The same decree also invalidated all orders and resolutions issued in the name, or on behalf, of the committee and proclaimed that the actions of officials who carried out the decisions of the committee "constitute a criminal offense and are subject to prosecution in accordance with the law."

Given the extraordinary nature of the situation, the need to provide a tough, specific assessment of the newly created committee, and the impossibility of giving careful consideration to all possible options, one cannot fail to be amazed by the precision of the juridical formulations and the references to prosecution procedures as stipulated by law. This first decree of the Russian president, consisting of three paragraphs, provided the requisite foundation for further legal action by the president and for the implementation of a series of measures restoring the violated interests of Russia's citizens. Importantly, legal responsibility for executing the decisions of the illegal committee rested only on officials. As a consequence, it was possible later to call to account those responsible for the enforcement of the information blockade, the deployment of military units within Moscow, and the seizure and occupation of several civilian installations, as well as the killing of civilians on the night of August 20-21.

As confrontations mounted, in his subsequent decrees the president's language became ever tougher and more decisive. In a decree adopted at 10:30 P.M. on the same day, August 19, the actions of the coup organizers were described as the "gravest of state crimes." The president's decrees were supplemented by an ordinance of the RSFSR Supreme Soviet Presidium that criminalized the actions of the committee members and also of all those who carried out their decisions, describing such actions unequivocally as "complicity in perpetrating a state crime, with all the ensuing consequences."[3]

During the night of August 19-20 there was a psychological, followed by a political, breakthrough. Barricades were built around the Russian Government White House, and certain military units went over to the side of the Russian administration, while reports began to come in of support by many local authorities for the Russian leadership. It became clear that Russia had a superiority of forces. As a result, the decrees issued by the president became still more decisive and strongly worded.

It is those political forces that have the support of the silent or of the most active majority that emerge victorious and, consequently, are able to legalize their supremacy by means of normative acts. Accordingly, the supremacy of political power was immediately reflected in the texts of RSFSR presidential decrees—politics were actively dictating law.

The elation and vigor displayed by the leaders of the democratic bloc, who had succeeded in enlisting reliable support against the reactionary coup, is completely understandable. Righteous popular wrath created highly favorable conditions for the concentration of power in the hands of the victorious president of Russia. Thus, Decree No. 61, dated August 19, appeared, transferring "all bodies of executive power in the USSR, including the KGB, Interior Ministry, and Defense Ministry of the USSR" to the direct jurisdiction of the popularly elected RSFSR president. This decree was followed by Decree No. 64, dated August 20 and entitled "Administration of the USSR

Armed Forces Located in the RSFSR under Emergency Situation Conditions"—Paragraph 1 of which provided that, as of 5:10 P.M. Moscow Time, August 20, 1991, command of the RSFSR armed forces located in the Russian Federation would be assumed by the RSFSR president.

Both these decrees are obvious instances of the RSFSR president exceeding his authority, and this conclusion remains unaffected by references to an emergency situation and descriptions of the committee's activity as criminal. With each successive decree that followed, such descriptions became more and more extensive and sounded increasingly persuasive in tone, including such lengthy addenda as "They embarked on the path of attempting the forcible overthrow of the constitutional system, thereby placing themselves outside the law."

Beginning in 1917, Russian history is rich in examples showing just what emergency measures can lead to, especially if such measures are formalized in normative acts. After all, the State Emergency Committee also referred to a crisis situation and the need to restore order and legality. Such measures constitute a highly alarming trend, even though it is difficult to argue against them in this instance.

However, it is to the credit of the president's legal advisers that both decrees included important provisions limiting the period during which special presidential powers were to remain in force. According to the first decree, they were to be valid "pending the convocation of an extraordinary session of the Congress of USSR People's Deputies," while according to the second decree they were to remain in force "until the operation of constitutional bodies and institutions of state power and administration in the USSR has been fully restored." This wording fulfills the function of a direction sign at a crossroads, one fork of which leads to the legalization of a totalitarian regime. On this occasion, we took the right road and were successful in avoiding such a regime.

So far, the subsequent development of the Russian legislative process does not seem to put in doubt this positive outcome. After USSR President Mikhail Gorbachev's return from house arrest in the Caucasus at the hands of the putschists, and following the arrest of the members of the State Emergency Committee, Russian President Boris Yel'tsin addressed a jubilant crowd at a mass rally. He announced that he had just signed decrees that, among other things, guaranteed the consolidation of Russian statehood—placing union-subordinate enterprises on Russian territory under Russian jurisdiction, transferring the All-Union Television and Radio Company to RSFSR government control, removing from office the chairmen of regional executive committees who failed to obey the Russian president's decrees, and ordering the drafting of a law for the creation of a Russian Guard. It would be completely unjustified to judge the victors over a reactionary coup on their behavior only hours after they had gained total victory. But what of their subsequent actions? Will the triumphant democratic policy-makers devise "their own democratic law"?

It should be noted that the Russian Federation was to take control of union-subordinate enterprises "with the exception of those whose administration has been placed under the relevant bodies of the USSR in accordance with current RSFSR legislation." Under Decree No. 66, dated August 20, 1991, the administration of the All-Union Television and Radio Company was temporarily transferred to the RSFSR Minister of Information and Mass Media, pending appointment of its chairman in accordance with the current legislation. Decree No. 69, dated August 21, ordered the dismissal of four top officials for giving direct support to unconstitutional activity. Decree No. 70, dated August 21, relating to the creation of a Russian Guard, contained only instructions to RSFSR Vice President Aleksandr Rutskoi to draw up corresponding proposals.

As long as established democratic legislative procedures continue to be observed, law will remain a restraining force and a stabilizing factor. Obviously, an attempted *coup d'état* is an illegitimate situation, and consequently the pendulum that had swung to the repressive and reactionary side inevitably then swung in the opposite direction, pulling behind it both politics and the law. Nevertheless, during the relatively short period that Russian statehood has been in existence, it has proved possible to create a supervisory juridical mechanism as part of the state's legislative institutions, and under normal conditions this will permit the preservation of the requisite balance between politics and the law.

As the Russian saying has it, the victors are not judged. Subsequent events demonstrated just how precarious was the temporary balance between politics and law: in the absence of any resistance, the Russian victors moved ahead rapidly, gaining new legal space. The Russian president's Decree No. 76, dated August 22, 1991, banning communist publications, was a particularly graphic violation of the proclaimed norms of legality. The decree's title speaks for itself: "On the Role of TASS, the *Novosti News* Agency and a Number of Newspapers in Misinforming the Population and the World Public about the Events in the Country."

The preamble to the decree states without qualification that TASS, *Novosti, Pravda, Glasnost', Rabochaya Tribuna, Moskovskaya Pravda, Leninskoe Znamya,* and other publications were actively engaged in a smear campaign against representatives of legal authority and had misinformed the people. This wording is an almost literal repetition of the phraseology used during the 1970s and 1980s in indictments against dissidents who had been charged under Article 190 of the Criminal Code—a very sad analogy indeed. Furthermore, although Part 3, Paragraph 1, of the decree recommends only that the Russian Federation Procuracy "give a juridical assessment of the activities of the aforementioned newspapers," the preamble to the decree states that all these publications had in fact "aided and abetted in the *coup d'état*," even though only the courts can decide the question of complicity in a crime.

Although this verdict was signed by the RSFSR president himself, the attempt was made to justify the measures by references to the provisions of Article 5 of the USSR Law on the Press and Mass Media, which states, "Following abuses of freedom of expression, in particular with the aim of calling for the forcible overthrow or transformation of the existing state or social order . . ." Part 1, Article 1, of the president's decree attempts to provide legal underpinnings for the closure of the publications in question by describing the measures as a "temporary suspension of publications following their active support of illegal and illegitimate activities and also propaganda by them in support of activities directed toward the forcible overthrow of the constitutional order."

Despite these statements, Part 2 of Article 1 of the decree destroys any illusion of legality, since it contains the demand to "transfer all the property and assets of the above-mentioned information media outlets to the jurisdiction of RSFSR state bodies." In this way, the publications that were out of favor with the RSFSR government were banned administratively, and under Article 1, Part 2, even the form in which they would be permitted to function subsequently was to be decided by the RSFSR Ministry of Information and the Mass Media.

However, the Law on the Press permits the suspension of a publication only "in accordance with a decision by its founder, or the organ that has registered the given information outlet, or a court ruling" (Article 13). It is appropriate also to recall Article 36 of the USSR Law on Information and the Press, which has never been annulled: "Any actions on the part of state or public officials designed to prevent or obstruct the legal professional activity of journalists, or any attempts to force journalists to disseminate or to stop the dissemination of information, shall be prosecuted and be punished by a fine of up to 500 rubles."

Since the regulations enforced were presidential decrees, what of the legal responsibility of the RSFSR president? At present there is no doubt that the RSFSR president is a "law unto himself," but the authority he exercises was granted to him by a legitimate body of power. Can the president be accused of usurping power, when he was provided with the relevant power under the RSFSR Constitution and the Law on the President of the Russian Federation? Under these laws, the only body that acts as a check on presidential power is the parliament, and at an emergency session the latter granted the RSFSR president extraordinary powers. Therefore, we had no one but ourselves to blame for the fact that a state of emergency remained in force. So that there be no doubt regarding the legitimacy of the RSFSR president's powers, the president issued Decree No. 75, "Certain Aspects of the Activity of RSFSR Executive Bodies," which over three and one-half pages enumerates the impressive list of powers enjoyed by the head of the executive branch in the RSFSR, with detailed references to the Russian Constitution and the Law on the President of the Russian Federation.

In particular, in addition to the right to issue decrees and ordinances binding throughout the territory of the RSFSR, and to appoint and dismiss the chairman of the RSFSR Council of Ministers (subject to the approval of the RSFSR Supreme Soviet) as well as ministers and heads of state committees and departments (on the initiative of the chairman of the RSFSR Council of Ministers), the president also has the right to "suspend the decisions of executive bodies on RSFSR territory and to dismiss from office the heads and officials of these bodies if they violate RSFSR legislation." Because "RSFSR legislation" is very often interpreted rather loosely as encompassing normative and regulatory acts, such legislation may also include acts issued by the president himself. Thus, the president is empowered to dismiss officials if they violate any of his decrees, and naturally he has the right to make such decisions at his own discretion. This situation may result in a real "coup," this time, however, in strict compliance with the RSFSR Constitution.

Significantly, the decrees issued on August 22, 1991, still attempted to provide substantiation or at least motivation for the decisions in question. For instance, according to the preamble of the decree on the activity of executive bodies, this decree was adopted "in the interests of strengthening state discipline, organizing the effective administration of the RSFSR national economy and ensuring uniform activity on the part of the executive bodies of the RSFSR," while the preamble of the decree banning communist publications refers to the "*coup d'état* in the RSFSR and the attempt at a forcible overthrow of legitimate power in the RSFSR," which revealed the "danger of monopolizing the mass media." Despite all the obtrusiveness of these attempts, there was at least an intention to convince the public that the measures that had been adopted were necessary. It is hard to judge just how successful these efforts have been, but in any event there has been no visible resistance. No one at the time condemned or even criticized the victors, and as a result, any need to provide justification for the decrees disappeared completely.

A subsequent series of ordinances issued by the RSFSR president on August 25, 1991 is remarkable for its laconic phraseology and crystalline clarity as well as the absence of any provision of ideological cover. Thus, the ordinance on the RSFSR customs (Ordinance No. 25, Paragraph 1, dated August 25, 1991) reads as follows: "Customs services located in the RSFSR will be placed under RSFSR jurisdiction. The RSFSR Council of Ministers will direct and administer the customs agencies." Ordinance No. 26, dated August 25, regulating the use of RSFSR state property in the city of Moscow, reads: "The RSFSR State Committee on Administering State Property will be granted the right, in coordination with the government of Moscow, to take control of non-residential premises, buildings and installations occupied in Moscow by the USSR Cabinet of Ministers, ministries, departments, and organizations of the USSR." Ordinance No. 27, Paragraph 1, dated August 25, streamlines the activities of fiscal agencies and banks in the RSFSR and reads: "All fiscal operations, as well as operations concerning foreign exchange and precious metals and stones conducted by the USSR Finance Ministry, the USSR State Bank (*Gosbank*) and the USSR Bank for Foreign Economic Activity (*Vneshekonombank*) will, as of August 25, 1991, be executed only with the approval of the RSFSR Finance Ministry, the RSFSR Central Bank and the RSFSR *Vneshekonombank*."

Having obtained the right to act "in the name and on behalf of democracy," Russia again rushed to occupy a place in the union pyramid after having wanted until shortly before the coup to dissociate itself from the union structure when it was striving for its independence. Taking advantage of its political victory, Russia was trying to bite off a bigger slice of the union pie, planting Russian flags on all the union "summits" that it had conquered, yet at the same time forgetting about the need to "ensure the economic basis" of its sovereignty and likewise forgetting that other republics had similar interests and the right to claim portions of the common pie that Russia now wanted to apportion single-handedly.

From this point of view, Decree No. 90, dated August 25, 1991, is especially revealing. The decree bears the title "The Property of the CPSU and the Communist Party of the RSFSR," and the text states without any preamble, reference, explanation, or substantiation: "Following the dissolution of the CPSU Central Committee and the suspension of the activity of the RSFSR Communist Party, I hereby order: 1) All property belonging to the CPSU and the RSFSR Communist Party, including real estate and movable property, monetary assets in rubles or foreign exchange deposited at banks or insurance companies, invested in joint stock companies, joint ventures or other institutions or organizations located in the RSFSR or abroad, shall be proclaimed state property of the RSFSR. CPSU property abroad will be distributed among the republics in accordance with agreement after signature of the Union Treaty."

It should be pointed out that the powers of the RSFSR president do not include the right to issue such declarations. It is evidently incomprehensible and illogical that the property of the CPSU, which belonged to all communist party members in the country, be appropriated by the Russian Federation as "RSFSR state property."

With respect to prospects for legality in the future, one must ask who is going to be so bold as to act as judge. At present there is a strong trend toward "legal lawlessness." What—or who—is capable of standing up to this development? First of all, there is the old rule whereby the "severity of laws is softened by the possibility of ignoring them." It is quite probable that many provisions of the RSFSR president's tough-sounding decrees will be "soft-pedalled."

Earlier, the uncontrollable lawmaking activity of the Russian president was carried on under the cover of the USSR president's decrees on the dissolution of the CPSU Central Committee and the USSR Council of Ministers, which also effectively ordered the transfer of control over the formation of new union bodies to the Russian government. As a result, the president of the Russian Federation was always able to invoke the need to ensure the implementation of the decrees of the president of the USSR. In his turn, the president of the USSR had been granted extremely broad powers by the highest legislative body, the USSR Supreme Soviet, including the right to proclaim a state of emergency.

Subsequently, the openly imperialistic claims of Russia, which had decided that it was "impermissible" for the autonomous republics within the RSFSR to participate in the signing of the Union Treaty and had raised the possibility of the revision of borders with neighboring states, contributed to the disintegration of the union. Opposition to the increasing "lawlessness" of the RSFSR president's decrees was to be expected on the part of some of Yel'tsin's loyal associates within his presidential team—or, at any rate, from the most farsighted and soberminded members of his entourage, who for purely pragmatic reasons were likely to attempt to persuade him to abandon some of his tough claims in the interests of good relations with the other republics of the Commonwealth of Independent States.

More generally, opposition was to be expected from the "democratic camp," and particularly from the liberal advocates of legality in its ranks, traditional critics of Yel'tsin who perceived the danger of absolute power as early as the Russian Federation presidential election campaign. Given the current situation, law will continue to be dominated by politics, and the nature of the legislation adopted in the Russian Federation will depend heavily on the balance of political forces. Inasmuch as the political pendulum has now swung to the more democratic and progressive side, it may be expected that after reaching its lowest point it will swing again in the opposite direction.

However, it is still not clear whether in fact the RSFSR president's lawmaking activity has passed through this critical lowest point. It would be sad to have occasion to observe in the future how action inevitably generates counteraction and to see a "superdemocratic" attack on the old bureaucratic system provoke a genuine coup—not merely an anticonstitutional putsch. In any event, the way in which opposition forces to the RSFSR presidency develop will demonstrate whether real political pluralism has emerged in Russia, or whether one monopoly of power has been simply replaced by another.

LEGAL ISSUES RELATED TO THE BUILDING OF DEMOCRACY IN THE REPUBLICS OF THE FORMER USSR

The existence of a law-based state is confirmed by a number of characteristics of the society related in particular to public life and relations between the state and the individual. These features include the separation of powers, the supremacy of law, the protection of individual rights and freedoms, etc. What is the situation in Russia today if such criteria are applied? Is Russia moving toward a law-based state?

First, the supremacy of law, or the subordination of the state and of politicians to the law, is clearly one of the most important characteristics of a law-based state. However, it is normally found only during periods of societal stability, and it is difficult to seek it in Russia at a time of radical change in the social system and of profound legal reform. Unquestionably, what now exists is the opposite—i.e., the virtually complete disruption of the existing legislative system—a war of laws, war between parliaments, war between parliaments and executive organs over the issue of governmental supremacy, and war between different government ministries, as well as wars between territories and regions and between cities. All of this results in competition among various normative acts.

As far as the criterion of the supremacy of laws is concerned, in view of the relative weakness of republican parliaments compared with the growing power of national presidents currently, Russia is not approaching—nor is it likely to approach in the near future—the ideal of a law-based state.

Yet in the area of the separation of powers, there have indeed been significant changes. However, one should not confuse the emergence of a multitude of different powers and what one might call a "dispersion of power" with a clear demarcation of the functions of legislative, executive, and judicial activity. On the one hand, formally speaking, separate systems of legislative and executive organs have been created. The powers of these organs have been defined and demarcated, and the principle of the separation of powers has been proclaimed in the new republican constitutions (or at least in the draft texts of these constitutions). On the other hand, the different authorities constantly endeavor to supplant one another. The executive power is acquiring ever more extensive functions with respect to the issuance of normative acts. As seen earlier, this development applies particularly to the Russian presidential cabinet, which has shown a pronounced tendency to govern by decree. At the same time, with increasing frequency, the parliaments adopt administrative regulatory decisions of very limited scope, because they do not trust the executive power. An example of this was the decree issued by Supreme Soviet Chairman Ruslan Khasbulatov regarding procedures for the registration of public associations and fixing registration fees.

It is clear also that a vertical separation of powers has taken place from top to bottom, and that as a result the hierarchical links of subordination of lower ranking organs to higher ranking bodies have been broken; in other words, the "administrative chain" has been destroyed. Thus, with regard to the criterion of the separation of powers, one can say that there is not a demarcation of powers, but a splitting of powers, indeed a splitting into excessively small pieces of power.

Turning to the criterion according to which the judicial power should constitute the supreme power, it must be noted that the Constitutional Commission, which existed as part of the central organs of power of the former union, proved incapable of playing any serious role during the putsch of August 1991 and instead endeavored to achieve a compromise, as a result of which this body became completely discredited. The Supreme Court, which also existed as a USSR institution, possibly may preserve a role for itself, but merely as an arbitration body for the resolution of disputes between members of the Commonwealth of Independent States, and then only if called upon to fulfill this role.

At the present time, the creation of judicial institutions is actively proceeding at the republican level. In Russia, a strong constitutional court has been established which possesses extensive powers. Valeri Zor'kin was elected chairman of the court. Zor'kin, a doctor of juridical sciences and a brilliant scholar and teacher, is known for his democratic views. The court began its activity by issuing a protest against the Russian president's decree on the fusion of the Ministry of Internal Affairs (MVD) and the KGB after the court had held the decree to be unconstitutional. As a result, the decree was annulled. This action on the part of the court constitutes an important indication of the role that the court can be expected to play in the future in the process of further construction of the institutions of the Russian state and of the country's judicial system in particular.

With respect to another criterion, the protection of the individual and of individual rights and freedoms, it has been proclaimed officially that the highest priority will be given to the inclusion of appropriate norms for the protection of the individual in virtually all normative acts regulating citizens' rights. However, the reform of criminal legislation has been proceeding only very slowly, and so far has barely affected the legislation on corrective labor camps and prisons. As a result, there has been a wave of disorders and open rebellions in penal colonies throughout the country.

The main problem is that no real mechanisms have been established to protect the population from the terribly destructive processes that are unleashed when social systems are revamped and national-territorial relationships are restructured. As a consequence, what in principle is a democratic and progressive process through which the former republics of the union are acquiring sovereignty has resulted in thousands of cases of death and injury caused by conflicts between different nationalities. Hundreds of thousands are losing their homes and their jobs and are forced to become refugees while the state is unable to provide them with vital necessities.

Under conditions of a market economy and privatization, if no social programs exist to support persons in poverty, it is virtually impossible to ensure the protection of the individual. As political activity declines and civil liberties consequently are accorded less importance, socioeconomic rights again acquire top priority, i.e., the right to work and to feed oneself, and the rights to housing, health care, and social programs.

The criterion of the protection of the rights of property owners is of great importance in a law-based state and provisions for this occupy a dominant place in the legislation of developed capitalist countries. However, in Russia, this issue so far has received unjustifiably little attention. The existence of a truly law-based state depends above all on social relations, and within the structure of such relations the social category of property owner (in Russian, *sobstvennik*) plays a major role.

The principal problem of privatization and, indeed, of the transition period as a whole relates to the difficulty of determining who, precisely, is the property owner. For instance, the USSR president issued a decree transferring all the property recorded as held by the USSR Academy of Sciences to the ownership of the academy. In itself, the question of whether the president has the right to take such action is controversial. But the question of property ownership is even more important: do the employees of academic institutes, research and design divisions, hotels, or other facilities belonging to the Academy of Sciences have the right to participate in privatization on a personal basis, and who represents the academy in negotiations with prospective purchasers—i.e., do the staff and the "workers' collectives" constitute the legal owner? Or is the owner the annual assembly of the Academy of Sciences, or the business office, or the administrations of institutes, research and design divisions, and hotels? Neither the Law on Privatization nor the decree referred to earlier resolves these issues, and thus the question of ownership remains open. As a result, virtually no privatization of the Academy of Sciences is occurring—science remains ownerless.

The view is often held that after a while a property owner will inevitably become an entrepreneur. Consequently, Article 1 of the Russian Federation Law on Enterprises and Entrepreneurial Activity states, "Entrepreneurial activity is the independent activity of citizens and associations based on personal or group initiative, and aimed at making profits." Accordingly, entrepreneurs and property owners are the most fitting social forces for supporting the construction of a law-based state. Property owners and entrepreneurs have stable interests; these interests can be predicted, and long-term legal regulation can be based on them. The encouragement of the growth of the property-owning class should be one of the lawmaker's principal tasks.

However, under currently prevailing conditions in the republics of the former USSR, lawmakers are simply unable to perform this task, or even to grasp its significance. The problem is that the membership of the republican parliaments today is not constituted by real politicians, but by scientists and academics, former communist party officials, police agents, and managers of state concerns, i.e., few persons who represent genuine property owners.

Moreover, the lawmakers are in a preprogrammed situation of conflict vis-à-vis the executive power, since at the present time, in reality, public officials and the executive power in general stand closer to the real levers of economic distribution than do lawmakers. In this sense, the executive power has a stronger orientation toward the creation of property owners, but on the other hand, with good reason, the lawmakers suspect the executive power of promoting its own selfish interests. This is the reason that legislation on property takes so long to be adopted, and that so far such legislation was initiated and supported mainly by the executive power. It was only relatively recently that legislative acts finally began to be adopted in this field under the pressure of necessity.

It is interesting to follow the brief history of legislation on property. A start was made in 1988 with legislation on "individual labor activity"—legislation that was, however, very limited and contradictory, indeed based mainly on prohibitions. Yet, this legislation was of exceptional importance insofar as it legalized individual activity in addition to state activity. This meant the destruction of the previous state monopoly on labor activity and on economic activity as a whole. Next, legislation on cooperatives was passed. Initially, regulations (*postanovleniya*) on four different specific types of cooperatives were adopted in 1987; then, in 1989, a USSR Law on Cooperation was passed that essentially provided the basis for the creation of private enterprises. Nevertheless, the law was a failure, since it did not fit into the legal system and was not supported by the existence of a proper legal status for private property.

In 1990, there followed the Sitoryan-Abalkin recommendations on small-scale enterprises, which almost entirely lacked a normative basis. However, they did provide the foundation for the registration of independent "economic subjects"—of which 15,000 had already been registered by local soviets by August 1991.

The Sitoryan-Abalkin recommendations also supplied the basis for the USSR Cabinet of Ministers Regulation on Small Enterprises, which recognized the automatic right to create such enterprises on application to the authorities, provided for the defense of entrepreneurs' rights in the courts, and made it impossible to refuse registration on grounds of expediency. To a large extent, this regulation provided the legal foundation for the development of an independent economy. Yet, a significant contradiction continued to exist between the scope for development of independent economic units and the still existing governmental systems that continued to preserve their control functions over the new "economic subjects" that were being created. For instance, an interministerial commission in Moscow continued to establish numerical limits and quotas for the registration of enterprises, although this was in direct contradiction with the regulation adopted by the Council of Ministers mentioned earlier.

At the same time, legislation was being adopted which furthered the decentralization of economic decision-making. In the spring of 1990, a law was passed on local self-administration and local economic activity. Under this law, the concept of "municipal property" was created, and also local authorities gained the right to introduce local taxes and to register local enterprises. The result was to provide additional support for the creation of local industry and independent private enterprises. Moreover, in the spring of 1990, the basic legislation on leasing (*arenda*) was adopted, applying both to enterprises and to land. However, little use was made of this law, since as before the legislation still avoided resolving the question of private property. Finally, after endless debate in parliament, the USSR Law on Property went into effect on July 1, 1990. Although the law carefully evaded the term "private property," nevertheless a general norm was established in accordance with which all forms of property enjoy equal rights, i.e., individual and family property, as well as state and collective property, so that private property effectively enjoys the same rights as other kinds of property.

Beginning with the last few weeks of 1990, the Russian Republic's Parliament began to be very productive. During the course of 1990 and 1991, laws were passed on enterprises and entrepreneurial activity, stock exchanges, bonds and shares, as well as on property and land. Importantly, the RSFSR Law on Land legalized the acquisition of land as private property. Thus, finally there is now legislation providing for the private ownership of land. However, the right to authorize the transfer of land to private ownership was granted to the local soviets, which establish their own rules and regulations in this respect. The private purchase of land still has not become widespread.

In view of these considerations, when it comes to the protection of the rights of property owners as a fundamental prop of a law-based state, there is still a great need for the rights of private entrepreneurs to be anchored in legislation. This becomes especially clear if one takes into consideration the constantly increasing taxes that are being imposed on the profits of private enterprises, now including the levy resulting from Yel'tsin's decree creating a Russian Federation "hard currency fund," for the benefit of which private enterprises are obliged to sell to the state at the official exchange rate 40 percent of their direct hard currency revenues.

PROBLEMS AND HOPES

According to Professor Vladimir Kudryavtsev, in theory, "Law is not the product of the arbitrary activity of the state. Law should satisfy the democratic criteria of equality and justice. A law-based state begins to exist when lawmakers understand the principle whereby the exercise of their will is limited by objective legal relationships having as their basis the freedom and equality of the members of the state." However, it is difficult for lawmakers to limit their will in view of such real legal relationships, since freely acting subjects exist neither in the area of politics nor in the area of economics.

The process of *perestroika* began with *glasnost'*, not with economic reforms, and consequently the first fruits of the new policies were freedom of speech and freedom of demonstration, association, and political activity. As a result, it was the persons most successful in these particular fields who got into parliament, and among them were very few representatives of independent business. Hence the politicians have only very vague positions on economic reform issues, although reforms in this field might help in establishing "real legal relationships," including relationships of importance for issues concerning the ownership of land, successive steps and procedures for privatization, and the basis for government price policy.

The consequence is that the state, in the form of parliament, continues to act arbitrarily and, due to inertia, still includes in many of the laws that it adopts mechanisms inherited from the past, i.e., prohibitions, provisions for central distribution, controls, and powers given to officialdom. It is not the law that is dominant, but politics—and politicians, such as Yel'tsin, Nursultan Nazarbaev, Leonid Kravchuk, or Gennadi Burbulis. These politicians subordinate legal developments to their concrete personal political interests and to the promotion of their political image in the eyes of tomorrow's electors.

Nevertheless, there is one definite and significant tendency in this rather chaotic development that gives one hope: administrative-command relationships are gradually being supplanted in daily practice by relationships based on mutual agreement. Due to the growing pluralism of political subjects and to the disintegration of the "center," administrative *diktat,* direct instructions from above, and pressure tactics are becoming less and less feasible. Whereas as recently as 1990 the "center" concluded agreements with the republics, now Moscow and St. Petersburg are forced to come to agreement with individual regions regarding deliveries of foodstuffs. A recent attempt to use administrative methods, i.e., the proclamation of a state of emergency in Chechen-Ingushetia, was a failure, and so Russia, it appears, now will also be obliged to reach an agreement with the Chechen Republic. The economic links between the different republics and regions are based on mutual agreement to an ever-increasing extent, while contracts between producers and consumers are becoming the normal basis of economic life.

The future of legal reform in the republics of the former USSR lies in the development and improvement of contract law legislation, just as the success of political reform depends on the skill of politicians to reach agreements and find compromises.

NOTES

1. V. I. Lenin, *Pravda*, no. 190, August 28, 1919, cited in V. I. Lenin, *Collected Works*, 5th ed., vol. 29 (Moscow: Progress Publishers, 1965), p. 553.
2. *The Socialist Legal State: Problems and Opinions* (USSR Academy of Sciences Institute of State Law, 1989).
3. See RSFSR Supreme Soviet Presidium Ordinance no. 1624-1, Paragraph 2, dated August 19, 1991.

—

Individual and Group Rights

Yelena Bonner

This chapter expresses my view of the new characteristics which are emerging on the part of the earth's surface that used to be called the Soviet Union. The disintegration of the Soviet Union was inevitable. It was caused by the fact that its totalitarian structure was incapable of prolonged survival, given the economic structure that had been provided. The first, timid attempt to change this economic framework was carried out under Alexei Kosygin. But it would be more accurate to say that change was never implemented: there was only the hope that this would be done. And not a single thought was ever given to changing the political essence of the state.

The tragedy of Mikhail Gorbachev and Gorbachev's entire team—the tragedy of *perestroika*—lay right there: they tried to change the economic system without changing its political essence. That is why they did not attempt to change the constitution in any real way. All the endless modifications to the constitution made after 1988 were aimed at strengthening the existing nature of the state. The only factor that really changed was the state of public consciousness. On the one hand, it could be considered a mistake on the part of the leaders that they permitted *glasnost'*; on the other hand, it could be considered a great victory on their part, and it is precisely thanks to this that they will enter the pages of history.

In the West, and even in Russia, the opinion is widespread that the peoples of the former Soviet Union are not ready for democracy. The inaccuracy of this view is demonstrated by the speed with which public opinion and public consciousness changed in our country. The elections of 1989, held on the basis of the 1988 electoral law, already reflected this aspect. Even though the electoral law was meant to handicap anyone outside the old *nomenklatura*—the party bureaucratic apparatus—new candidates successfully broke into political life. Their numbers were small—only about ten percent of the deputies were followers of the new thinking. However, the podium provided by the Council of People's Deputies became a school for the entire country, and the audience gained a great deal from hearing these new personalities speak out. But the main boon was the entry of political figures who began to enjoy the trust of the population. In a country that for 70 years had lived by lies, finally something honest had appeared. Incidentally, the phenomenon of Andrei Sakharov was founded precisely on this factor of trust. The people and the new leaders began to understand that the government and the whole system were not only incapable of producing *perestroika,* but incapable of producing anything at all. The system was impotent. This realization provided the impetus for the disintegration of the union and for the rise of national liberation forces in all the republics.

At the same time one has to understand that the new forces which were formed were not necessarily democratic. Moreover, the more pressure from the center that these forces came under, the more of a right-wing coloration they acquired. The best example of that is provided by events in Georgia during the last three years. These include the election of Zviad Gamsakhurdia as president; violent anti-Russian sentiment—not just anticommunist feelings; and the development of fascist tendencies, not only with regard to Georgia's own dissidents, but also vis-à-vis national minorities. Consequently, we have the case of the attempted genocide of the Ossetian people in the autonomous republic of South Ossetia. A similar process is now occurring in Azerbaijan, encouraged by Gorbachev's consistent policy after 1988 of supporting Azerbaijani nationalism. In February 1988, the request of the parliament and government of Nagorno-Karabakh that the region be transferred from Azerbaijani sovereignty to Armenia was brusquely rejected, and subsequently the Azerbaijan government implemented a policy of massive violations of human rights and forcible deportations of the Armenian population.

It has to be said that the old structures of agitation and propaganda still work extremely effectively, and that until very recently, the whole world, including a large part of the intelligentsia in Russia, saw the events in the region as a purely Armenian-Azerbaijani conflict. This misconception resulted in a desire to stand aside or to take up a political position of neutrality with regard to what was occurring, but there has never been a conflict between the two states of Azerbaijan and Armenia, and there still is none.

This tragedy has occurred not because of a conflict between states, but rather because Azerbaijan violated human rights by attempting to deny the Armenians in Nagorno-Karabakh the right of self-determination.

Here we come to the problem of the incompatibility between one of the generally accepted human rights and a principle of international law; consequently, contradictions are encountered in trying to implement this particular right. In the 1936 Soviet Constitution, the "great sage" Stalin simultaneously proclaimed two principles: the inviolability of borders and the principle of the self-determination of peoples. It seems now as if the entire world community has seen fit to adopt Stalin's "model" in this particular respect—however, not consistently. It was in accordance with the principle of the inviolability of borders that the world community took action against Iraq's aggression in the Persian Gulf. This was an appropriate step. However, similar action should have been taken several years earlier against the Soviet Union when it violated the borders of Afghanistan. Moreover, the world community did not consider it possible to defend the Kurds, since it held that to do so would amount to interference in the internal affairs of the Iraqi state as opposed to the defense of human rights.

Another example is Yugoslavia. In the summer of 1991, the parliaments of two republics voted for independence. Had we wanted to defend human rights as laid down in the Universal Declaration of Human Rights, and the rights of peoples, we should have recognized these states immediately. However, the international organizations that are supposed to be concerned particularly with peace in Europe—the United Nations, the Conference on Security and Cooperation in Europe (CSCE), and the EEC—considered this none of their business. It was not until civil war broke out and there was bloodshed that attempts finally began to be made to bring about a ceasefire. At the present time, the West is adopting a similar attitude toward the new states of the former Soviet Union and their peoples.

The Commonwealth of Independent States was organized too rapidly. The leaders of the republics were forced to move so quickly because they were afraid of yet another provocation on the part of Mikhail Gorbachev. However, their hastiness prevented them from paying attention to the need to work out clear principles for the creation of a truly democratic community. In order to avoid the impression that I refer to Gorbachev's provocative activity without due evidence, I cite as an example the aim of such political movements as Nina Andreyeva's communist movement, whose goal was to preserve a single unitary Soviet Union, this terrible, totalitarian state.

In the conspiracy we called "putsch" (the abortive August 19, 1991, coup), the goal also was to preserve a unitary, indivisible USSR. Vladimir

Zhirinovsky's extremist, chauvinistic movement, as well as similar groups of this type, aimed to restore this centralistic state. Gorbachev made repeated attempts over two years to achieve the same objective of preserving a unitary Soviet state. These various efforts led to three different versions of a union treaty, the last of which was due to be signed on the very day on which the people of Moscow put an end to the putsch. However, scarcely had Gorbachev recovered from his experiences in Foros in the Crimea (where he had been placed under house arrest by order of the putschists), when he attempted to work out yet another union treaty.

Consequently, the states that wished to create a commonwealth were forced to hurry. I do not think that the commonwealth in its current form is likely to survive very long. However, this does not bother me in the slightest, because the commonwealth is not based on democratic principles. Moreover, the individual member states have been unable to adopt criteria for dividing up the army, currency reserves, and so on. This is the reason for the crises that have arisen, such as the one concerning the Black Sea Fleet.

I consider Boris Yel'tsin to be a positive force, since in my view the process of the disintegration of the Soviet Union into individual states is a positive development, and the Russians and the Muscovites under Yel'tsin's leadership successfully defended this trend at the time of the August 19-21 putsch. Moreover, in general I consider that it is not a question of whether presidents and heads of state are good, bad, or just average—everything depends on the democratic counterweights that society establishes. In this respect, Russia is still a strange state—it was the first of the republics to set up a constitutional court, but the country still lacks a constitution. I could cite a lot of examples of such internal contradictions, not only in relation to the development of Russia, but also of other former Soviet republics. I consider Armenia to be the most democratic of the new states—not only because completely new public personalities gained power, but because the Armenian parliament adopted a democratic agrarian law and transferred the land to the peasants as early as February 1991. So far, no other parliament in any of the successor republics has taken such a step.

Russian society clearly contains potential dangers to democracy—for example, Zhirinovsky and his party. When I see him interviewed on television or speaking at public meetings in Moscow, I get the feeling that we are seeing the theater of the absurd, but then I cannot help but think that those who gathered in Munich beerhalls in the 1920s resembled Zhirinovsky, and that as a result we got World War II and genocide. Consequently, I believe that we have to take him seriously. The *Pamyat'* movement represents another potential danger. I am grateful to the Russian people for the fact that the movement still has only limited support, but the grave economic state of the country, the threat of unemployment, and ever-decreasing hopes that we will be able to cope with the situation may increase the influence of *Pamyat'*.

Currently, there is much discussion of various forms of government, including even the restoration of a monarchy in Russia. However, I believe it is unrealistic to think in terms of the establishment of monarchies in any of the successor states. Incidentally, perhaps my thinking has been conditioned by stereotypes, but I do not like the restored name of St. Petersburg. And it is interesting to find that the majority of former Leningraders don't like St. Petersburg, either. The referendum on the name change was held at a time when the population rejected everything that remained of the old communist system. At that point we did not really ask ourselves whether such changes corresponded to our basic concepts or not. The renaming of the city illustrates a current danger—the danger that our democratic leaders depend, to a greater or lesser degree, sometimes indeed to a considerable extent, on the electorate's state of mind at any given moment. The result of this dependence is that they remain silent at times when they ought to speak out, tending to fawn to the crowd. In my opinion, St. Petersburg is an inappropriate name for the city. They should have given it a Russian name—Peter, or perhaps Petrograd. Somehow, I just can't bring myself to say of my children that they were born in St. Petersburg.

Basic criteria for the formation of the commonwealth will need to be established in the future, but the main principle according to which the states of the commonwealth should be brought together, if they are to develop in a democratic way, is the right of self-determination of peoples. Today, this problem is particularly acute in Azerbaijan, where genocide of Armenians is being attempted; in Georgia, where genocidal measures against the Ossetians are underway; and in Moldova, where the right of self-determination calls for the establishment of a Slav Dniestr Republic. There is also the difficult problem of the Volga Germans. Here, justice requires the restoration of a historical right. But in the process of establishing historical justice, one ought not to infringe the rights of those who now live in a given territory— e.g., Russians in the former Volga German republic. It is a matter of achieving a fair balance.

A similar problem gave rise to a conflict between Sakharov and the leaders of the Crimean Tatars. Sakharov considered the demand of the Crimean Tatars to return home to be justified, indeed mandatory, and advocated that the state provide assistance for this. On the other hand, he considered the Crimean Tatars' demand for an independent state to be legally unjustified, because at the present time there is a population of 3.5 million

Slavs in the Crimea. Even if almost all the Crimean Tatars were to return, they would amount to only 700,000, or, at most, one million. All decisions must be based on the principle of self-determination, but the realization of this principle must be based on the free expression of the will of the majority of the people in a given region. It is the task of the democratic community to establish procedures for determining this, whether by referendum or some other means of expressing the people's will.

Yel'tsin has stated with brutal frankness that there can never be a German republic on the Volga, but he has also said that one could be established in areas where there is a 90 percent German population. I think that this figure is too high. Decisions should be made on the basis of a simple majority or a plurality. Ninety percent is too much. An important consideration when the question of creating new states arises has to do with the possible presence of national minorities in the given territory, and with consequent action consonant with the principle of self-determination in ensuring the full observance of their rights. In saying this I ask the world to pay particularly close attention to the Baltic states. Beginning in March 1990, I personally welcomed the self-determination of Lithuania and the creation of all the independent Baltic states. But now it is clear that we need to follow the situation in these countries very closely, since otherwise there will be infringement of the rights of minority peoples in the Baltic republics. It is the task of the United Nations, the CSCE, the mass media, and world public opinion to put pressure on new states not to violate human rights.

The creation of states is one solution to the problem of nationalities not only in the former Soviet Union, but in Afghanistan and Pakistan as well. I believe that this is a general principle irrespective of whether the resulting state is large or small. If any group of people exercises the right to self-determination and votes in a democratic fashion to establish its own state, it has the right to an independent state, no matter what the size of its population or its territory.

On the threshold of the 21st century, we must endeavor to bring about a situation whereby every nationality is able to live in its own country and possess its own territory—living in peace with its neighbors as Luxembourg lives next door to France, a nuclear power. Just as each single individual is worthy of enjoying all human rights, so each and every people, irrespective of its size, is worthy of all the rights of statehood. If these principles are adopted and implemented consistently, territorial disputes could become a specter of the past. No state or leader of a state has the right to make claims to territory, whether it be on an historical or any other basis, except for self-determination. According to the Universal Declaration of Human

Rights, the land, air, water, and all natural resources belong to the people who live on the given territory. If the principles of human rights are followed, territorial issues could be struck from the world's agenda.

The theory of governance holds that communities with small populations are more difficult to govern than larger, unitary, more tightly administered communities. This theory constituted the basis of the policy of strengthening the Soviet center that the West followed for seven years. However, this policy made it possible for the center to steal the country blind—virtually to exhaust its gold and foreign currency reserves. Associations such as the Movement for Democratic Reforms, which had Aleksandr Yakovlev, Eduard Shevardnadze, and Arkadi Vol'sky (chairman of the Industrial Union) as its leaders, succeeded in privatizing and gaining control of everything that was worth having, without others becoming aware of these actions. Consequently, whatever the intentions of the G-7 and other international organizations were, the result has been that the people of the former Soviet Union—the new independent states—have been reduced to beggary. In Russia we are very soon going to have our own Rockefellers, J. P. Morgans, and top 200 families.

It is sometimes asserted that the existence of numerous small states in Europe led to World War II. In my view, the principal cause was the excessive trust that the West placed in the regimes of Hitler and Stalin. Now, it is terrible that a third world war could very well occur as a result of the West placing excessive trust in the changes that have been taking place in the former Soviet Union over the course of the last seven years. In this regard, I believe that we should all give thanks for nuclear deterrence. Moreover, we ought to consider whether it is realistic to attempt to achieve the goal of complete nuclear disarmament, indeed whether that is not a dangerous objective. This was certainly Sakharov's view.

The establishment of a nuclear-free planet can only be a very remote goal. Perhaps, indeed, it will be to the world's benefit only when there are no more states left in the world that resemble the regime of Saddam Hussein. Unfortunately, most Western politicians, whether they are democratic in their views or not, as well as the majority of democratic leaders in the former Soviet Union, are afraid to express this view openly. As a result, excessive hopes and unjustified illusions are created which mislead the population.

I believe that today the formulation of universal principles binding all states is an important task incumbent on the United Nations and the CSCE. We need to adopt such principles now, looking ahead to the 21st century. Not only the right of peoples to self-determination, but also ecological issues and security from war, which indeed are important constituent principles of the fundamental right to life—all these are rights that must be defended. To provide a brief definition of what I would call the supreme ideology of human rights: it consists of the unstinting defense of individual human rights in all countries, everywhere in the world, irrespective of religious belief, social position, skin color, or any other factor, and of the right of all peoples to self-determination, irrespective of the size of their population or the size of the territory they occupy.

The question of self-determination will also arise very acutely with regard to Russia itself. However, I do not believe that there is any likelihood of a civil war. That the possibility of a civil war ever arose in some regions is the legacy of Gorbachev's policies and his unwillingness to resolve problems in a parliamentary way. Examples of this are the legacy bequeathed to us in Nagorno-Karabakh and Ossetia, as well as the question of the Dniestr Republic. Imperialists such as Eduard Shevardnadze and Aleksandr Yakovlev try to frighten the West with the threat of civil war and the danger of the misuse of nuclear weapons, since this serves their purposes, but these warnings do not correspond to reality.

I remain concerned about the continued existence of the state security organs, the former KGB. It is doubtful that this institution can be transformed into something that will correspond to the essential nature of a democratic state. However, earlier I had excellent—almost friendly—relations with the (then) Russian Federation security minister (V. V. Ivanenko), as well as with one of his aides, who let me read the files on my parents. They also allowed me access to the files on many officials of the Comintern, for which my father worked. Moreover, I had a very good relationship with Vadim Bakatin, who was briefly in charge of the KGB, and I believe he made a genuine effort to find the dossier on Sakharov, which was stolen by the KGB. Here I am talking of individuals, but it seems to me that the security ministry as an institution is still not capable of being transformed into something worthy of humanity.

In conclusion, I will stress that it is incumbent on Russia—indeed Russia's historic role, and not a question of imperialism—to become the first republic to ensure the recognition of human rights, including the right to self-determination. If it is not the first to undertake this mission, then our hopes to see the democratic development of Russia will have proven to be in vain. Further, I believe that Russia also has the obligation to help the peoples of other independent states to defend their rights. The area of the defense of human rights is the only domain in which Russia can permit itself to act as Big Brother. Russia should consider it its duty, indeed a question of honor, to defend the Armenian people in Nagorno-Karabakh and the Ossetian people as well. For the same reason, I believe that the basis for the existence of the commonwealth should be above all the attitude of its member states toward human rights, and the admission pass for entry of a state into the commonwealth should be guarantees of human rights. A return by the union to its previous form will destroy its durability and ruin its prospects for democratic development in the future.

The West should follow a consistent policy of developing relations with republics that guarantee human rights and should withhold aid from, and curtail relations with, countries in which human rights are violated. It is clear that, after a moment of confusion following the breakup of the Soviet Union, Western politicians have begun to give consideration to following such a policy—evidence of this is Secretary of State James Baker's Princeton speech, as well as the EEC meeting in Brussels. Today, the West has a phenomenal opportunity to aid the development of democratic structures in the new states of the former Soviet Union. It will be unforgivable if the West lets this chance pass. To fail to take advantage of this opportunity would be to permit the development of the most terrible form of nationalism—fascism—in the former Soviet republics. In none of the republics is such a possibility excluded—including Russia.

Human Rights: Established or Precarious?

Richard Schifter

On August 19, 1991, the world heard the grim news from Moscow that Gorbachev had been replaced by an "Emergency Committee" that counted among its members the three men who commanded all the country's security forces—namely, the military, the KGB, and the militia (ordinary police) and special action detachments.

For most of its history, the ability of the communist party leadership to govern the far-flung Soviet state had rested on the support provided by these three pillars of armed might. They had been united almost always. Only once, in July 1953, had the military leadership been pitted against the secret police. The military had triumphed then, with the arrest of Lavrenti Beria and his subsequent execution.

However, on August 19, 1991, Defense Minister Dmitri Yazov, Interior Minister (thus chief of all militia forces) Boris Pugo, and KGB head Vladimir Kryuchkov were together. They issued their orders and expected that they would be obeyed as had been the tradition in the country, both under Bolshevik and czarist leadership. Students of Soviet politics and history throughout the world shared that expectation.

Yet within two days the coup collapsed and its plotters were arrested. It has been suggested that the coup plotters were inept, drunk, and poorly organized. This may have been true of some of them, but it was surely not true of the mastermind of this effort, the KGB's Kryuchkov, a careful, meticulous professional. The fatal flaw in his plan, indeed, was his assumption that the security forces would follow the orders of their united leadership. But they did not. Illustrative of the response of a very large part of the Soviet security forces was the action of the Alpha Group, a KGB special strike force trained for rapid action against hostage takers. When ordered to move on the Russian government's White House to arrest Boris Yel'tsin, they took a vote on whether to carry out the order and decided unanimously to disobey it.

The Alpha Group's decision, of course, was of critical importance. But the Alpha Group was not alone. Throughout the entire complex of security forces, the coup leaders faced disobedience. Only once in this century had the country experienced such a mass breakdown of discipline. That was in February 1917, when a hungry, defeated, and demoralized army which was no longer prepared to follow orders helped bring about the fall of Czar Nicholas II.

The sharp decline in military discipline and the resulting unraveling of the czarist empire—in the third year of a war in which one military disaster had followed another—were understandable and even predictable. But nothing even remotely resembling the calamitous conditions of 1917 existed in 1991, and yet the security forces failed to follow orders. How did this truly incredible change in behavior evolve? What caused the highly disciplined security forces to engage in massive disobedience when their leaders sought to overthrow the constitutional order? What had eroded the iron discipline that Lenin had inculcated in his movement and in all its organs?

There were, of course, a great many long-term trends that came together in recent years to effect significant change in the Soviet Union. But just as one man, Vladimir Lenin, served as a catalyst in making the Bolshevik revolution, so one man, Mikhail Gorbachev, was the catalyst in unmaking it. And in both instances, personal qualities played a critical role. History will remember Mikhail Gorbachev kindly, as the person who released the prisoners of the Gulag, who let people speak their minds and practice their religions, who tore down the iron curtain and the fences that surrounded the country, who indeed brought the evil empire to an end.

When pondering the question of the reversibility of recent changes in the former Soviet Union, one must indeed explore the Gorbachev phenomenon. In the absence of an introspective autobiography or definitive historical studies of recent Soviet history, we are limited to an examination of developments in the Soviet Union as they appeared to those who watched from outside. This chapter is written from the vantage point of an observer who was engaged in human rights work on behalf of the United States government.

The United Nations Human Rights Commission, which meets annually in Geneva, has for many years provided an important platform for the discussion of human rights questions. Where the Soviet Union stood on the issues under debate at the commission was best illustrated by the fact that the Soviet delegation was headed in the late 1970s and early 1980s by Valerian Zorin, who for his work in 1948 had acquired the sobriquet of the "butcher of Prague."

Zorin saw to it that his delegation lived up to his reputation. No opportunity was missed to scotch any serious consideration of human rights issues by the commission. Every effort was made to introduce extraneous matters into the agenda or, if the debate did indeed turn to human rights questions, to focus exclusive attention on those countries which were on the Soviet blacklist: South Africa, Israel, Chile, El Salvador.

Invariably, verbal duels between Soviet and United States delegations erupted at each of the sessions of the United Nations Human Rights Commission. Toward the end of one of these sessions, a French reporter asked me about this contest between the superpowers. I remember responding that in my view the debate had no direct relationship to our respective military capabilities. It had everything to do, I said, with our outlook on life. It was a contest between the thinking of philosophers such as Locke or Voltaire on the one hand and Lenin on the other hand.

As each side tried to make debating points, we may very well have thought that we were engaged in mere public speaking exercises and that our presentations had no practical results. It was only years later that we found out to our surprise that our presentations did have an effect, at least with regard to some representatives of the Soviet bloc. A high-ranking Bulgarian diplomat told me in 1990: "I attended the CSCE Madrid meeting in the early eighties. We heard what your side had to say and we of course were aware of what we were instructed to say. Living in the Western world, we gradually came to the conclusion that what you were saying made good sense and that what we were instructed to say was simply not true. And when we came back to Sofia, we shared our thoughts with colleagues in our ministry. It should not have surprised anyone that it was the Foreign Ministry that took the lead in overthrowing Zhivkov."

Bulgarian Foreign Ministry officials were not the only groups or individuals in the Soviet bloc to be reached by the democratic message. Nor were the outspoken dissidents in communist countries unique in their understanding of the severe shortcomings of the regimes under which they lived. It is now clear that after Nikita Khrushchev's anti-Stalin speech in 1956 communism was never again what it had been before this speech. In the years that followed, Khrushchev opened the system wider and let in more fresh air. Hard as he may have tried, his successor, Leonid Brezhnev, was never quite able to put the genie back in the bottle. On the contrary, Brezhnev's "era of stagnation" led to increased disillusionment with the system among many Soviet intellectuals.

Not all who lost their faith had lost faith in communism, however. Many of them had lost faith merely in the incumbent leadership, which was so clearly inept and corrupt. They hoped for a better day, in which true communism would be reborn under better and more honest leaders.

There is every reason to assume that Mikhail Gorbachev was a faithful communist on the day that he took the reins as General Secretary. He had been reared in the Leninist faith and believed in it with heart and soul. The wrong people had been in power, he thought. Their greed and selfishness had corrupted the system. What was necessary was to return to the purity and idealism of the Founding Fathers (most particularly of the sainted Vladimir Lenin).

It was thus with a strong ideological commitment to communism and faith in the teachings of Lenin that Mikhail Gorbachev took power in the Soviet Union. There are those who, pointing to Gorbachev's speech after his return to Moscow from the Crimea in August 1991, insist that he never changed. In the Soviet Union, by contrast, the small remnant of communist believers regards him as the worst of traitors. Which of these assessments is right?

Lenin had read Machiavelli's *The Prince* and was influenced by it. He had come to the conclusion early that in order to create the ideal society to which he had dedicated his life, he had to resort to lies, deceit, defamation, and ultimately to torture and killings. In his mind, the means were fully justified by the altruistic end for which he strove.

In his August 1991 speech, Gorbachev told how shocked he was by the rudeness of the delegation which had brought him the demands of the coup plotters. In these extemporaneous remarks, he also said that he had not been raised to treat people that way.

Gorbachev's casual remark about his upbringing explains a great deal about developments in the Soviet Union in recent years.

Character attributes of personal decency, and not an understanding of the democratic world, are what Gorbachev brought to his position of leadership. But he also brought in as a close associate a man who had lived in the Western world and had come to understand it—Aleksandr Yakovlev. Eduard Shevardnadze, a person very much of Gorbachev's character mold, soon joined them. Though Shevardnadze had not had any previous significant contacts with the outside world, as Foreign Minister he quickly developed them.

Outside the small circle of intellectuals in good standing with the leadership, the ascent of Gorbachev to the position of General Secretary of the Soviet communist party, and thus *de facto* head of government, did not have any significant immediate impact on the totalitarian character of the system of government. The secret police continued to function as it had in the past. Political prisoners remained in the gulag, indeed others were still sentenced for such "crimes" as "anti-Soviet agitation and propaganda" or "defamation of the socialist system." Abuse of psychiatry, in particular the commitment to psychiatric institutions of perfectly sane persons who had run afoul of the system, continued unchecked. Religion remained repressed. Emigration remained restricted. The total number of Jews, Armenians, and ethnic Germans (the three minority groups most anxious to leave the Soviet Union) permitted to emigrate remained at the low levels that had prevailed since 1982.

In November 1985, about six months after Gorbachev had come to power, the first Reagan-Gorbachev summit took place in Geneva. The president and many in his party were greatly impressed by the new, vibrant Soviet General Secretary and hoped that, following the summit, this new leader would move the Soviet Union toward a more open society. But as the months passed, there was no indication of significant change in the Soviet Union. The State Department's annual report on human rights conditions in the Soviet Union published in February 1986 stated, "Soviet performance in the realm of human rights fails to meet even the most elementary of accepted international standards." The report went on to characterize grimly the state of human rights in the Soviet Union in this first year of Gorbachev's leadership. It painted a vivid picture of the Soviet Union that Gorbachev had inherited from his predecessors:

> The state and party control the mass media and seek to prevent the free flow of information and ideas from abroad. Voluntary organizations, if allowed to exist, must submit to state or party supervision. Trade unions are strictly subordinated to the party and act as agents of the Government in implementing economic policy and assuring labor discipline. They are not collective bargaining agencies for workers. Religious believers in an officially atheist State must submit to State supervision or face harassment or imprisonment. Freedom of movement is neither guaranteed by law nor respected in practice. Many infringements of human rights are carried out by the KGB and police authorities, whose actions are not subject to effective appeal.

The regime confines those attempting to exercise their rights to prisons, labor camps, or psychiatric hospitals. Mistreatment of political prisoners continued in 1985. Beatings, inadequate food, clothing, and shelter, heavy manual labor, unsatisfactory medical care, isolation, extended interrogation, and threats against prisoners' families are characteristic abuses. Many prisoners are denied the right to correspond with their families or to receive family visits. Some are arbitrarily confined to special psychiatric hospitals or to the psychiatric wards of regular hospitals where they are often subjected to cruel and degrading treatment and administered doses of powerful and painful drugs to punish and intimidate them rather than to treat a medical condition. The authorities also continue to exile prisoners to remote areas of the Soviet Union or force them to emigrate. Every year a number of persons die in prisons and labor camps because of the harsh conditions and inadequate medical attention.

Persecution of individuals who attempt to express themselves outside state-controlled channels continued during 1985. Human rights monitors, religious believers, proponents of greater cultural and political rights for ethnic minorities, and peace activists were subject to arrest and imprisonment. Jewish, ethnic Germans, and Armenian emigration remained at severely restricted levels, despite the desire of many thousands of persons to emigrate.

Moreover, there was no indication of change in the state of affairs described above throughout most of the following year, 1986. When the third follow-up meeting of the CSCE convened in Vienna in the fall, the United States delegation and other delegations representing Western democracies took the floor to denounce the continued systematic repression in the Soviet Union of the rights that the participants in the conference had promised to respect when they signed the Helsinki Final Act on August 1, 1975.

It was in the last month of 1986, 21 months after he had taken office, that the world received the first clear signal of change in the Soviet Union under Gorbachev. Andrei Sakharov, the intellectual guiding spirit of the Soviet Union's political dissident movement, who had been banished in 1980 from Moscow to Gor'ki (Nizhni Novgorod), was invited by the General Secretary personally to return to Moscow. There were other moves and announcements around this time which suggested a possible change in outlook, but most foreign observers remained skeptical. Gorbachev, it seemed, had decided to engage in a number of public relations stunts. There was still no indication of any basic change in the character of government in the Soviet Union. The State Department's annual report for 1986 summed up the situation as follows:

Those who attempt to exercise their rights face a risk, trial, and imprisonment, or internment in a psychiatric hospital. Human rights monitors, religious believers, peace activists, and proponents of greater cultural and political rights for ethnic minorities were all subjected to arrests and imprisonment in 1986.

By the time these words were published in early 1987, the first changes which had been hoped for under Gorbachev's leadership appeared to be underway. Research into the records of the Politburo will presumably reveal the nature of the decisions taken by the Soviet leadership late in 1986 and the reasons therefor. None of these decisions was ever publicly announced. However, in early 1987, substantial numbers of pale, emaciated, recently released prisoners of conscience were permitted to return to their hometowns. About the same time, the number of exit permits granted to Armenians, ethnic Germans, and Jews began to increase appreciably. And a few months later it became clear that the Soviet Union was no longer prosecuting citizens for "anti-Soviet agitation and propaganda," nor were there any new cases reported of the commitment to psychiatric institutions of political dissidents or religious believers.

Furthermore, in the summer of 1987, Moscow was treated to an unusual spectacle: Crimean Tatars, members of an ethnic group that had been expelled from their Crimean homeland by Stalin in 1944, demonstrated in Moscow, calling for permission to return to their native land. Their appeal was not granted, and the demonstrations were ultimately stopped. However, the Tatars had been allowed for weeks to call attention to their plight, and when they were finally detained, they were not put on trial—as might have happened only a year earlier—but simply were put on a train that took them back to their homes in Central Asia. Summing up the situation of human rights in the Soviet Union, the State Department human rights report for 1987 described the new developments as follows:

As we look back at human rights developments worldwide during the year 1987, there is no doubt that the attention of a great many observers focused on developments in the Soviet Union. Was Mikhail S. Gorbachev in this third year of his stewardship of the world's first Leninist dictatorship, bringing about fundamental change, or were the changes merely cosmetic? The answer to this question, asked by so many observers, is that neither adjective fits. The changes were more than cosmetic and less than fundamental. The Soviet dictatorship, concentrated in a small elite group and operating through a single recognized party, remained in place. The secret police and its comprehensive network of informants remained the principal pillar on which the state edifice rests. A majority of political prisoners remained in jail. But, as our report on the USSR points out, there was *some* relaxation of totalitarian controls. Some political prisoners were released. The Soviets announced moves to end the truly barbarous practice of abuse of psychiatry. Emigration levels for ethnic Germans, Armenians, and Jews were higher than those of recent years, although totals for Soviet Jews fell far short of those of the 1970s. Plays and films could be seen that dealt with the realities of Soviet life more honestly than had been allowed in a long time. On the other hand, we regret to say, the hopes and expectations voiced in the spring of 1987 as to rapid additional progress were not fulfilled by the end of the year. We need to see what 1988 will bring.

We need to find out from official records, and possibly also from the key decision makers, what moved the Soviet leadership to effect this first significant set of changes in the mode of government that were carried out in early 1987. Did they reflect a commitment to a more open society, or were these steps taken to accommodate the West, in particular the United States, in order to improve the Soviet Union's international standing? It would seem that while the release of prisoners and the end of new commitments of dissidents to psychiatric hospitals may very well have reflected a genuine interest in a less repressive society, the increase in emigration was evidence of nothing other than an interest in better relations with the United States.

That the latter was in fact true was shown by the alacrity with which Soviet authorities responded throughout the year to American complaints about the guidelines for the issuance of exit permits. For example, at the beginning of the year, prospective emigrants had to furnish with their applications the consent of both of their parents, as well as their siblings, to their emigration. The requirement to submit statements of consent from siblings was abandoned in the course of the year. Also, at the beginning of the year, only long-term "refuseniks" could qualify to have their cases processed. New applications were generally not accepted. Later, when they began to be accepted, every applicant had to furnish an invitation from a first-degree relative living in the country to which the Soviet citizen would travel. In midyear this legal requirement was abandoned for emigrants to Israel. In each instance, the Soviet Union had responded to U.S. expressions of concern.

As the year 1987 progressed, the term *glasnost'* came to be identified with the Gorbachev regime, reflecting its new willingness to allow greater freedom of expression. In the speeches that Gorbachev delivered in the course of the year, he spelled out his political goals. Rejecting the "period of stagnation," the label affixed to the rule of Leonid Brezhnev, and condemning Stalinist tyranny, Gorbachev appeared to associate himself with the liberalization efforts of Khrushchev and to suggest a return to what seemed to be characterized as the purity of the days of Lenin. Gorbachev thus made clear his continued commitment to Leninism, in other words, the dictatorship of a party elite and a collectivized command economy. Though opposition to the system would continue to be prohibited, there was to be free discussion within the context of the system. Ideas for improving it would be considered. Citizens were encouraged to criticize inefficient bureaucrats. Corruption and the abuse of authority were to be eliminated. The secret police would remain on guard, but would be less inclined to intimidate men and women of dissenting views who did not really appear to be a threat to the state.

This kinder and gentler communism with which Gorbachev's name now became associated was not endorsed by the entire leadership. Toward the end of 1987, it became evident that a tug of war was going on within the Kremlin. Yegor Ligachev was mentioned as the leader of the anti-Gorbachev group.

The concerns over possible retrenchment—which a good many advocates of Soviet liberalization expressed toward the end of 1987—ripened into fear that the Gorbachev period had come to an end when, in early 1988, the newspaper *Sovetskaya Rossiya* published a letter from a Leningrad teacher, Nina Andreyeva, which denounced the liberalizing trends and clearly espoused a return to Stalinist verities. The letter would not have been printed, it was said, if it had not been authorized. The fact that it evidently had been authorized would suggest that the opposition to Gorbachev had won the upper hand and that, after little more than a year of liberalization, the country was about to return to the rigidity of old.

A few weeks passed, and then, to the surprise of a great many observers, *Pravda* published an editorial sharply denouncing the Andreyeva letter and calling for an acceleration of the reform effort. The publication of the Andreyeva letter, it was now clear, had not been a sign that the Ligachev faction had won. Instead, putting the letter and the *Pravda* editorial together, it was now evident that a factional split within the leadership was being aired in public. Since a *Pravda* editorial trumped a letter in *Sovetskaya Rossiya,* it was also evident to the readers of Kremlin tea leaves that the Gorbachev faction remained on top.

After the weeks of uncertainty and the fear of regression aroused by the Andreyeva letter, the *Pravda* editorial resulted not only in a sigh of relief from many of those who had welcomed the Gorbachev approach. Significantly, it was followed by a further relaxation of governmental controls. A once monolithic press began to reflect substantial differences in opinion. The cloud of fear which had caused people to remain silent began to lift as citizens throughout the Soviet Union began to speak more freely. In the summer of 1988, a communist party conference was held, and its proceedings, including debates, were televised. In the fall, Gorbachev obtained changes in the Soviet constitution which provided for the creation of a genuine legislature whose members were to be chosen in genuine elections. And in December, in a speech to the United Nations General Assembly, he indicated for the first time a doctrinal deviation from Leninism when he suggested that the political seers of one age could not simply determine policies for another age. Summing up these developments in the Soviet Union in 1988, the State Department human rights report observed:

> We still cannot say that there has been a fundamental shift in the Soviet Union's approach to human rights, but there is no doubt that the changes in evidence in 1988 have profound implications, as advocates of significant systemic reform appeared to have gained strength.
>
> By the end of 1988, all persons in the Soviet Union who had been sentenced under the articles of the criminal codes which punish dissenting political or unauthorized religious activity had been set free. Plans for amendment or repeal of the so-called political and religious articles have been announced. Abuse of psychiatry has been made a punishable offense. Freedom to leave the country temporarily has been significantly expanded. Armenians, ethnic Germans, and Jewish emigration has increased further, as has the emigration of Pentecostals. Plans have been adopted for elections which, though not completely free and open, are no longer to be the farce they have been heretofore.
>
> At the same time, the ability of opponents of reform to slow down progress, the existence of a powerful and pervasive secret police force, and the supremacy of the communist party remind us of the fact that institutional guarantees to protect the rights of the individual against unbridled state authority are still needed. Soviet reformers speak of the importance of respect for the rule of law and have underlined the vital importance of creating an independent judiciary, but that is still in the future. Nonetheless, the recognition of the need for action to secure the rights of individuals, and the fact that the defects of the existing system are now openly discussed, offer a basis for cautious hope of a better day.

In retrospect, it is now clear that in the year 1989 Gorbachev departed from the Leninist path. There is no evidence that on this occasion or on any other he moved deliberately, after thoughtful analysis of the implications of his actions. Instead, we are left with the impression that he was driven both by pragmatic considerations and by his personal attitudes. He recognized that the system he had inherited was inefficient and incapable of keeping up with the Western world. He also appeared to have increasing disdain for the police state and its mindlessness and brutality.

Lenin's basic concept of the structure of the state was that all governmental functions should be subordinated to the party and that the party should be run from the top down. The changes that Gorbachev put into effect in late 1988 and early 1989 reversed this process: On March 26, 1989, elections were held for the Congress of People's Deputies, which in turn was to elect the Supreme Soviet. Though flawed in many respects, these elections gave the citizenry of the country the first opportunity since November 25, 1917 (when the ill-fated Constituent Assembly was elected) to choose their representatives in a parliament. In metropolitan areas, the elections were free and fair, while the old-line communist party machine continued to control areas of lesser population density. Where the elections were indeed free and fair, the reform candidates invariably emerged victorious.

The Congress of People's Deputies met in May 1989, and governmental affairs, once shrouded in secrecy, were now publicly debated. The Supreme Soviet was elected and installed in office. Freedom of speech and the press was established. Whereas all forms of organized activity had once been the sole prerogative of the communist party and its subsidiaries, associations of various types now organized themselves throughout the country, totally free of party control. By the middle of the year it was clear that a leadership which only three years earlier had tight control over all public life in the country had surrendered it voluntarily. This action was an historically unprecedented move. Also in the course of 1989, the government ended its official espousal of atheism, and by December, when the Ukrainian Catholic Church was allowed to register, the activity of all denominations wishing to function in the Soviet Union had been authorized.

Summing up the events of 1989, the State Department reported:

> The spectacular events in what was once known as the Soviet satellites tended to overshadow remarkable steps taken by the Soviet Union in the direction of an open society. Elections to the Congress of People's Deputies, though rigged in some areas, were genuine contests in others, and resulted in the election of numerous opponents of the old order. The Supreme Soviet, chosen from members of the Congress, became a legislative branch relatively independent of the executive. There was further progress regarding freedom of expression, of association, of assembly, and of religion. Many restrictions on emigration were relaxed.

What the State Department's report also pointed out, however, was that although the Soviet leadership had made a significant turn toward an open society, there were lower-ranking bureaucrats in office who persisted in the old ways:

> Though reformers strengthened their hold on the top echelon of the Soviet Government, "new thinking" has failed to penetrate many parts of the Soviet bureaucracy. Incidents of autocratic use of power continued to be reported. The absence of a legal tradition and of legal institutions empowered to protect the rights of individuals add to the leadership's difficulty in getting its reform policies fully enforced. The creation of an independent judiciary remains critically important for the enhancement of respect for human rights in the Soviet Union.

Further steps to dismantle the one-party dictatorship continued during most of 1990. In February, the communist party was deprived of its monopoly. Though there was now a multitude of political organizations, three camps came clearly into evidence: 1) the supporters of Gorbachev, who continued to press for reform at a moderate pace; 2) reformers who identified with Boris Yel'tsin, who urged much more radical action, particularly regarding economic reform; and 3) opponents of reform, whose leadership remained in the shadow.

With the country rapidly leaving its Leninist past behind it and evolving toward democracy, the focus of concern shifted toward the economy. Radical reformers pressed Gorbachev increasingly for fundamental changes. In turn, Gorbachev, uncomfortable with the rapidity of change which was urged upon him and also concerned about bringing the more conservative elements along, hesitated and became deeply resentful of the advocates of radical reform. It was at this point in late 1991 that Gorbachev took the fateful step of breaking sharply with the radical reformers. Reaching out to the reactionaries, he replaced the reformist Interior and Justice ministers with persons identified with "old thinking." In December, Eduard Shevardnadze took a step which truly shook observers. He resigned as Foreign Minister, expressing deep concern over the threat of a new dictatorship. Shortly after, there were reports that Aleksandr Yakovlev, the third member of the Gorbachev leadership group, was being eased out gradually. Progressives were purged from leadership of the electronic media. News-oriented television programs that reflected new thinking were replaced by the traditional, dull recitals of the government line. This latest retreat from *glasnost'* was the clearest evidence to the whole world of Gorbachev's capitulation to the hard-line elements in the regime.

That these elements could exercise armed might was demonstrated in early 1991, when clashes between Soviet troops and Latvian and Lithuanian civilians resulted in casualties. The world took note of the fact that Gorbachev, who dissociated himself from these occurrences, had not been able to prevent them and was either unable or unwilling to discipline the responsible military officers. The State Department's report for 1990, which covered also the events of early 1991, noted:

> In the Soviet Union in 1990, vast numbers of citizens continue to exercise newly won political rights, including freedom of expression, assembly, and religion. Hundreds of thousands were permitted to emigrate. However, reforms were unevenly implemented in the country as a whole, and many were not as yet secured by law or buttressed by an independent judiciary. Toward the end of the year and in early 1991, the central government's moves to reassert authority over the republics, particularly the use of military force in Latvia and Lithuania, raised concern over the future of the recent reforms, with dangerous implications for the entire country.

In the early months of 1991, it became increasingly clear that the still nebulous forces of reaction were not satisfied by the concessions that Gorbachev had made to them. They were now committed to deposing Gorbachev. In April, the hard-liners decided to move for Gorbachev's ouster as President and as General Secretary of the Communist Party, the first move to take place in the Congress of People's Deputies and the second in the Central Committee of the Communist Party. They hoped to gain the support of the Yel'tsin supporters for the first of these efforts.

It was at this point that both the reform groups recognized that, to use Benjamin Franklin's famous expression, if they did not hang together they would hang separately. The Gorbachev and Yel'tsin forces decided to enter into a truce. This truce made it clear to the Gorbachev opponents that they could not prevail in the Congress and the Central Committee and caused them to give up the idea of ousting Gorbachev constitutionally, although it did not prevent them from continuing their efforts to undermine him. He ignored the various signals that should have been clear to him and failed to wake up to the reality until the delegation which presented him with an ultimatum to surrender power appeared at his Crimean dacha on August 18.

During the following 48 hours, the Russians were tested and successfully met that test. The last vestiges of a system established and maintained at the cost of millions of casualties expired with the deaths of three persons. Tragic as this circumstance was for the three families affected, the relatively peaceful demise of Bolshevism was expected by no one. The new "mode of civility" which provided the basis for the acts of mass disobedience by the security forces was indeed Gorbachev's most important legacy. It may very well be that if the confrontation had occurred a year earlier, the mass disobedience of orders issued by the top leadership of the army, police, and KGB would not have occurred, and the attempted coup would have been successful. By holding the forces of reaction at bay as long as he did, Gorbachev appears to have allowed the time needed for the Soviet Union's organs of repression to corrode.

The end of Bolshevism, regrettably, has not ushered in an era in which democracy and respect for human rights are fully assured in the successor states. A return to Leninism is now most unlikely, but the institution of nationalist-militarist dictatorships is distinctly within the realm of possibilities. In fact, even though belief in communist ideology appears to have evaporated throughout the former Soviet Union, some of the republics have not yet made the transition even to the trappings of democracy.

There is no doubt, however, that the leaderships of the two largest successor republics, Russia and Ukraine, which together contain about 70 percent of the population of the former Soviet Union, are fully committed to the institution of democracy. What is in doubt is whether they will succeed. There are intellectual elites in both republics that fervently believe in a form of government which derives its authority from the people in free elections and which respects individual liberty, but it is by no means clear that this is a sentiment shared by the population at large. Well aware of the economic success of the democratic West, many Russians and Ukrainians today may be prepared to give the democrats more time to institute a system that provides not only fundamental freedoms but also significantly reverses the economic downward slide. However, at a certain point their patience will end. For democracy to succeed in the republics that once constituted the Soviet Union, it is critically important that an economic upturn begin soon.

Attention has been focused on Russia. The future of the democratic experiment in that country will affect in the first instance its own population, which constitutes more than half the population of the former Soviet Union. It is likely to have an important influence on the other successor republics as well. Concern has been expressed in recent months over some failures by the Russian government to live up to the highest standards of freedom of the press. This may very well reflect the inability of some observers to see the forest for the trees. The underlying problem in today's Russia is the absence of a democratic legal culture. All the republics need institutions authorized to enforce democratic legal principles and capable of doing so. And they need to teach their citizens how such institutions can be used effectively to attain the desired result. Establishing legislatures that write democratic laws and having the executive branch of the government try to live within the law is half the job. The other half is to establish an independent judiciary which can be called upon to restrain the other branches of government if they exceed their authority.

The institutions on which democracy thus rests, a legislature capable of writing democratic laws, an executive branch which will seek to remain within the framework provided by these laws, and an independent judiciary that can compel the other branches to adhere to basic democratic principles, are all still embryonic in the former Soviet Union. Progress toward a democratic culture, in terms of public support of the democratic idea and an understanding of how a democracy should function, is furthest advanced in metropolitan areas such as Moscow, St. Petersburg, and Kiev. In areas more thinly populated, there is less support for, and understanding of, democratic principles. Authoritarian habits persist in the rural areas, particularly on collective farms. Much more is required to lay a solid foundation for democracy in such communities than the fine tuning of freedom of the press.

To be sure, democracy did not spring full-blown from the heads of the writers and thinkers of the Enlightenment. Democracy evolved over centuries in England and over many decades in France. The information revolution has, however, caused a sharp acceleration in the rate of social change in many parts of the world. One of the reasons why the ideas of democracy have established themselves more solidly in the metropolitan centers of the former Soviet Union is that these conurbations have been more closely in touch with the West, through the media or through travelers, than have other areas. Given the end of censorship and other restrictions on freedom of expression, the ideas which once circulated in the metropolitan areas through *samizdat* can now spread to Chelyabinsk or Omsk—and, ultimately, throughout the entire former USSR.

It is appropriate to recall that the Franco dictatorship, established in the 1930s with the support of Hitler and Mussolini, outlasted the Berlin-Rome Axis by thirty years. Yet in the 17 years that have elapsed since Francisco Franco's death, Spain has evolved as a vibrant democracy.

The example of Spain should be a reason for hope that a similar evolution can take place in the former Soviet Union, or at least in those republics in which the leadership has committed itself to democracy, foremost among them Russia. (Others appear to include Ukraine, Armenia, and Kyrgyzstan.) In seeking to determine whether the present trend to an open society in Russia is reversible, we need to note some important differences between Spain in 1975 and Russia in 1992.

When Franco died, he left behind him a country whose traditional agricultural base was functioning well and which was making substantial progress in the development of industry. Although government played an important role in the country's economic life, many enterprises were independent and thus able to play a role in the opening of Spanish society in the post-Franco era. The continuing upward trend in the standard of living added to the country's stability as it gradually, but without undue delays, replaced the government's authoritarian structure with democratic institutions.

By contrast, in recent years, the people of Russia have suffered a substantial drop in their standard of living as the command system unraveled without being replaced by a workable alternative. The continuing economic crisis has undoubtedly weakened the ground on which the country's present leadership seeks to erect a democratic governmental framework.

Russia's economic decline, social disintegration, increase in criminality, and general disillusionment made the Soviet Union ripe for the coup attempt of August 1991. As noted earlier, that coup failed because its leaders assumed that the men under their command would follow orders as they had always done. Therefore, they did not consider it necessary to engage in careful preparation, move down the chain of command, and bring key personnel at all levels into the conspiracy before the first overt move was made. They indeed were unaware that the old command system had corroded. If another coup is attempted, its leaders will undoubtedly study the lessons of August 1991. They will undertake a great deal of preparatory work. Key installations throughout the country will be seized simultaneously. Key personalities supporting the democratic cause are likely to be arrested and possibly killed.

But who would engage in such an elaborate plot? Who has the capability of putting together an effective organization that can move promptly, efficiently, and ruthlessly against Russia's democratic leadership? An organization exists which can play that role and may turn out to be the Achilles' heel of Russia's democracy. *This organization is Russia's secret police.*

In the United States, many casual observers of the Soviet scene viewed the KGB—the most recent acronym for the Soviet secret police—as an amalgam of the Soviet equivalents of the FBI and the CIA. The KGB has indeed discharged many of the functions performed in our country by our foreign intelligence and federal police agencies. But it has played, and continues to play, a much broader role, a role rooted in tradition. Russia's secret police has not only been the premier organ of repression which has served Russia's rulers since Peter the Great, but it has also become a political force in its own right. Beyond that, in the close to 300 years of its existence, Russia's secret police has not only established itself as a permanent fixture of the governmental apparatus, but become an integral part of the country's public life. It is presumed to be ever-present and all-knowing and has tried to live up to its reputation.

It was Peter the Great, influenced by the earliest experiences of his reign, who decided not to shrink from the utmost brutality to safeguard his life and his throne. To provide him with the security that he thought he needed, he established the so-called Secret Office and, by an ukase issued in 1702, gave that office the authority to enforce the country's laws by pursuing persons suspected of treason "by word or deed." Under the leadership of Peter's trusted close friend, Fedor Romodanovsky, the Secret Office established a network of informers and relied on internal spying and denunciations to ferret out suspects. These suspects would then be tortured to obtain confessions and information and more often than not would ultimately be killed.

For less than one year—out of the 290 that have elapsed since the ukase of 1702—has Russia been without a secret police organization. The Provisional Government established after the democratic revolution of February 1917 did abolish the *Okhrana,* the name by which the secret police was known at the time Nicholas II abdicated. However, following the Bolshevik coup in October, Lenin reestablished the secret police under the leadership of a man who soon acquired worldwide notoriety, Felix Dzerzhinsky. Named the "Extraordinary Commission for Combating Counter Revolution and Speculation," or *Cheka* for short, it began to operate with a ferocity reminiscent of Peter's days. The critical role it played in maintaining the Bolsheviks' power was stated bluntly by Lenin: "The *Cheka* is putting into effect the dictatorship of the proletariat, and in this sense it is of inestimable value. Outside of force and violence, there is no way to suppress the exploiters of the masses. This is the business of the *Cheka* and in this lies its service to the proletariat."[1]

By 1921, the Bolsheviks had consolidated their grip on power and the *Cheka* terror temporarily subsided, but the organization was well in place and had established a *modus operandi* that, as it had demonstrated, enabled it to succeed in its mission. At a cost of millions of lives, many of them victims of the *Cheka,* all organized opposition to the Bolsheviks had been destroyed. The fear the *Cheka* had engendered throughout the country did indeed, as Lenin had prescribed, enable the Bolsheviks to establish and maintain their one-party state.

It was under Stalin that the secret police came to the forefront again. The acronyms had changed from *Cheka* to OPGU, GPU, and NKVD, but the methods had remained the same. With the opposition to the Bolsheviks destroyed, Stalin enlisted the NKVD in his effort to purge the party of any individual whom he did not consider personally loyal to him. Thus, in the 1930s, a new blood bath, a new terror, was begun, in which the secret police was elevated to the position of Prætorian Guard of the leader and became the instrument through which the leader governed. It was the power vested in it by Stalin which gave the secret police the status that it possesses to this day.

Given this power, it was not surprising that when Stalin died in 1953 his Minister for State Security, Lavrenti Beria, made a bid for the supreme leadership position. Only through the intervention of the Soviet army was Beria checkmated, arrested, and subsequently executed. (At least these are the data contained in the semi-official versions of events which have surfaced.) But the resultant reduction in the power exercised by the secret police did not last long. In fact, its quick comeback following the arrest and execution of some of its top leaders demonstrated its resilience and the discipline with which the lower echelons were able to close ranks in times of trouble. By 1964, the secret police, now known as the KGB, spearheaded the successful effort to oust Khrushchev and replace him with Brezhnev. And in 1982, the KGB was able to have its own leader, Yuri Andropov, succeed Brezhnev as General Secretary of the Communist Party and *de facto* head of government. It is generally assumed that after Andropov's death the KGB played an important role in advancing the political fortunes of Andropov's protégé, Mikhail Gorbachev. The KGB leadership clearly did not anticipate where Gorbachev would ultimately lead the country. Only when it viewed itself as betrayed by Gorbachev did the KGB ultimately turn against him.

Following the failure of the coup attempt, the realization appears to have dawned in Moscow that something had to be done with the secret police. Two days after the coup's collapse, Gorbachev gave formal approval to the appointment of Vadim Bakatin, a man with the capability and commitment to clean house, as the KGB's new head. Bakatin, who had served as Soviet Interior Minister (and been removed from office in November 1990 by Gorbachev as a concession to the reactionaries) promptly made his position on the KGB clear in a public statement, "You are sending me to a department which I have said on more than one occasion should be eliminated. So it turns out that I have come to destroy the Committee for State Security."[2]

As he went about that task, the government which had placed him in authority was rapidly disintegrating. A few months later, as he looked back at his short period in office, Bakatin had this to say:

Everybody keeps saying that Bakatin has torn down the KGB structure. For goodness sake, this is not so. If you come to Kazakhstan, not a single hair has fallen from the head of any official in Kazakhstan. Or to Kyrgyzstan: I just got back from there. Everything is still as it was. The situation is the same in the Moscow department, and in the Kemerovo one. That is all the capillaries at the bottom and the structure have remained the same.[3]

This candid admission should be seen as a warning to all supporters of the democratic cause in the former Soviet Union. The termination of the Soviet Union was not accompanied by a dissolution of the secret police. On the contrary, each of the KGB organizations has continued in existence at the republic level. Yel'tsin did not appoint Bakatin as head of the Russian KGB, or AFB, as it is now called. There has been little effort to cleanse the secret police of Russia, or of any of the other republics, of the staff which for decades has carried out the task of repression. Yel'tsin, like the pre-coup Gorbachev, has settled for a KGB leadership which has kept the "capillaries" in place.

Thus, 290 years after Peter's ukase, police officials imbued with the spirit of the Secret Office continue to ply their trade. To be sure, there are some functions the KGB has performed which would indeed be performed by a central police organization in a democracy, such as counterespionage and the pursuit of persons suspected of involvement in corruption, terrorism, or organized crime. But the KGB also served as the country's political police. Staff members who hold down jobs to this day in the successor organizations, in command positions as well as in the ranks, were responsible in the recent past for the arrest of persons for "anti-Soviet agitation and propaganda" (penalty: seven years at hard labor plus five years of internal exile) or "defamation of the Soviet system" (penalty: three years' imprisonment). They were also, in many cases, responsible for framing citizens so that they would be convicted for ordinary crimes that they never committed, or for obtaining psychiatric findings which permitted the dispatch of perfectly sane persons to hospitals for the mentally ill. Many KGB officers were involved in surveillance of dissidents and religious activists and in "dirty trick" operations, including such childish ones as damaging the tires on the cars of the U.S. Embassy's human rights officers.

The young poet Irina Ratushinskaya (who was released in 1986 after having served three years of a sentence of seven years' hard labor and five years' internal exile for her poetry—deemed to constitute anti-Soviet agitation and propaganda) has told of her exit interview with the head of the KGB detachment at her labor camp. Commenting on her premature release, this officer told her that he disapproved strongly of the decision to set her free, which had been made at the highest level of government. However, he consoled himself with the parting observation that some day Ratushinskaya was going to be back in the camp.

In light of the American experience with the CIA, it has been suggested that one way of warding off a threat to democracy from the secret police is to place the latter under legislative oversight. It is conceivable that such a move could help bring the foreign intelligence operation under effective control. But this agency is not the source of the threat to Russia's new democratic system. It is the domestic arm of the former Soviet KGB that should cause Russia's democrats the greatest anxiety.

Concerned about crime, and in particular about corruption, the new leaders hesitate to move resolutely against the secret police. They want to use that organization's talents to serve their perfectly laudable goals and seem confident that they will be able to keep it sufficiently in check to prevent it from undermining the state. However, they use it at their peril.

Acting alone, the secret police is not likely to be able to overthrow a democratically elected government. It would need allies, particularly among the military. However, if economic conditions do not improve, there will be enough disgruntled elements throughout the country who could be gathered to execute a more efficiently organized coup than the botched effort of August 1991. And it is the secret police that would have the knowledge, skill, and finesse to rally all these disaffected elements together and plan the effort to reestablish a dictatorship.

If economic conditions in Russia continue to deteriorate, it will be difficult to maintain democracy. If they improve sharply and rapidly, the democratic cause in Russia will be much safer. However, there is the possibility that Russia's immediate economic future may fall between these two extremes, stabilizing and then improving fairly slowly. It is in that setting that the continuation of democracy in Russia would depend on whether the secret police is able to manipulate events.

It follows that there is really only one option available to protect Russian democracy: to follow the Bakatin prescription and dissolve the secret police. The secret police requires careful investigation. KGB members who were guilty of crimes should be prosecuted. Those who were engaged in questionable activities should be retired. Only officers who can demonstrate that they were not involved in politically oriented activities should be retained in police work. These officers with clean records could be transferred to the police functions of the republican interior ministries. And these ministries in turn should shed responsibility for police work of purely local import, letting local communities establish their own police forces, with the republican police force focusing only on those crimes which require a coordinated effort at the republic level.

After four years of rapidly accelerating and almost unbelievable progress toward a more open society in the Soviet Union, Eduard Shevardnadze startled the world on December 20, 1990, with his emotionally charged speech in which he warned that a dictatorship was coming. The devils of which Shevardnadze warned then showed their true colors eight months later. They were beaten back but have not been exorcised. To accomplish the latter—and to remove the sword of Damocles, which now hangs over the former Soviet republics—is one of the greatest challenges confronting the leaders of the democratic forces in these republics.

NOTES

1. Quoted by David Shub, *Lenin* (Garden City, N.Y.: Doubleday, 1948), p. 326, from *Yezhenedel' nik Chrezvychainoi Komissii* (Moscow), November-December, 1918.
2. Russian Television Network, 2000 GMT, August 28, 1991; FBIS-SOV-91-168, August 29, 1991, p. 42.
3. Yevgeniya Albats, "KGB-MSB-MBVD: Substantive Changes?" *Moscow News*, January 13, 1992, p. 5, cited by J. Michael Waller, "Who Will Control the Former KGB, And When? Opportunities and Challenges for Russian-U.S. Cooperation," unpublished paper delivered at the American Bar Association conference, "Intelligence in a Post-Cold War World," Washington, D.C., May 1, 1992.

Part III: Pluralism in the Media

The "Independent Media"

Nicholas Daniloff

For seven decades, Moscow imposed a high degree of uniformity on the Soviet media by using a rigid censorship system, KGB intimidation, and, most importantly, widespread self-censorship inspired by fear. Now that these factors have largely disappeared from Russian life, it is reasonable to expect that diversity and independence will be the rule for newspapers and broadcasting in the future. But can we be sure?

Russia today is in economic chaos and political confusion. People are crying out for a firm hand to restore order and predictability. Suppose President Boris Yel'tsin decides to impose rule by state of emergency and rein in the critical press? Suppose Yel'tsin fails to deliver on promises of a better life and is overthrown by a new junta? Suppose the post-Yel'tsin leaders do not feel bound by legal or constitutional niceties? The questions will then arise whether media independence will survive and whether the present diversity in journalism is really irreversible.

To arrive at a judgment, three secondary questions need to be asked:

- How independent and courageous is Russian journalism today?
- How well or poorly does Russian law protect freedom of the press and broadcasting?
- What factors, if any, might cool the determination of the new Russian rulers to reinstitute strict media controls?

The unsuccessful coup attempt in August 1991 clearly demonstrated that the Russian press had developed an uncommon vitality and independence and was not about to be frightened by moves to restrain it.

In the first hours of the August 19-21 coup, junta members announced that they were taking control of the mass media (Directive No. 1, Paragraph 8) and banning critical newspapers (Directive No. 2, Paragraph 1). By secret instruction, they ordered the KGB and military to take control of Central Television and to seize television centers in the Baltic states—media that would certainly be adversarial.[1]

Vice President Gennadi Yanaev and the other conspirators apparently expected that the media, on the whole, would obediently follow the precedent set during the 1964 coup against Nikita Khrushchev: attack the fallen, and trumpet the call of those newly arrived in power. As events would show, the junta misjudged the situation, although its members were not totally wrong in identifying the press that might be supportive. *Pravda, Izvestia,* and other "reliable" organs prominently published the conspirators' directives. Even the press service of the Soviet embassy in Washington, normally loyal to Mikhail Gorbachev, put out the junta's statements as routine press releases. What the junta did not expect was the fierce, instantaneous resistance which developed among political opponents, notably Russian President Yel'tsin and Leningrad mayor Anatoli Sobchak, several key officers of the military and KGB, and influential editors and writers of the banned press.

The prohibited press, "infected" by *glasnost'*, struggled from the start. Independent-minded journalists were determined to collect the news, then to battle to make it public. Many journalists acknowledged later that they were fearful until they saw resistance developing. They knew that this was the first great test of freedom of the press in a fledgling democracy and that it must not be abandoned without a fight.

"I first heard of the coup," said Alex Korgun, a junior editor of *Komsomol' skaya pravda*, "from Radio Liberty early in the morning of August 19. I rushed in to the office, getting there about 7 A.M. Immediately we began organizing a chronology, drawing on reports from our own correspondents and supplemented by well-wishing citizens who called in on their own. This chronology was posted in the corridors for all to see and to share with their friends and contacts. When a top editor announced to the staff that the newspaper was among those banned by the junta and would not be coming out, one of the younger reporters shot back. 'No! We've already published! Look at the corridors!' Was our editor surprised!"[2]

The editors of *Komsomol' skaya pravda* were determined to get the word out. They welcomed passersby, allowed them to enter the premises and read about the events. They encouraged journalists to tell their friends. They faxed their running chronologies to 35 Soviet and foreign newspapers, including the *New York Post*.[3] Similarly, the independent news agencies Interfax and Postfactum went to work on even more ambitious chronologies. Drawing on hundreds of correspondents across the nation, the two agencies reported on provincial reaction.

Their dispatches revealed confusion across the nation. Many high officials—local communist party leaders as well as local council members—adopted a wait-and-see attitude. Others, such as Krasnodar council chairman Nikolai Kondratenko, supported the junta and rejected Yel'tsin's appeals. Still others rallied openly to Yel'tsin. In Moscow, the widow of academician Andrei Sakharov, Yelena Bonner, called on all the people to "defend freedom."[4]

Under the leadership of editor-in-chief Vitali Tret'yakov, the employees of *Nezavisimaya gazeta* developed a novel approach to circumvent the publishing ban. They typed up a two-page edition and ran off 1,000 photocopies. They posted these leaflets in subway cars, on buildings at major intersections, at bus stops, churches, and schools: anywhere that influential people might pass.[5] "Most people understood we could use civil resistance to stop the coup," said *Nezavisimaya gazeta* reporter Yuri Leonov.

Vladimir Vesinsky, another reporter for the same newspaper (and a Nieman Fellow at Harvard University in 1991), recalled that the newspaper's printing plant was seized by 20 soldiers with assault rifles. The troops were supposed to silence the newspaper, but failed.[6] Vesinsky managed to telephone word of events to Portuguese television in Lisbon, to *El Espectador* in Bogota, and to the *Milwaukee Journal,* where a Nieman colleague worked.

One of the most original acts of resistance was thought up by the editors of 11 banned newspapers—*Argumenty i fakty, Kommersant, Kuranty, Megapolis ekspress, Moskovskie novosti, Moskovsky komsomolets, Nezavisimaya gazeta, Rossiiskaya gazeta, Rossiiskie vesti, Stolitsa,* and *Komsomol'skaya pravda.* They banded together to create a crisis sheet called *Obshchaya gazeta,* or *The Common Newspaper.* This novel enterprise denounced the coup as illegal in its very first issue and printed Boris Yel'tsin's appeals. To respect Russian (as opposed to Soviet) legalities, the editors registered the newspaper with the authorities. Their application was accepted and they received certification No. 1054. They managed to print their broadsheet in editions of 500,000 copies using the presses of *Kommersant,* which were not seized by soldiers loyal to the plotters. Free copies of *Obshchaya gazeta* were carried by volunteers to Russia's other major political city, Leningrad (St. Petersburg), where they were handed out and plastered on street corners, much as in Moscow.[7]

Despite the censorship imposed by junta representatives in Leningrad, employees of the independent North-West Information Agency continued to go to work. "We gradually pieced together the fact that there was resistance," wrote journalist Yelena Zelinskaya afterwards. "Yel'tsin had appealed to the Russian people; barricades were erected in Moscow; meetings were being held in Leningrad. By 1 P.M., it was clear that the Russian people did not intend to give up the democracy movement without a fight. The horror disappeared. Now it was time simply to work."[8]

Independent broadcasters, also banned by the plotters, reacted in a manner similar to the writing press. *Ekho Moskvy,* a low-power station sponsored by Moscow University and the Moscow City Council, proved to be daring. Although it was knocked off the air several times by the plotters, *Ekho Moskvy* managed to come back with the connivance of several Ministry of Communications officials. The radio station, which prides itself on its independent reporting, kept nine million Muscovites well informed about the troop and tank movements and the general course of events. "We listened to *Ekho Moskvy* all the time," said Isabella Babich, a Moscow housewife. "It was terrific. It was at least two to three hours ahead of the information being put out by Radio Liberty."[9]

The Russian Television Company, which had started up for the first time in early summer, was effectively prevented from transmitting by the junta. Nevertheless, its staff went out on the streets with video cameras and tape recorders to collect the news. Like their writing colleagues, they hoped that they would eventually break the ban. In the Far East, the independent TVK television station in Petropavlovsk-Kamchatski evaded the prohibitions. Using information received from the independent Russian Information Agency, this station condemned the coup and delivered to the public Yel'tsin's appeals.[10]

One factor which the plotters seemed to have entirely overlooked was the activity of Soviet stringers for the Munich-based Radio Liberty. During the Cold War years, of course, *"Svoboda"* was looked upon by Moscow officials as an enemy radio station that was financed by the CIA and intent on destabilizing the Soviet government. More recently, under *glasnost',* Soviet officials were willing to allow Radio Liberty to draw on the services of some two dozen Soviet citizens. When the coup began, Andrei Babitsky, Mikhail Sokolov, and Dmitri Volchek rushed to the RSFSR Government White House and managed to phone Radio Liberty with up-to-the-minute reports. Thus, Russian voices in Moscow were talking to Russian listeners throughout the Soviet Union, thanks to a foreign radio station broadcasting from Munich. After the coup, Yel'tsin authorized permanent accreditation in Moscow for Radio Liberty. Accreditation was approved under the Russian Federation press law while Soviet central government officials prevaricated.

Similarly, Artyom Borovik, an editor of the magazine *Sovershenno sekretno,* an organ of the detective writers' association, was able to give commentaries from the White House to CBS News in New York. The son of APN correspondent Genrikh Borovik, Borovik spent many years in Manhattan and was able to deliver his observations in perfect English. Diane Sawyer of ABC also slipped into the White House and transmitted a dramatic film clip of Boris Yel'tsin in his headquarters.

This Soviet-American "overlap" was given yet another dimension by Cable News Network, which played a key role in political developments. Since March 1990, CNN has been available in many Moscow government offices, hotels, diplomatic missions, and private apartments that have parabolic antennae. A 100-watt Ministry of Communications transmitter had been beaming a UHF test signal prior to introducing cable service for Russian viewers.[11] From the roof of the CNN bureau at 15 Kutuzovsky Prospekt, cameras would zoom in on events in front of the White House and broadcast these events live to the whole world as well as to the Moscow public. Within 90 minutes of the coup announcement, CNN had a live satellite feed on its way to Atlanta and the world. The CNN coup reports, led by Steve Hurst, stayed on the air for more than a month.

Knowing the power of television, the plotters had ordered strict control of state broadcasting beginning at 4 A.M. on the first day of the coup. Interior Minister Boris Pugo specifically instructed Central Television executives to prevent Leningrad mayor Anatoli Sobchak from appearing on the air. These orders were cunningly subverted through intentional delays. Not only did Valentin Lazutkin, the first deputy of Soviet Central Television, contrive to allow Sobchak to appear; he also permitted the main national evening newscast, "*Vremya,*" to do a two-and-one-half-minute piece on Yel'tsin's rousing call to resist, delivered on the first day from atop tank No. 110.[12]

Other influential figures, sensing a lack of will among the junta members, took actions that defied the plotters. Dean Yasen N. Zasursky of the School of Journalism of Moscow University told a meeting of the Gannett Freedom Forum in Moscow, at noon on the first day of the coup, that the takeover was illegal and would likely collapse. The same day, he telephoned Northeastern University in Boston to urge that the undergraduate journalism exchange between the two universities go ahead despite events.[13] Shortly after the attempted coup, Zasursky published an article in *Izvestia* asserting that if

President Gorbachev were to be covered by newsmen as thoroughly as the American president, future coups could be avoided.[14]

These examples suggest that Russian journalists today are no longer the automatons of the old Soviet propaganda machine. They are fiercely independent and prepared to go to great lengths, much like their Western colleagues, to get the news and to get it out.

The August coup lasted only three days—a short period that did not seriously affect the morale of independent journalists. If the *putschisty* had been able to maintain themselves in power for a month, the outcome for the independent press might have been far different. Similarly, a long, insidious attack on the critical Russian press, including denial of supplies, economic pressures, lockouts, refusals to register new journals, harassment, and possible arrests of editors, might dampen the ardor of crusading newsmen. This possibility of whittling down the press by "salami tactics" raises a second question: how well does the law protect the Russian press from the whims of leaders under pressure?

During the weeks after the August putsch, President Yel'tsin accomplished his own coup over the Soviet central government. On more than one occasion, he rode roughshod over fairness and even legality. With regard to the press, he and his cohorts fired several warning shots. First, Yel'tsin banned the communist party press at the same time that he suspended the communist party. When reform-minded editors pointed out the antidemocratic nature of this action, Yel'tsin backed off from his original stand. The newspaper *Pravda* was allowed to reorganize itself and register as an independent newspaper.[15] However, financial difficulties subsequently forced it to suspend publication early in 1992.

In October 1991, a second incident caused consternation. The Russian Ministry of Press and Mass Media castigated *Nezavisimaya gazeta* and *Moscow News* for reporting discussions within the Russian government over a possible nuclear conflict with Ukraine. Yel'tsin's government was apparently concerned that such reports might cause public disorder and complicate relations with the West. Information Minister Mikhail Poltoranin told the newspapers that a second warning would result in closure. Rather than trying to kill the message, Poltoranin was using the primitive approach of attacking the messenger. A former liberal journalist, Poltoranin is reputed to be a Yel'tsin loyalist, more interested in protecting his boss than in the philosophy of a free press.[16]

Meanwhile, in St. Petersburg (then still Leningrad), Mayor Sobchak reportedly ordered television chief Viktor Yugin to prevent television gadfly Aleksandr Nevzorov from going on the air. Nevzorov, a supporter of using armed force in Lithuania in January 1991, apparently had offended Sobchak with snide remarks about Sobchak's wife, calling her "the lady in silks."[17] "We, of course, expected repression," Nevzorov told *Pravda* later, "because the present rulers greatly dislike our principle of not toadying to any authority. Our team was expecting the democrats to make a strike, but we did not think it would be sudden and underhanded." Earlier, editor Vitali Tret'yakov had voiced similar views in *Nezavisimaya gazeta*: "The democrats very quickly start to manifest the same intolerance of any kind of criticism as their predecessors the communists did. The democrats loved us when we criticized the communists, but they can't stand it when we go after them."[18]

The trouble, of course, is that Russia has no tradition of tolerating dissent or, in the formulation of U.S. Supreme Court Justice Oliver Wendell Holmes, of protecting the "expression of opinions we loathe and believe to be fraught with death." The political leaders of Russia tend to believe that the newly liberated press should be actively supportive of democracy. At any rate, it should not criticize the leadership.[19] In the absence of a free press tradition, the Russian Law on the Press (Law on Mass Media Information, adopted in 1991), which was written by Yu. M. Baturin, M. A. Fedotov, and V. L. Entin, represents a considerable achievement. It prohibits prior censorship and requires access to information. But at the same time, this law is loaded with provisions that can be used to restrain the press, both before and after publication.[20] Most notorious is Article 4, which explicitly prohibits "abuses" of the mass media. This article makes it illegal to publish state, commercial, or other "specially protected secrets." The law prohibits calls to overthrow the government by force or to incite social, class, or national intolerance. Likewise, the law forbids the dissemination of war propaganda, or incitement to commit other "criminally punishable acts." The broad nature of this article is entirely "Soviet" in its approach. It reflects that major concern of decades of Soviet jurisprudence: to protect the state from outraged citizens, not to protect citizens from the abuses of power.

Nor is Article 4 the only catch-all which could be used against overly independent media. Article 13 presents various reasons for refusing the required registration of new media, or, worse still, declining to accept and consider a registration request. Among the reasons for such a refusal is the presumption on the part of the authorities that the requesting media organization might engage in the "abuse of free mass information." Operating without registration, of course, would be considered illegal and would subject the organization to closure.

Broadcasting is always vulnerable to regulation because the finite number of broadcast channels invites a government to create a system to maintain order among the available frequencies. A licensing system naturally suggests reasons why licenses may be refused, including the possibility, as provided under the Russian law (Article 33.1), that the original license was issued as a result of deception, trickery, or bribery. Article 43 prohibits the publication of information given on a confidential basis. This is bound to be a slippery area because it would appear to create an imprecise enlargement of secrecy classifications. Furthermore, no attention is paid in the press law to defining the term of secrecy. Is an item considered secret this year to be considered secret a year from now? A quarter-century from now?

Other extraordinarily broad prohibitions are included under Chapter VII, which lays down responsibility (see Articles 58, 60, 61, 62) for violating various provisions of the law. Enumerated are several score reasons for taking action against the media, such as operating without legal registration or publishing in violation of rules relating to pornography, advertising, and campaigning.

Apart from these legal considerations, a number of other factors make the critical press vulnerable to pressures by an embattled Russian government. Most newspapers, for example, do not yet own and operate their own presses. These presses today belong to the state and are subject to restraint by the government. Furthermore, newsprint is a deficit commodity. Even under the new system of free prices, the Russian government may find ways to ration or otherwise limit supply. And finally, there is a possibility of an economic squeeze: the Russian Ministry of Communications is threatening to raise the charges for transmissions (faxes, telexes, and telephone calls), thus imposing an additional burden on the poorly financed independent press.[21]

These difficulties come at a time when newspaper and book readership is decreasing. The Russian public is tiring of sensationalism, and the rising price of subscriptions is having a negative impact. Renewals for 1992 are falling, and 18 of the most popular newspapers reportedly have lost a total of 18 million readers.[22]

A government under stress, with little historic experience with press freedom, is likely to place some conditions on the media. The media may not be ordered to propagandize unrealistic goals or false achievements. But officials are likely to insist that the free press should be "supportive" and in any case should do nothing "disruptive" or "seditious." Not surprisingly, a law to prohibit criticism of the Russian president has been under consideration in the Russian parliament, since desire for such restraint is common in the former Soviet Union, which had adopted an all-union law to this effect. Similar measures have been adopted in the Baltic states and Georgia.

"I doubt that the government of Boris Yel'tsin would try to choke off press freedom altogether," Sergei Sholokhov, a television personality of St. Petersburg's well-known "Fifth Wheel" program, has observed. "He understands only too well that his political power depends on his ability to communicate through the press and especially television."[23] Sholokhov makes an important point. In any country, television magnifies the voice and power of politicians. Anatoli Sobchak's appearance on television during the coup, for example, convinced many that the plotters had failed on their first day and that the reformers had won. Furthermore, a number of other considerations could oblige Yel'tsin or his successors to move slowly in reining in the press. These might be called Pandora's Four Genies:

• *Free Thinking.* One of Gorbachev's lasting contributions is that he succeeded in diminishing fear in Soviet society. He also drew attention to the need for legality and due process. The result is that people today feel freer than ever to reveal their private views in public and to act on them.

During the coup, key officers of the military and the KGB refused orders by the junta to arrest and isolate the chief resisters. The KGB knew where Yel'tsin was throughout the crisis but would not detain him. The Alpha Group, ordered to storm the White House where Yel'tsin and his supporters had holed up, refused to move. Similarly, the critical press refused to bow to the orders of the Yanaev clique.[24] Furthermore, polls taken by *Argumenty i fakty* during the August coup showed that the public at large generally believed that the junta acted illegally. Of 1,438 persons polled on August 20 in four different major cities, 62.5 percent said that they considered the coup to be illegal. [25] In Russia today, there is a new appreciation of legality and democracy. Freedom of expression, press, and religion is viewed as part of that democracy.

• *Memory of Evil.* Allied to the first factor of free thinking is the painful historical memory of lawlessness and gross abuse of human rights under Stalin. The details of the Soviet holocaust are reasonably well-known to the population. The inevitable conclusion is that single-party rule, or rule without a legal opposition, is likely to result in ghastly mistakes. Therefore, it is necessary to have a free press which will provide a wide variety of views and suggest corrective approaches. This memory of evil may well act as a check on unconstitutional actions.

• *The West.* In announcing his conditions for diplomatic recognition of members of the Commonwealth of Independent States, President Bush made explicit the attitude of the West: Russia and the associated states must develop in a democratic manner if they want help and support. Any acute or prolonged crackdown on the free press could spark fears in the West that a return to the Stalinist past was underway.

• *The Economic Imperative.* Russia and the associated states are today in a desperate economic situation. They can expect reasonably generous humanitarian help for the immediate future. But quick fixes will not be enough. Medium-term and long-term rebuilding programs must be undertaken.

To receive adequate aid, Russia will have to guarantee a certain level of openness. Gone are the days of "give a kopek, get a ruble." Western nations and international financial institutions will insist on a high degree of frankness and mutuality in business dealings. If Russia is to benefit from a new beginning with the West, it will have to discard many of the secretive reflexes of the Soviet and czarist past.

Pluralism in the Russian media is now a fact of life. Russian journalists today are more vital and independent than ever before. But their freedom of action is not without limits, and their independence is likely to be challenged from time to time.

The legal boundaries of the free press in Russia are yet to be defined with clarity. The current Russian law on the press prohibits prior censorship, but at the same time offers the new Russian rulers plenty of opportunity to restrict overly critical journalists.

Russian officials may sporadically assault the press, but they are likely to move slowly in initiating a systematic crackdown. A host of reasons will argue for restraint on the part of the leaders, including the recognized value of a free press in well-established democracies and the dependence of the new rulers on a credible and independent press to articulate their policies.

As editor Vitali Tret'yakov of *Nezavisimaya gazeta* observed, very much in the spirit of Thomas Jefferson and James Madison, "I hope that the Russian authorities will have sufficient common sense to take a sensible attitude toward the problems of the press. In any case, it should be remembered: first the freedom of the press is destroyed, then those who shattered it."[26]

NOTES

1. *Pravda,* August 20, 1991, pp. 1, 2.
2. Personal interview with Alex Korgun in the offices of *Komsomol'skaya pravda,* Moscow, September 5, 1991.
3. *Ibid.*

4. See *Putch, khronika trevozhnykh dnei* (Moscow: Progress, 1991), pp. 17-187.

5. *The Wall Street Journal* (New York), August 22, 1991, p. 1.

6. Vladimir Vesinsky, "Moscow During the Abortive Coup," Nieman Reports (Harvard University) 45, no. 4 (Winter 1991), p. 31.

7. See *Obshchaya gazeta* (Moscow), nos. 1 and 2. Information also from interview with Alex Korgun, September 5, 1991.

8. Yelena Zelinskaya, "Leningrad Publication's Resistance," Nieman Reports (Harvard University) 45, no. 4 (Winter 1991), p. 31.

9. Personal interview with Isabella Babich in Moscow, September 5, 1991.

10. *Putch, khronika trevozhnykh dnei*, p. 77.

11. Personal interview with CNN Vice President Stuart Loory, Moscow, September 7, 1991.

12. Stuart Loory and Ann Imse, *Seven Days that Shook the World* (Atlanta: Turner Publishing, Inc., 1991), pp. 99-102.

13. Personal conversations with Dean Yasen N. Zasursky in Moscow, September 1-12, 1991.

14. Zasursky, *Izvestia*, September 5, 1991, p. 2.

15. The fate of *Pravda* was discussed in the Moscow central press between August and November 1991. See *Izvestia*, August 24, 1991, p. 2; *Rossiiskaya gazeta*, December 19, 1991, p. 2.

16. Daniel Sneider, "New Russian Leaders Threaten Curbs on Independent Press," *The Christian Science Monitor*, October 31, 1991, p. 3.

17. *Pravda*, November 30, 1991, p. 2.

18. *The Christian Science Monitor*, October 31, 1991, p. 3.

19. A typical comment on the "duty" of the free press to support democracy was offered by Yevgeni Velikhov, the well-known physicist and political leader, on the Moscow-Boston Space Bridge, WGBH, November 2, 1991.

20. See text of the law published in a special edition by *Rossiya*, journal of the RSFSR Supreme Soviet Presidium. The Russian parliament approved the new press law with amendments on December 19, 1991. On December 24, 1991, *Pravda* reported that the authors of the law charged that freedom of the press was threatened by certain amendments. Yu. M. Baturin, M. A. Fedotov, and V. L. Entin explained that the amendments would prohibit the use of concealed cameras for collecting information and would oblige journalists to identify confidential sources on demand of prosecutors.

21. Russian Television Network, "*Vesti*" program, December 20, 1991, FBIS-Sov-91-247, December 24, 1991, p. 26.

22. *Moscow News*, no. 47 (November 24-December 1, 1991), pp. 4-5.

23. Personal interview, Andover, Vermont, November 24, 1991.

24. Loory and Isme, *Seven Days That Shook the World*, pp. 82ff.

25. *Obshchaya gazeta*, no. 2 (1991), p. 3, citing results of a poll conducted August 20, 1991, by the All-Union Center for the Study of Public Opinion.

26. *Pravda*, November 1, 1991.

—

Press Freedom: New Dangers

Vitaly Korotich

Some time ago, the chief editor of one of the principal Russian literary monthlies asked for help in finding an American purchaser for his magazine. Russia's new political leadership had announced that it planned to provide subsidies for a number of periodicals, but unfortunately, his monthly was not included in the list of privileged publications. Consequently, there was little prospect of the journal surviving, which would have been a great pity, since it was one of the most liberal Russian-language literary monthlies. The editor cursed the government freely over the telephone, thus confirming that *glasnost'* had indeed been successful in freeing persons of their constant fear of the government. He was acting in a new way, unafraid of saying what he thought.

The government also demonstrated that it accepted the new rules— periodicals are now being crushed by economic methods, not by censorship. The tears shed by the Russian editor resembled the tears of American editors facing bankruptcy; this shared experience brings colleagues from the West and the former Soviet Union closer together. There will be a lot of bankrupt-cies. Whereas before the (Soviet) press existed entirely as a government operation and the mouthpiece of the communist party, now its Russian successor has achieved the freedom it had sought for so long. To the limit of its ability, the government is endeavoring to restrict this freedom, just as governments in the majority of countries, including the countries of the Free World, have done. Who will survive? Probably very few.

By the most modest estimates, about one-third of Russian periodicals were expected to be defunct by the end of 1992. In the summer of 1991, the Committee on Publishing Houses and the Press had registered 1,773 all-union periodicals, i.e., periodicals that are distributed over the entire country. Of these, 803 belonged to state organizations, 233 to editorial boards and publishing houses, 291 to public organizations, 27 to party organizations (mainly the CPSU), 19 to religious organizations, and 241 to private individuals. These were the official registration statistics. Naturally, the former CPSU, in reality, controlled a lot more than just 30-odd publications. Chances are high that a number of publications received money from the former KGB. A lot of anti-Semitic, semifascist periodicals also had funding sources that would not have been indicated on registration forms.

After the so-called August putsch—this comical attempt at a *coup d'état* can hardly be called a serious effort to seize power—the entire communist press was prohibited. At the same time, the state entity that had gone under the name of the Soviet Union began to disintegrate rapidly. Similarly, the command function of such publications as (the until recently omnipotent) *Pravda* declined, while the authority of national republican newspapers and magazines, which had always had to take a back seat politically, began to grow sharply. Managers of periodicals had to begin to think seriously about how many staff members they could afford to keep—it would be ludicrous to try to return to the times when that same *Pravda* maintained over 700 journalists in its Moscow offices alone, many of whom scarcely did any real writing at all. Moreover, thanks to their bottomless budgets funded by the party, *Pravda* and the other communist party newspapers and magazines had been in a position to maintain an enormous corps of correspondents abroad. All the publishing houses with relatively modern printing equipment belonged to the party, which established arbitrary prices for their services.

Ogonek, of which I was the editor, paid completely different charges compared with the party publications, and also had to pay a far higher price for newsprint. Despite this, the profit that we produced was neatly confiscated by the *Pravda* Publishing House, which had assumed responsibility for distribution of the magazine and pocketed all the income from subscriptions and newspaper-stand sales. We were the first organization in the country to disband the magazine's party organization. We then began to fight for our independence. The sanctions that were imposed on the magazine initially were only financial, but nevertheless they were difficult to withstand: for a while, *Ogonek* staff members were paid only one-third of equivalent *Pravda* staff salaries; also, honoraria to authors were far lower than those paid by any of the communist publications. It was impossible to compare staff perks with the system of privileges enjoyed by the staff of the government press, since *Ogonek* staff received no perks at all. This is all in the past tense, however. The property of the communist periodicals and publishing houses has been nationalized, and *Ogonek* has become something of a privileged weekly, since the Yel'tsin government has granted it a very substantial subsidy for the purchase of newsprint.

That privilege, however, may be cause for concern, with the possible creation of a new group of "faithful servants," although the individuals who have been awarded such subsidies thus far probably will not perceive them as an advance in return for future loyal service. However, the result is that the situation of the press now has an important new aspect: some periodicals will be given additional income, while others receive nothing. New injustices are created, because the national leadership is attempting to create a "pocket press." Probably, this will not be the last instance of an official relapse into communist thinking. Totalitarian power—and today the country is moving rather steadily in the direction of a new totalitarianism, since it is unlikely that the planned market reforms can be carried out under democratic conditions—is now leaving the independent press very little chance of survival. The Law on Mass Media that was adopted by the now defunct parliament in 1991—assuming that it is replaced by new legislation—will not bring new freedom.

Many people have already grown tired of hearing the very word "freedom" used without adjectives, and more and more frequently the word is combined with "responsibility" and "understanding of the moment"—almost in the same way as it was in earlier times. One gets the impression that the old Leninist dictum has been resuscitated: "To live in the society and to be free from the society is impossible." However, this idea remains topical in every country where there are political leaders who dream of an obedient crowd and journalists who will organize this crowd for them. The communists leaders, so it seemed, had realized this dream. From 1918 to 1990, the most brutal censorship in history raged in Russia. Although initially introduced as a "temporary measure," it remained in force for many decades and reduced the nature of the journalistic profession itself to a shameful bureaucracy implementing directives issued by the political leadership.

I brought to the United States a number of notebooks that contained the instructions given to the editors of the country's main newspapers and magazines at regular conferences held by the CPSU Central Committee. Everything is in there, from rebukes for those who had made critical statements without prior approval to direct instructions to ignore particular events. For example, one look through the runs of Soviet newspapers and magazines for 1988 (the very time in which *perestroika* was at its height!) makes it evident that reference, in any context, to the twentieth anniversary of the crushing by Soviet tanks of the Prague Spring was forbidden. The censors watched carefully to ensure that no mention of this event was made. When *Ogonek* produced a piece on the group of Muscovites who organized a protest in 1968 on Red Square against the Soviet intervention in Czechoslovakia (and as a result ended up in court), the material was taken away and held for an unconscionable length of time, until finally, with great effort and ingenuity, the staff managed to publish it. And this occurred at the height of that very same *glasnost'* that, in the eyes of the West, was resolving so many Soviet problems.

Today Russians resemble the heroes of Ken Kesey's novel *One Flew Over the Cuckoo's Nest,* who are told that from now on they can live just the way they want. After making this announcement, the doctor departs—leaving the patients to decide for themselves how to get by, now that the intimidating nurse in charge of them has gone. During the course of many decades of persecution and repression, we lost the sense of common measure with the remainder of humanity. Now, our way back will be complex and dangerous, because we are only beginning to learn what is normal for almost everyone else.

To return to the problems of the mass media, one must remember that in Russia the creation of the truly professional journalist is an ongoing process. It is only now that chasing after news has become an important task, since previously all the information came from the authorities. To seek out news oneself was dangerous, unfashionable, and unpopular. Moreover, there is the concept of news selection and journalistic responsibility for determining the criteria for selection. This, too, is an aspect with which few journalists are familiar. Living and working under democratic conditions is more difficult in many respects than being squashed by a dictatorship.

Today, writers in the former Soviet Union are being forced to understand that modern journalism is impossible without democratic norms. Learning what democratic legislation is needed, as well as writing and safeguarding these laws—all this is work in which we are at least 50 years behind the rest of humanity. Alas, the habits of violence and the habits of freedom produce completely different kinds of citizens. Another hurdle consists of the need to bypass a mass of journalists, politicians and parliamentarians who have internalized the reflexes of a completely different system and are endeavoring to apply these reflexes to the construction of the institutions of today's world.

Many seek fast tracks, and consequently facile approaches. Russian media now are entering a period of semiserious newspapers and tabloids, since commercially these are the most profitable. Indeed, a new, facile type of serious publication has been created, on the lines of the Moscow newspaper *Kommersant* for businessmen. This weekly does provide a certain amount of information that is needed by the business world, but it frequently supplies the data in such a tendentious or simply superficial form that it is incapable of serving as serious guidance for business people. But so far there are no other reliable sources of guidance. The London *Financial Times* is still only in the process of creating a Russian-language edition. As a result, the business world is obliged to subscribe once a week to something that is a cross between the *New York Post* and *The Wall Street Journal*. Each newspaper and magazine survives or perishes on its own. The creation of cartels, trusts, corporate associations, and empires in the publishing world of the former Soviet Union has not yet even begun. A Soviet Citizen Kane is still far from opening his first office.

At the present time, the country's journalists are still at the crossroads between the old and the new system, without knowing exactly what future itinerary will be followed. As late as the 1920s, publication associations dominated the country's journalistic life, but then the communist party began to stifle each periodical separately, leaving each isolated to this day. However, the situation in the newspaper world is no worse than in any other area of life that was mutilated by the party. Simply, *glasnost'* and the press have become one of the most conspicuous areas of Soviet life, and the problems they confront disturb very many persons.

The Leninist dictum that newspapers should fulfill the functions of collective agitator, propagandist, and organizer at the service of the government—that they should serve as anything but a source of information—has suited more than one generation of political leaders. Within the Soviet Union, all that was ever permitted was uniform propaganda that eliminated the expression of any thought at variance with it. In earlier times, the justification given for this was that socialism was being built in one country.

Today, however, from time to time, there are voices—and they are becoming louder and louder—claiming that it is time to put screws on the press in view of the difficulties everyone is experiencing, although the banning in Georgia not so very long ago of all publications that were critical of the government is an extreme phenomenon. In Russia everything is happening in a highly civilized way, but nevertheless the trend is very alarming and an ever greater cause of concern. On January 11, 1992, the Stockholm newspaper *Dagens Nyheter* wrote, "The new Russian government under Boris Yel'tsin views the mass media as an important propaganda instrument in the implementation of the economic reforms which were launched at the beginning of the year. With the aid of the press, television and radio, the government must consciously strive to create a positive 'image' of the reforms and of leading reformist politicians." The press is constantly "assigned tasks," and the lofty, patriotic significance of these tasks is carefully explained. There are quite a few editors in Russia ready to serve any master who will feed them well and treat them leniently. This is a dangerous situation.

Lenin was a political cynic who considered that political aims justify any methods. The people who have come to power in Russia today are a lot more honorable than Lenin, but at the same time they are not such skillful exponents of demagoguery; neither do they have at their disposal a variety of instruments in their political arsenal. Since they have been taught nothing different, they are automatically prepared to treat the press in the old way—as a connecting link between the political leadership and the masses who need to be led. So far, the press has not developed new mechanisms for self-defense. The very thought that it may have to defend itself from such a liberal leadership as the present Russian government seems to many to be inimical to the spirit of reform itself.

Since the movement for the defense of human rights has virtually ceased to function, and political dissidence likewise no longer exists as such, it will be very difficult to devise and effectively implement nongovernmental methods of monitoring the observance of civil rights and freedoms. The new political opposition in Russia is predominantly fascist-communist, i.e., it combines extremists of both the left and the right. Issues related to the defense of human rights are of absolutely no interest to such people. Worse, they advocate restricting human rights. With the rise in crime and the weakness of governmental administration, many so-called "ordinary people" are drawn to what in America is termed "law and order," and show openly that they are tired of all the democratic talk.

The present situation is similar to the environment in Russia during the weeks preceding the October 1917 *coup d'état,* or in Germany at the end of the 1920s. There is an enormous number of tabloids, increasing governmental autocracy, and a popular weariness of helpless democrats. This situation does nothing to contribute to the authority enjoyed by the free printed word. The number of publications propagating conflict between different nationalities, anti-Semitism, and racism in complete violation of the law is multiplying. So far, the government has not brought itself to haul a single one of these publications into court, nor has it ordered a single investigation of their funding sources. Moreover, the questions of where the many millions of rubles in the accounts of the communist party and the KGB disappeared to, and to what use these funds are being put today, remain unanswered. In fact, there are still more questions than answers regarding the fate of the resources that belonged to these organizations.

The state of democratic institutions in a ruined economy is especially miserable. It is impossible to reduce economic issues to the price of newsprint or printing costs. The delivery system is becoming a vital problem. The communication links between the various republics of the former Soviet Union are inadequate, and sometimes this creates obstacles to the free exchange of information. When, as is happening, many former union republics proclaim independence without always properly understanding the meaning of their own declarations, connections between the different portions of the old Soviet Union break down. In particular, no one knows what the appropriate postal rates should be.

Moreover, many of the new non-Russian governments are simply not interested in having the Russian press available in their republics, since traditionally Russian publications have always been very influential. Subscription rates established during the fall of 1991 no longer correspond to costs. Inflation has disrupted the system, and the former centralized delivery arrangements no longer function at all. Even persons who conscientiously took out 12-month subscriptions for 1992 (and these annual subscribers always provided the majority of newspaper and magazine readers) receive their publications intermittently, and it appears that, in many instances, they may cease obtaining them altogether. The press of the former USSR has never been in a more difficult situation than now.

It is not only the links between the different republics that have been interrupted. In addition, the necessary new communication channels between Russia and foreign countries have not been established. The old network of correspondents, in many cases staffed not with journalists but with intelligence operatives, no longer exists, but there is simply no money to set up a new network on the same broad scope. Radio and television also are in an extremely difficult situation. This applies particularly to the electronic media in the newly created independent republics, which undoubtedly will sink into a destructive provincialism even faster than is desired by their noisy nationalistic regimes—governments that as a rule are interested not in broad links with the world outside, but in their own provincial preoccupations, which they sedulously present as patriotic.

It is very characteristic that in Georgia the nationalist opposition forces began their resistance with burning down television centers, while in the Baltic region the famous events of 1991 revolved around publishing houses and television studios. The media still exist in conditions of political uncertainty and instability, and in many cases are perceived, for good reason, not as channels of objective and unbiased information, but as powerful weapons in the struggle for power. In the course of announcing the new Russian government's policy of providing subsidies for periodicals to a total amount of seven billion rubles, Mikhail Poltoranin, Minister for Press and Media, stated, "A policy of state favoritism will be carried out in respect of publications working for the revival of Russia" (*Trud,* January 14, 1992). What can a free press and governmental favoritism have in common?

Russia today is in a very difficult situation. The danger exists that totalitarian tendencies may again arise both in Russian political life and in the country's mass media. Whereas in earlier years it was possible to separate the analysis of different aspects of Soviet life, today it must be recognized with maximum clarity that all the different manifestations of life in Russia form an integrated whole, and that democratic processes will never follow a simple and easy course.

The Impact of Foreign Broadcasts

Savik Shuster

The three classic Russian-speaking radio broadcasters—BBC, Radio Liberty, and Voice of America (VOA)—have often played a crucial role during the turbulent postwar decades, mainly due to their influence within the political and cultural elite of the USSR. However, during the three days of the August 1991 coup attempt, their impact spread across all social strata and acquired critical importance.

In the pre-Gorbachev era, people turned to foreign radio stations when a drastic change in the leadership occurred, mainly to discover who their new leaders were. Then, during the Gorbachev period, listeners to Western radio wanted to know above all why the changes at the top had occurred. The three days of the existence of the State Committee for the Implementation of the State of Emergency, that brought with them the beginning of the post-Gorbachev era, radically changed the concerns of the foreign radio audience in the USSR, as well as of the Soviet people in general.

Two related phenomena support this thesis. First, the Russian Broadcast departments of the BBC, Radio Liberty, and VOA found that they were the only nationwide information sources reporting on the countermeasures being undertaken by the opposition led by Boris Yel'tsin. Second, according to the results of an opinion poll carried out by the independent Soviet institute *Vox Populi* in September 1991, during the three days of the attempted putsch, 32 percent of the population of Moscow listened regularly to Radio Liberty's Russian Broadcast Department, 18 percent to the BBC, and 15 percent to the VOA. For the first time in the postwar history of the USSR, therefore, foreign media were literally reaching the masses. Moreover, for the first time during a crisis at the top, the Soviet people were indifferent to the new power holders, and interested instead in what the opposition was doing. This change in popular attitude toward the "men in the Kremlin" was of course largely due to the surprising amateurism of the coup's leaders, who failed to cut the lines of communication and hence of information. This first glimmering of a critical faculty in the public mind, enabling it to distinguish between legitimate and illegitimate governments, points to a new trend in Soviet political behavior.

Radio Liberty played a vital role during the attempted coup. For years, during jamming, Radio Liberty ran neck and neck with the BBC and behind VOA in the ratings, according to admittedly imprecise research at the time. However, during the coup, Radio Liberty's Russian Broadcast Department was demonstrably the leading international broadcaster. On August 27, President Boris Yel'tsin signed a decree accrediting Radio Liberty in Russia, an act unprecedented in international journalism. "Every family in Russia listened to Radio Liberty during those three days," said Yel'tsin in an exclusive interview with Radio Liberty on August 23. Mikhail Gorbachev, the first leader (in or out of power) of the USSR to give an interview to RFE/RL, paid tribute to the station: "I want to take this opportunity to say that in those days in Foros most of my information came from the BBC and Radio Liberty."[1] Radio Liberty remains firmly in first place among foreign radios broadcasting to the former Soviet Union. Radio Liberty's Russian Broadcast Department draws a much bigger listenership than the Radio Free Europe/Radio Liberty (RFE/RL) native language services. Before drawing any firm conclusions, however, one should attempt to understand the reasons for this success.

At the time of the coup attempt, the Russian Broadcast Department's 60-minute nightly news show "In the Country and in the World" (CW) had a scrupulously selected, tried and tested network of freelance reporters covering practically the entire territory of the USSR, a network that could be considered, without too much exaggeration, the fastest and sharpest reporting operation out of the Soviet Union. Even now, when the USSR no longer exists, this practice of on-the-spot live reporting, routine in the West but new for the vast Soviet radio audience, makes Radio Liberty unique. It is instructive, therefore, to describe the history of the CW program, which understandably went through the same phases as Gorbachev's *perestroika*.

Until jamming was lifted from Radio Liberty in November 1988, there was little incentive in Munich to search for new forms of broadcasting. Western press reviews and staff commentaries were the dominant elements in the Russian Broadcast Department's programming. Meanwhile, Soviet society—and especially its politically active stratum—was rapidly evolving. The policy of *glasnost'*, or openness, proclaimed as it was by the sole permitted political party, the CPSU, consequently was discriminatory and biased. It was, however, instrumental in creating alternative information sources throughout the Soviet Union. Grass-roots opposition movements, democratic and otherwise, were sprouting all over the country, each one sure to have its own press center, however effective. A new offshoot from the mainstream of Soviet society, though incoherent and uncoordinated, had appeared—a younger generation that had been liberated from the "bugged telephone complex," and began to use the telephone as a means of communication and a straightforward working tool.

Nevertheless, these strictly internal changes were often so subtle and slow that many of them could not be perceived promptly by radio broadcasts working far away from their target areas. At the same time, other political developments were shaping Radio Liberty's attitude to *perestroika* and influencing its editorial policy. In December 1986, Andrei Sakharov was freed from exile and allowed to return to Moscow. Jamming of Western radios was gradually being lifted, first in January and May 1987 from the BBC and VOA, then later from Radio Free Europe's Polish Broadcast Department. In May 1988, the Soviet troop withdrawal from Afghanistan began. Members of the Soviet political and cultural establishments visiting the West were becoming much less apprehensive about meeting Radio Liberty staffers, although most of them still insisted on talking "off the record." It was becoming clear that in its programming Radio Liberty's Russian Broadcast Department needed a new, more journalistic and less propagandistic approach.

Listeners in the Soviet Union yearned for information on the aspects of democratization that the central electronic and print media would not cover even in conditions of *glasnost'*. They also needed to hear the pioneers of the democratic movement who did not have access to CPSU-controlled television and radio. Foreign radios, especially Radio Liberty because it was not a voice of government, had a unique chance to fill the information vacuum and become quasi-domestic information sources. In the case of Radio Liberty's Russian Broadcast Department, this theoretical proposition became reality in November 1988—the time of Gorbachev's memorable visit to the United Nations, when jamming was finally lifted.

Perestroika entered a new phase of rapid democratization, which reached its peak in March and April 1989, when the elections to the USSR Congress of People's Deputies took place. In November 1988, I was appointed

managing editor of "In the Country and the World," which still remains
Radio Liberty's only live program. It was clear what needed to be done.
Radio Liberty's Russian Broadcast Department required a group of talented
and resourceful freelance reporters who could cover events more quickly,
thoroughly, and objectively than the Soviet media. These people also had to
be daring enough to be willing to get involved with Radio Liberty, for the
KGB would undoubtedly open a file on each of them. As it turned out, there
was no shortage of people with the courage to work for Radio Liberty, but
guts—alas!—do not imply talent. Communism survived mainly because
there was no journalism. The classic breed of reporter, who, as the saying
goes, "needs no more than a good pair of shoes and a fine nose for horse
manure," was extinct in the Soviet Union. The ever-growing number of
independent news agencies and newspapers was relentlessly publishing
unchecked news items; their reporters were no better trained than their
colleagues in the official communist media to dig for the truth.

The CW Munich team had no choice but to select its freelancers in the
USSR by trial and error. Yet the number of errors had to be kept to a minimum
in order not to damage the reputation of Radio Liberty. It was decided to
proceed in stages, always bearing in mind the final goal of creating a group
of radio journalists working to the highest Western standards. Moreover, we
were working with a deadline, since the Soviet team had to be in place by
the time of the March 1989 elections. We began by commissioning a weekly
press review from the best staff members of the independent publications in
Moscow, regardless of their political orientation. In such a way we selected
a small number of young people who could write well. Next, we asked them
to attend unofficial gatherings and demonstrations, carefully comparing their
reports with those published in the Western press. The same procedure was
followed in Leningrad, Kiev, and the Baltic republics.

At the same time, we conducted scores of telephone interviews from
Munich with personalities across the Soviet political spectrum. In January
1989, Boris Yel'tsin gave his first interview to CW. This interview was not
merely a journalistic scoop, but a decisive psychological breakthrough.
Communist party officials no longer hesitated to give interviews to Radio
Liberty, and our freelancers began to lose the feeling of working "in the
underground." By the spring of 1989, CW could count on a dozen literate,
enthusiastic young reporters who had none of the inhibitions of the older
generation, with its almost automatic reflex of self-censorship, and who had
acquired healthy "manure detectors."

During the early stages of setting up the correspondent network, the senior
staff of the Russian Broadcast Department was adamantly opposed to the

attempt. It was a generational conflict, the average age of staff members of the Munich Russian Broadcast Department being above 50 and of the Soviet freelancers under 30—a conflict between radio journalists formed in conditions of jamming and those who began their careers after jamming was lifted.

Dramatic clashes were about to take place in the Soviet Union. In Tbilisi, on April 9, 1989, Soviet military units attacked unarmed Georgian demonstrators. The casualty count was shocking: twenty dead and many hundred injured. Because of CW and its correspondents, Radio Liberty's coverage of the tragedy was the fastest and frankest of all the Russian-language media. Radio Liberty was the first to report the final results of the March elections to the USSR Congress of People's Deputies, including the results in Yel'tsin's constituency. The Soviet media were bewildered. How was it possible at such distance? It was achieved thanks to our correspondents and to Western methods of covering elections that the CW team adopted in organizing the program. This success put a stop to the generation clash in Munich. Subsequently, Soviet military assaults against unarmed persons in Baku in January 1990 and in Vilnius in January 1991 completed the "finishing" of the CW correspondents, making them ready for the August 1991 coup attempt. The effectiveness of our program's correspondents was attested to by KGB Chairman Vladimir Kryuchkov, who responded as follows to an official inquiry from Yuri Ryzhov, then chairman of the Supreme Soviet Science Committee, as to why I was not allowed to enter the USSR:

Committee of State Security of the USSR
June 20, 1991 No. KL-8462

Comrade Yu. A. Ryzhov
Chairman, USSR Supreme Soviet Committee of Science

Dear Yuri Alekseyevich,

Your enquiry concerning so-called "black lists" maintained by the USSR Committee of State Security has been considered.

The Soviet Union, like any other state, in conformity with the current law of the Union of Soviet Socialist Republics "Legal Status of Foreign Citizens in the USSR" (USSR Supreme Soviet Enactment No. 836 of June 24, 1981), does not permit the entry of foreign citizens into its territory in cases in which it threatens the country's security interests. In this connection, the USSR KGB, like the corresponding services in Western countries, maintains a register of such persons. Canadian citizen S. Shuster is refused entry into the USSR in accordance with Paragraph 3, Article 24 of the aforementioned law on the grounds that since 1988 he has been an employee of Radio Liberty's Russian Service, the activities of which are aimed solely at undermining Soviet constitutional order, and that he prepares and broadcasts programs aimed at discrediting our system and the President of the USSR, [and] directly organizes and co-ordinates the activity in our country of Radio Liberty's so-called "freelance correspondents," which represents interference in the internal affairs of our country on the part of a representative of a foreign organization.

(Signed) V. Kryuchkov
Chairman of the Committee

Yet despite all his seeming understanding of the threat that Radio Liberty correspondents were posing to the system in the USSR, Kryuchkov, one of the key plotters in the attempt to ensure its preservation, did nothing to neutralize them on the morning of the putsch, August 19, 1991. I must confess that I was pleasantly surprised when, in the early morning hours, I reached all our Moscow reporters by telephone and found them safe in their homes. This meant that we could go on the air, though nobody could tell how long they and their telephones would remain free. They did not try to conceal their concern, and I did not try to sound reassuring.

In Moscow we deployed rapidly. Our two political correspondents, Andrei Babitsky, 27, and Mikhail Sokolov, 29, found a desk and a telephone on the eleventh floor of the RSFSR Supreme Soviet building, the "White House." Our best writer, Dmitri Volchek, 27, spent the three days and nights of the putsch on the streets and the squares, describing the reactions of ordinary citizens. The oldest of the team, Mark Deich, 47, who regularly reports on the doings of the extreme right, continued his coverage. CW economics and labor correspondent Karen Agamirov, 30, performed a double duty, never leaving home; he kept up continuous contact with the activists of the miners' movement and coordinated the link between Munich and the rest of our correspondents nationwide. The hardest task fell to Mikhail Bombin, 39, in Riga, where the local coup leaders captured the telephone center. He found a reliable courier ready to carry his tapes to Moscow, which allowed us, albeit with a 12-hour delay, to keep our listeners informed on events in Latvia.

No matter how uncertain and tense the state of affairs in the provinces, it was in Moscow, or more precisely in the White House, that the fate of the country was being decided. Every person, whether conservative or not, sensed it, but the farther away they were from the capital, the less citizens knew about the steps being taken by Boris Yel'tsin, his staff, and the Russian Federation Supreme Soviet. All the liberally inclined electronic and print media were banned; Central Television, received in every home, was broadcasting the State Emergency Committee's decrees, as well as a film version of *Giselle*. Given this dearth of information, Radio Liberty's Russian Broadcast Department became one of the heroes of the three-day drama. This was the consequence primarily of the correspondent network already described, but also of the Russian Broadcast Department's advantage as the only Western broadcaster which was on the air 24 hours a day.

During the coup attempt, CW produced, on average, a live program every four hours, each one opening with a telephone bridge between Munich and the RSFSR Supreme Soviet building. Our two men in the White House described the atmosphere, gave accounts of Supreme Soviet sessions, interviewed political leaders and other well-known personalities, gave details on developments in Foros in the Crimea where Mikhail Gorbachev was being kept hostage, and reported on the movements and mood of the KGB and Red Army troops. They also read President Yel'tsin's decrees. Inevitably, the most important part of the news show was based on information from White House sources. Subsequently, during the heated debates about who had been where and done what during the coup, Radio Liberty's Russian Broadcast Department was criticized for having become the mouthpiece of Yel'tsin and his entourage. One of the most liberal papers, *Nezavisimaya gazeta,* probably inspired by the polemic in the United States over the role of CNN in Baghdad during the Gulf War, initiated this discussion. However, nobody—not even the most conservative papers—dared pursue it, because, I suppose, arguments in justification were lacking. The roles of CNN in Baghdad and of Radio Liberty in the Moscow White House are comparable to the same extent that Saddam Hussein might be compared to Boris Yel'tsin. I am certain that if the CW team had been able to place a reporter in Kryuchkov's headquarters, we would have been just as impartial in relaying information from this source.

Be that as it may, by proclaiming the state of emergency on August 19, 1991, and ousting the legally elected President of the USSR, the eight-member committee headed by Vice President Gennadi Yanaev had unceremoniously breached the newly adopted constitution. Under these circumstances, Russia's Parliament building, the White House, symbolized the last political resort of the *Rechtsstaat*. In such a black-and-white situation, any pretense of impartiality would have been self-defeating, not just for Radio Liberty but for any news organization functioning in a political democracy and mediating between the citizens and the powers-that-be. There was but one side to support, and the choice had to be made long before the popular attitude became known.

Shortly before noon on August 19, President Yel'tsin made an appeal to the citizens of Russia calling for an indefinite strike: "We have to do with a rightist, reactionary, unconstitutional *coup d'état*." This statement opened the first edition of the CW program. In a live interview from the White House, Rasul Mikhailov, a member of the parliamentary committee for *glasnost'*, reported on his experiences in the capital and the provinces. He had driven to the Ostankino TV tower, but access to it was blocked by special Interior Ministry troops. "We have lost the ability to receive and distribute information," he said. Rasul Mikhailov then called the TV center at Makhachkala, capital of the autonomous republic of Dagestan, where he had previously worked. His former colleagues told him that the official Russian state channel had been closed down immediately after the announcement of the state of emergency. He was also told that TV journalists had been ordered to collect laudatory statements on the State Committee. "I am sure that the White House telephone lines were bugged," added Mikhailov. "As I was talking to the Chairman of the Ryazan' city council, a former colonel of the airborne troops, I told him that a Radio Liberty correspondent was standing next to me and was ready to tape an interview. The telephone line immediately went dead."

The first Radio Liberty stringer reports on the situation in Moscow were rather pessimistic. They found that the most popular local radio station, "Moscow Echo," had been shut down by the KGB. Liberal newspapers were being harassed. The initial polls carried out on the streets reflected divisions in public opinion. The dislike for Mikhail Gorbachev was so great that many of those questioned greeted with malicious satisfaction his removal from office. Russian parliamentarians, members of democratic parties and movements, kept saying in interviews that the democratic forces had been taken by surprise; those of them who had witnessed the January 1991 coup attempt in Vilnius placed their hopes in the inhabitants of Moscow, taking their example from the Lithuanians and flocking to defend the White House. In fact, they spent the last hours of the morning discussing whether to appeal to the people to come and defend the Parliament building. Later, Yel'tsin personally read this appeal on radio.

Around noon, a spontaneous mass meeting against the reactionary plotters took place on one of the central squares, Manezhnaya Ploshchad'. During the six years of Gorbachev's *perestroika,* the square had become a point of convergence for democratic forces. Given the tense and unpredictable situation in the city, the rally had a stormy start. "Down with the traitors! Down with the State Committee!" was the dominant slogan. Promptly armored personnel carriers surrounded the square. A Radio Liberty correspondent reported: "The military behaved very correctly. Soldiers and demonstrators began fraternizing. Punks and pacifists occupied two of the armored vehicles. It was an idyllic picture." In fact, it was the first tangible sign of a changing tide.

Vladimir Zhirinovsky, the notorious Soviet protofascist who won 10 percent of the vote in the June 1991 Russian presidential election, showed up on the square and was nearly lynched by the excited crowd. Before taking to his heels, Zhirinovsky gave an interview to Radio Liberty: "I fully support the State Committee. The proclamation of the state of emergency was the natural thing to do. The chauvinist leaders of Georgia, Moldavia, and Lithuania should quickly leave the country," he stated.

At the same time, the Radio Liberty correspondent in Vilnius described a relatively calm situation in Lithuania with Vytautas Landsbergis, the parliament chairman, firmly in control. The only act of aggression on the part of the Soviet Army was the seizure of a radio station near Kaunas which had been the sole source of information during the January coup attempt in Vilnius. Since that time, Lithuanian central television had been in the hands of the military.

During the course of August 19, alarming news kept coming in from Riga, headquarters of the Baltic Military District. The district commander, General Anatoli Kuz'min, trumpeted in an official statement that power in the Baltic republics was in his hands. By the dawn of August 20, the military had captured Riga's television center and the main telephone exchange. Latvia was practically cut off from the rest of the country. The Radio Liberty correspondent there sent his report by courier to Moscow. It included an interview with the so-called "black colonel," Viktor Alksnis. "We shouldn't take the negative reaction of the West too seriously," he said with an elated expression. "Remember Tienanmen. They shouted for a while and then stopped."

From the first, it was obvious that the speed with which workers in remote industrial areas responded politically to the state of emergency was going to decide the fate of Yel'tsin's administration in Moscow. The attitude of the miners, whose strikes had seriously undermined the credibility of Gorbachev and his government, would be vital. "I am not counting on the intelligentsia," said Yelena Bonner in a telephone interview to Radio Liberty in the early morning of August 19. "We must rely on the working class." It was also evident that time was becoming a decisive factor. Besides the episode of soldier-protester fraternization on Manezhnaya Ploshchad', Radio Liberty correspondents reported several other instances of irresolution on the part of the troops during the early hours of the coup. In the end, the Army's position depended on whether it would be ordered to open fire against unarmed people marching in the streets of Russian towns. The reaction of the miners to Yel'tsin's appeal for a general strike was of crucial importance.

They reacted swiftly. Immediately after Yel'tsin's appeal during the first day of the coup attempt, the chairman of the Council of Workers' Committees of

Kuzbass (a heavily industrialized area in Siberia), Vyacheslav Golikov, said in an interview to a Radio Liberty stringer: "It's a *coup d'état!* The miners will never support the State Committee." Valentin Kopysev, the chairman of the workers' committees in Vorkuta in the Northern Urals, was categorical: "We support Yel'tsin's appeal and are ready to strike." The Ukrainian coal miners also spoke against the proclamation of the state of emergency. In the early evening edition of the CW program, Radio Liberty reported the beginning of strikes in the Siberian city of Novokuznetsk.

Nevertheless, as a whole the picture was far from rosy. A member of the Miass city council in the Urals, Vladimir Mandrygin, told a Radio Liberty correspondent that, in general, opinion in the town was favorable to the State Committee: "It seems that people were waiting for the state of emergency," he said in dismay, "perhaps they don't really understand what's happened and don't see the consequences."

On the evening of August 19, the situation was still unclear in Novosibirsk, the Siberian regional *oblast'* capital. The city council had unanimously voted a resolution in support of Yel'tsin, whereas the rather conservative regional council was hesitant. However, a Radio Liberty correspondent reported, "Even the CPSU members in the council are beginning to favor the President of Russia." In Khabarovsk also, one of the largest cities in the Far East, the political picture was blurred. "We'll wait for the session of the USSR Supreme Soviet, see what they decide and then make up our minds," Vladimir Tolmachev, Chairman of the City Executive Committee, said in an interview for Radio Liberty.

It must be borne in mind that people in the USSR were not given the opportunity to see the international press conference given by the eight members of the State Committee on August 19. The trembling hands of Gennadi Yanaev, the sight of Interior Minister Boris Pugo incessantly wiping the sweat off his glasses, the mocking questions of journalists, and the senseless replies of the plotters—all this might have influenced voters and elected officials in the provinces. The CW program tried to make its radio report on the press conference as visual as possible.

Obviously anxious to reassure the crowds defending the White House, Boris Yel'tsin hurried to announce that "proletarian" Novosibirsk, Sverdlovsk, Chelyabinsk, Kemerovo, and Khabarovsk were on his side. This amounted to a clear signal to the army: either shoot your compatriots, or join us. At the same time, a number of democratic members of parliament were dispatched to military units to conduct "agitprop" among soldiers. The first news came from the Chebarkul armored division based near Miass. The soldiers constantly listened to Radio Liberty and remained undecided, while the divisional commander insisted that he would continue to carry out the orders of the defense minister. The MPs played a vital role in convincing a few subunits of the crack Tamansk division, stationed near Moscow, to join the ranks of Yel'tsin's supporters. The Radio Liberty correspondent in the White House broke this news at 10:30 P.M. "The Army has split," he reported.

By the end of the first day of the coup, the thousands of people who responded to Yel'tsin's appeal and came to defend the White House had a hero to worship—Major Sergei Evdokimov of the Tamansk division, who brought with him 30 tanks to defend democracy. "The score at the moment is 30-10," the Radio Liberty White House correspondent reported at midnight. At the same time, the All-Union Council of Servicemen's Parents distributed an appeal. "We mothers appeal to you, officers, soldiers, marines: do not be part of the *coup d'état*," ran this statement read on Radio Liberty by Zinaida Lednyova of the Council's Presidium. In the early hours of August 20, during the first edition of the CW, Aleksandr Rutskoi, the Vice President of Russia, read a personal statement: "As a colonel, as a Hero of the Soviet Union, as an Afghan veteran, I appeal to your hearts and minds: join us."

No doubt Rutskoi knew that he would not gain a mass response from the soldiers. The war in Afghanistan showed that a Soviet soldier would carry out orders, no matter how criminal. His statement was really aimed at disorienting the troops psychologically. Meanwhile, the vice president had convinced two renowned Afghan veterans to switch sides: General Pavel Grachev, Commander of Airborne Troops—now the Russian Defense Minister—and his deputy, General Aleksandr Lebed'. The military equilibrium remained rather fluid. CW ran an unconfirmed report on the refusal of a helicopter unit to provide support for a KGB assault on the White House. "If this first night passes quietly, we may avoid general bloodshed," said General Konstantin Kobets, chairman of the White House defense committee. The night did indeed pass relatively peacefully, but in the morning it became known that Generals Grachev and Lebed' had been put under house arrest by the State Committee.

No matter how much Yel'tsin and his closest aides despised Gorbachev, they understood from the start that he represented the principal constitutional tool in their hands and that this instrument could slip away from them at any moment. The USSR president's fate was the subject of almost every interview and statement released by RSFSR officials. Consequently, the whereabouts of Gorbachev were widely discussed on the streets and squares of Moscow, despite his unpopularity. In this respect, Radio Liberty, which had been very critical of Gorbachev's most recent decisions, committed its most serious mistake. During the first hours of the coup, Radio Liberty continued to run a commentary, always ending with the words: "Farewell, President! Forgive us, Mikhail Sergeyevich!" According to the monthly *Moskva* (January 1992), the commentary provoked a bitter reaction among people in and near the White House: "We believed in victory and were ready to fight to the end, but in Munich they began to hold a funeral service for us." Fortunately, before the day of August 19 ended, a Radio Liberty correspondent learned that Gorbachev was alive and under house arrest.

At 3 P.M. on August 20, Sergei Stankevich, the deputy mayor of Moscow, provided some sensational details on how Gorbachev and his family had been prevented from flying back to Moscow from the Crimea on the presidential plane. Their return was scheduled for August 19, three days before the signature of the Union Treaty, but shortly before sunrise two tractors blocked the runway at Bilbek near Foros. The orders were given by General Mal'tsev, chief of staff of the USSR Air Defense Forces. At 4 P.M. on August 19, the order was given not to let any plane, ship, or vehicle approach the presidential *dacha*. CW repeated Stankevich's report several times in order to let the country know that Gorbachev had been betrayed by his closest aides, including his personal secretaries and security guards. And it came as no surprise that the chairman of the USSR Supreme Soviet, Anatoli Luk'yanov, a friend of Gorbachev, was the "Richelieu" of the coup. The acting chairman of the RSFSR Supreme Soviet, Ruslan Khasbulatov, said in an interview for Radio Liberty after a meeting with Luk'yanov during the morning of August 20: "He exhibited striking duplicity."

As the number of strikers in the Urals and Siberia swelled by the hour during the second day of the coup, it became evident that the plotters' house of cards was falling apart. The Mayor of Leningrad, Anatoli Sobchak, forced his way onto local television and called for a political general strike. A Commission for the State of Emergency was established in the city on August 19, but two of its members only found out about this from the television news. Sobchak even succeeded in convincing the commander of the Leningrad military district, General Viktor Samsonov, to refrain from bringing troops into the city. "The situation here is much better than in Moscow," reported the Radio Liberty Leningrad correspondent. "Newspapers are on the stands, local radio stations are beginning to function normally."

CW also received a curious report from Vilnius: On August 20, the Central Committee of the Lithuanian Communist Party remained dumbfounded by the decisions of the State Committee in Moscow. Many inexplicable things were happening, such as the official Central TV news show

"*Vremya*" broadcasting the texts of Yel'tsin's decrees. But one thing was being emphasized in every straw poll taken by the CW team on the streets: vodka was still being sold only for coupons. "If the State Committee were serious, they certainly would have freed the sale of vodka," was a typical response.

In an atmosphere of obvious drift, a huge anticoup demonstration took place near the White House at noon on the second day of the coup attempt. Shortly afterward, Yel'tsin announced that 70 percent of Russia's territory was behind him. Naturally, the unarmed defenders felt confident during daylight and hastened to speak out and do as much as they could before sunset. Tension began to grow during the afternoon of August 20 as rumors of an imminent assault spread across Moscow. At 5 P.M., Yel'tsin signed Decree No. 64, under which he appointed himself Supreme Commander of USSR Armed Forces on the territory of Russia. The soldiers organizing the defense of the White House that night harbored no false hopes: "If they decide to attack, we can hold out ten minutes at most," Zakir Kadyrov, an officer who had fought in Afghanistan, told a Radio Liberty correspondent.

The climax came at 10 P.M. on August 20. Firing began in the vicinity of the White House. There were dead and wounded. CW went on the air immediately. Radio Liberty reported, "Just now the MPs decided to tell people to leave the area surrounding the White House. This decision was taken to avoid bloodshed. The MPs themselves will stay here. They don't want to give the impression of fleeing. We must say goodbye!" During the course of the following hour, Radio Liberty's two White House correspondents continued to describe what they saw from a window on the 11th floor. At 1:30 A.M. on August 21, the Patriarch of Russia, Aleksi II, finally condemned the coup, saying, "Those who raise their weapons against unarmed people commit an unforgivable crime." Radio Liberty broadcast the text immediately. The culminating event came unexpectedly at 1:55 A.M. "A second miracle occurred this very minute," said a Radio Liberty correspondent. "The first miracle happened on August 19, when the people who went to arrest Yel'tsin were 20 minutes too late. A few minutes ago a Russian diplomat called from Tallinn to tell the RSFSR authorities here that the State Committee had ordered the withdrawal of troops from Moscow."

This news was correct, and for all practical purposes the *coup d'état* was over.

Radio Liberty's audience increased remarkably during the three days of the coup attempt. Crowds gathered around shortwave receivers in the streets and backyards of Kiev, Riga, Kaliningrad, and many other cities far from Moscow. During a recent journey that I made through the Caucasus, the words "Thank you for what you did during the putsch" were re-echoed in Grozny, Baku, Yerevan, and Tbilisi.

Radio Liberty's potential could be exploited much further. It is my firm conviction that neither the Voice of America nor the BBC is capable of contributing to the cause of democracy in the former USSR to the same extent as Radio Liberty. The information and analysis provided by Radio Liberty are most frequently perceived as Western in a broad sense, rather than as advocating the interests of any given country. Moreover, it would not be unrealistic to imagine Radio Liberty becoming the "Voice of the West" with all the Western allies contributing to its support. Radio Liberty could play an especially valuable role now that the threat of ultrachauvinist forces coming to power in Russia has become real. The demonstrations organized by these forces in Moscow, beginning in February and March 1992, have shown how willingly the old communists and the new fascists formed an alliance in order to exploit mass discontent with the economic policy of President Yel'tsin's cabinet.

The "red-black fusion," as Russian democrats call it, is already affecting the political situation in a number of republics of the former USSR: in many of them, the Russian populations feel harassed by local nationalist governments and, in reaction, see in extreme Russian nationalism a solution to their troubles. (In Moscow, this has become even a "red-brown alliance," in which demonstrators carrying Stalin icons sometimes link arms with (neo) fascist *Pamyat'* and Zhirinovsky adherents, some giving the Hitler salute.) This new political symbiosis of the two once-conflicting ideologies of nationalism and internationalism to retaining or regaining power, the "Milosevic approach" (in the words of the UN Secretary General's Special Envoy, Giandomenico Pico), may be observed in almost all countries where communism had been the ruling ideology, from Afghanistan to Germany. Die-hard communists, like Milosević in Belgrade, invoke national chauvinism as a tool for retaining power. Western democracies need to acquire safety devices, and Radio Liberty could serve as one of them. Its impeccable reputation and its nongovernmental status could help make it the universal voice of democracy. If such were to become Radio Liberty's role, it should be sponsored jointly by the parliaments of the Western Allies.

On the other hand, now that Radio Liberty has become part of the journalistic establishment in most republics of the former USSR—the bureaus in Moscow, Kiev, and Minsk are functioning, and correspondents have been regularly accredited—the danger is rather high of its becoming platitudinous. Radio Liberty editors believe that they must fight for survival by competing in a free information market in the former USSR. As a result,

Radio Liberty risks becoming too deeply involved in internal political intrigues and unavoidably defending the interests of one particular lobby rather than the values of democracy. On the other hand, were Radio Liberty to withdraw from the competition by keeping aloof from fierce internal controversies, this might result in superficiality. Radio Liberty might distance itself from political life in the former USSR, laying emphasis exclusively on entertainment and culture.

I am convinced that, in order to avoid these pitfalls and become the authentic voice of the West, Radio Liberty must change its profile radically. It has to become a CNN-like radio, putting greatest emphasis on coverage of current events, which is very poor, as well as biased, in the CIS and the Baltic states. At the present time, governments in every republic place the question of media control very high on their agenda and try to censor every word of criticism. I was struck by a comment made by Gorbachev after his interview with me.[2] When the microphone had been switched off, Gorbachev came up to me and said: "Report everything, let everybody have their say, talk about everything, and keep working until they start jamming you again." "Jamming?!" I couldn't conceal my surprise. "Yes, jamming," Gorbachev repeated loudly. He was obviously exaggerating, trying to show that Boris Yel'tsin was even worse than he who had lifted jamming from Radio Liberty. However, there was a grain of truth in his words: since Leonid Brezhnev's years, there has not been such strict government control of the media, particularly the electronic media.

So far, Radio Liberty is uncensored, unjammed, and listened to by millions. Russian is the *lingua franca* in the geopolitical space of the former USSR, and it would be a grave mistake not to draw a lesson from the success of the BBC after the disappearance of the British Empire. In the collapsed Soviet empire, rent by war and poverty and torn by political incompetence and power struggles, Radio Liberty could become a universal provider of information on the lines of the BBC. A final argument in support of this point of view would be that many years will pass before television finally triumphs in the media battle and before the peoples of the former republics of the Soviet Union become dependent on television as their main source of information. Radio has come into its own in the Commonwealth of Independent States.

NOTES

1. Gorbachev refers to the dacha in the Crimea where he was detained during the August putsch (interview with the author in Munich, March 8, 1992).
2. See footnote 1.

Part IV: The Role of Religion

—

The Orthodox Church
and a Pluralistic Society

Kent R. Hill

Does Orthodoxy support the creation and nurturing of a pluralistic society, or is it hostile to pluralism's very existence? This will be the major focus of this chapter. Though the chapter often focuses on the Russian Orthodox Church, major parts are based on a discussion of Orthodoxy in general and on practices of the Orthodox Church in other parts of the world. In this way, the fuller dimensions of Orthodoxy's relationship to pluralism begin to emerge.

THE CHALLENGE OF CREATING A DEMOCRATIC, PLURALISTIC SOCIETY

In the Commonwealth of Independent States, the former Union of Soviet Socialist Republics, much is in turmoil. Streets and metro stops are being stripped of their communist names and given back their prerevolutionary designations. Leningrad is now St. Petersburg again. The statue of the dreaded head of the early secret police of the Soviet state, Felix Dzerzhinsky, has been removed from its lofty pedestal in front of the KGB. The grand communist experiment of over 70 years has been judged a colossal failure, but what is less clear is what will rush in to take communism's place.

There is much talk of "democracy" as the alternative to "totalitarianism," and "capitalism" as the antidote to the economic dead end of "socialist communism." But as the heady days of euphoria pass in the wake of the failure of the August 1991 coup and the dissolution of the Soviet Union early in 1992, and the realities of economic decline and inflation inflict themselves on a population already beaten down by communist exploitation, it is more and more obvious that it will take far more than the demise or defeat of communism to produce democracy or economic prosperity. This applies also to religious freedom and pluralism. One cannot simply return to the pre-1917 Russian Empire to achieve these worthy ends, for the society of that day had not yet achieved them.

Democracy in the West has been the product of a long evolution of religious and political forces. Furthermore, democracy is far more than majority votes. It requires the protection of minorities against the arbitrary whims of majorities, the notion of inalienable human rights, and the separation of powers.

In addition, certain virtues are required to sustain democracy: initiative, diligence, tolerance, the ability to compromise, a willingness to balance rights with responsibilities, and a genuine respect for the rule of law. These are virtues that were systematically eroded during totalitarianism's reign.

It is not true that Russians and other peoples who have been part of the Soviet Empire are historically predestined to live always under authoritarianism. Russia was, after all, evolving towards a constitutional monarchy in the half century before the Bolshevik Revolution. Even in the Western "democratic" societies, women did not receive the right to vote until this century.

One of the most important questions facing Russian society and other societies in the former Soviet Union is what role the Orthodox Church will play in shaping the political contours of their postcommunist world. More particularly, will the Russian Orthodox Church support a pluralistic society or will it resist this development as something which is not in its own interests or those of Russian society?

ORTHODOXY AND RUSSIAN HISTORY

It is critically important that one recognizes at the outset that the Russian Orthodox Church is inextricably woven into the history of Russia and the other Slavic peoples of the former USSR. This fact has profound implications for the future of pluralism in the postcommunist Commonwealth of Independent States.

Historians have long recognized that religion, along with language, is a key factor in national identity. Russian history is inseparable from Orthodoxy. As the 19th-century playwright Aleksandr Griboyedov put it: "A

Russian feels fully Russian only in his Orthodox church."[1] In 1917, the Orthodox Bishop Ukhtomsky made a revealing statement to Aleksandr Kerensky:

> It is not the Church which should fear separation from the state, but the state [which] should fear its separation from the Church . . . To separate the Russian State from the Church would mean the separation of the nation from its conscience, its deprivation of moral foundations.[2]

Many believe that more than seven decades of communism did indeed deprive Russia of her "moral foundations," and that this was closely linked to an attack on religion and, more particularly, an assault on Orthodoxy.

Orthodoxy is a critical ingredient in Russian nationalism. To the extent that communism is seen as having been hostile to Russian nationalism, the reaction against communism means a new emphasis on Orthodoxy, for cultural and political reasons as well as for religious ones. Even political leaders who continue to identify themselves as atheists—for example, St. Petersburg mayor Anatoli Sobchak or Russian Republic President Boris Yel'tsin—find it in their own best interests to court the favor of the Orthodox Church.

There is no doubt that the rise of Russian and Ukrainian nationalism is and will continue to be intimately connected with Orthodoxy. Thus, the prospects for pluralism in these areas will be influenced to a significant degree by Orthodoxy's attitude toward pluralism.

THE ACHILLES HEEL OF ORTHODOXY: RELATIONS WITH THE STATE

The Achilles heel of the Orthodox Church is church-state relations. There is a disturbing historical tendency among the Orthodox, and not just in Russia, either to seek to use the state to advance the church's own interests above those of other religious confessions or itself to be subservient to the state so that it loses significant independence. This is not to pick on the Orthodox. Catholics and Protestants have their own Achilles heels, and both have passed through significant periods of their history when they too did not handle relations with the state with sufficient discretion or courage.

Roman Catholics in the Middle Ages, for example during the early 13th century and the pontificate of Innocent III, often sought to control the state. But they eventually came to accept the necessity, and later the wisdom, of the separation of church and state. The Protestants have had their own brushes with theocracy, as with John Calvin in Geneva. The "two kingdoms" theory associated with Lutheranism often relegated virtually all authority in the secular world to the state, but insisted that there was a religious realm in which the state had no right to intervene. American Christians of different denominations were compelled at first by circumstances, and later by conviction, to support full religious freedom for one another.

The point is that, after a long, historical process, Catholics and Protestants have emerged basically supportive of pluralistic societies and now believe in the importance of churches remaining independent from the state. The concern expressed in this chapter is that the Orthodox have yet to arrive at that moment in their history, in either theory or practice.

It has become fashionable in recent years to criticize the notion that Cæsaropapism—the view that secular rulers control the church—is an accurate description of the relationship of the Orthodox Church to government authorities. Traditionally, the judgment was made that the Byzantine emperors controlled the Eastern Orthodox Church from the sixth to the tenth centuries. Aristeides Papadakis, who in general does not find the term Cæsaropapism to be sufficiently nuanced, nevertheless asserts that the Byzantine emperor's

sacrosanct status in eastern Christendom had no parallel in contemporary medieval Europe. His right to interfere in the church's institutional structure was unlimited.[3]

The emperor chose the patriarchs and forced one-third of them to resign. In the area of doctrine, however, the Eastern Orthodox Church did maintain its independence.[4] Nevertheless, in the academic debate over the appropriateness of the term Cæsaropapism, we are now in danger of underestimating the degree to which the Orthodox Church was not, and is not, independent of the state.

Indeed, the relationship of the Orthodox Church to the czarist authorities from the time of Peter the Great in the early 18th century, and the pattern of co-option and collaboration so typical of the Orthodox Church in many countries under communism in the 20th century, again raise the issue of whether Orthodoxy is not peculiarly susceptible to subordination to secular authorities. It should be noted that Peter the Great borrowed some of his ideas for controlling the church from German Protestant models at a time when important segments of the Protestant Church were anything but independent of the state. But as so often has proven to be the case, Western influences imported into Russia have a life of their own, many times taking on a character ultimately more extreme and less tempered than the fate of these ideas within the Western context.

Deep within Orthodox theology and thought, dating to the conversion of Constantine to Christianity in the fourth century, is the notion of "symphony," i.e., a close working relationship between church and state. However, this idealistic notion of "symphony" has not spawned a rich tradition of profound political treatises on political subjects. It is interesting that during the 1991 Gulf War, the Synod of Bishops of the Orthodox Church of America declared in its statement on the war that "the 'just war theory' does not reflect our theological tradition."[5] This refusal to identify with a rather well-developed church tradition dating to the Fathers, regarding situations when the use of force is allowable, without anything else to put in its place as a means of navigating these tough moral issues, leaves the Orthodox Church in an untenable position. In a similar way, the theoretical relationship of church and state is not well-developed in Orthodox thought. The idealistic "symphonia" so often talked about has frequently been, in fact, a "false symphonia" in the view of the well-known historian of the Russian Orthodox Church, A. V. Kartashev.[6] It is necessary to stress that the assertion that there is a major weakness in the Orthodox tradition should be balanced by a recognition of the church's remarkable strengths, including worship, liturgy, and a profound appreciation of the Patristic Fathers.

The phenomenon of "autocephalous" churches in the Orthodox world is a powerful reinforcement of the Orthodox Church's intimate link with nationalism. (In the Eastern Orthodox world, an "autocephalous" Orthodox Church is governed by its own national synod.) For example, this phenomenon can be clearly seen in the political histories of both Bulgaria and Serbia. Not surprisingly, political leaders have invariably favored "autocephalous" status for the churches in their region. It has often followed that these political leaders seek to make this "autocephalous" church a branch of government, thus co-opting the church.

As Father Anthony Ugolnik, himself an Orthodox priest, recently put it in an analysis of the Russian Orthodox Church and politics:

> There are inbred impulses to accommodate to any authority: hence the patriarch has a tendency to act too swiftly to support what he perceives as the emerging strongman.[7]

An example of this comes from the Romanian patriarch Justin in 1980:

> A warm word, coming from the heart, is also owed to the first citizen of the country, our highly esteemed Nicolae Ceauşescu; as a brother of the holy soil of

our Fatherland, he carries the torch of love for the nation, which warms the hearts of millions upon millions of people, in robust arms which fashion the image of a new Romania, the image of a free, independent . . . Romania. . . . Highly esteemed President of the Republic, that is why we all treasure you, why we all honor you, why we all love you.[8]

Or consider the words of Russian Orthodox Patriarch Aleksi in 1949, on the occasion of Stalin's 70th birthday:

Stalin is the first amongst the fighters for peace among all the nations of the world . . . he is our leader, whose charming personality disarms any who have met him by his kindness and attentiveness to everybody's needs . . . by the power and kind wisdom of his speech.[9]

On his trip to the United States in November 1991, Patriarch Aleksi II offered the following partial, limited explanation and apology for the church's silence and accommodation:

Defending one thing [the institutional existence of the church] was necessary to somewhere else [sic]. Were there any other organizations or any other people among those who had to carry responsibility not only for themselves, but for thousands of others, who in those years in the Soviet Union were not compelled to act likewise? Before these people, however, to whom compromises, silence, forced passivity or expressions of loyalty permitted by leaders of the church in those years caused pain, before these people, and not only before God, I ask forgiveness, understanding and prayer.[10]

His words angered many because he failed to acknowledge that many did not capitulate as the Orthodox hierarchy did. In an open letter the Association of Concerned Christians of America, a group of Catholics, stated:

While the final sentiments of apology are most laudable, the introductory statement should be placed in a historical context. Notables such as Andrei Sakharov, Cardinal Josef Slipyi and Nathan Scharansky head the list of millions of individuals who chose to suffer exile, torture, and death for their religious, ethical or national principles rather than capitulate to "compromise, silence, forced passivity or expression of loyalty."

Among the "organizations" that made the choice of martyrdom versus survival were the Ukrainian Catholic, Ukrainian Orthodox Autocephalous churches, and many Protestant believers who chose to follow Christ's example rather than that of Judas or Peter.[11]

There are notable Orthodox figures who refused to capitulate in the face of state intimidation: the Solovki bishops in the 1920s, Alexander Solzhenitsyn, Father Gleb Yakunin, and many other Russian Orthodox dissidents, most of whom are still viewed with considerable suspicion or outright hostility by the church hierarchy. In some ways, *glasnost'* has been less in evidence in the Russian Orthodox patriarchate than anywhere else in Russian society or government.

Another factor which makes it less likely that the Orthodox Church will emerge as the champion of pluralism is the historical precedent in Georgia, Romania, and Russia of a "state church." Thus, the Orthodox have little or no experience of full religious freedom within the framework of church-state separation and guarantees of nondiscrimination against minority religions. Nor do they necessarily want to acquire this experience. As Father Artyom, a Moscow priest, said in late 1991:

The most dangerous thing for Russia is religious and spiritual pluralism. Moscow isn't a Babylon for second cults, for protestant congregations who resemble wild wolves rushing in here or Catholics like thieves using their billions to try to occupy new territory. Democracy is an idol that will be broken like communism was.[12]

To be sure, such a rabid statement would never be found in any public communiqué from the patriarchate leadership, and yet there are indications that some within the hierarchy are profoundly uncomfortable with the advent of full religious freedom for all groups. A high-ranking senior Soviet human rights leader reported to a prominent American leader of an evangelical mission that he had been approached by senior people in the patriarchate with the suggestion that a "state religion" be reinstituted such as existed under the czars. The Soviet official, a nonbeliever, responded that his colleagues were interested in granting freedom to all, not just to the Orthodox.

ORTHODOXY AND PLURALISM

Of the three major Christian confessions, the Orthodox are perhaps the least inclined towards theological ecumenism. Before proceeding any further, it must be made clear that this discussion does not concern the reservations that the Orthodox Church recently expressed regarding the World Council of

Church's fidelity to basic Christian beliefs. On the contrary, it is to the Orthodox Church's great credit that she raises such issues; serious believers among other Christian confessions have also been greatly disturbed by both the leftward political orientation as well as the theological slippage that crops up from time to time in ecumenical organizations.[13] Serious Catholics and Protestants have far more in common with the Orthodox, who view the Catholics and Protestants theologically with some suspicion, than they have with members of their own confessions who have no qualms about joining hands "ecumenically" with theological heretics so long as they have the "politically correct" position on nuclear weapons or achieving justice in this world. In fact, for many in the old-line Protestant world or the ecumenical world, "theological heresy" is a category which no longer seems to exist; only "political heresy" is of importance.

Sadly, in the eyes of many, and for very understandable reasons, the term "ecumenical" has become identified with political liberalism and radicalism. Ironically, it was precisely the Orthodox Churches' pliability in the hands of the communist authorities that allowed them to be used in repeated propaganda blitzes for peace and justice, organized by the Kremlin, which further eroded respect internationally and at home for the Orthodox Church. The Orthodox Church, and registered Protestant leaders from the communist world as well, repeatedly denied in world ecumenical meetings for almost three decades that there were serious problems for believers in communist countries.[14] However, this chapter focuses on Orthodox theological attitudes towards non-Orthodox Christians.

For many serious Orthodox believers, it is an open question whether there is salvation outside the Orthodox Church. Their position in some ways is not unlike Catholicism pre-Vatican II, though some would argue that even before Vatican II there was considerably more Catholic tolerance towards Christians of other faiths than that which may be found among Orthodox leaders today.

It should be noted that members of other churches have been, and sometimes still are, intolerant of the Orthodox. Some fundamentalist Protestants have talked as if Catholics and Orthodox are not Christian at all. Some Ukrainian Catholics are extremely hostile and unfair toward the Orthodox. And, of course, there are Christians in all three confessions who treat one another with genuine respect as members of the same family of God. Nevertheless, it is the author's position that there are particularly serious problems within the Orthodox Church regarding its attitude toward, and treatment of, Christians of other confessional affiliations. If this observation is indeed true, then it will certainly be relevant for a consideration of pluralism in societies in which Orthodoxy is a powerful force.

In coming to terms with powerful Orthodox reservations about pluralism, it is helpful to consider their very strong feelings about what they call "proselytism." Recently, this issue boiled up in Romania, Georgia, and Russia and resulted in considerable Orthodox anger against both Catholics and Protestants. To be sure, the line between evangelization and proselytism is not always clear. Usually, the term *proselytism* is used to describe an aggressive attempt to convert committed adherents of one religious perspective to that of another, while *evangelization* is understood more broadly to mean the attempt to convert unbelievers. In a truly free society, even proselytism must be legal, although it may not be considered by some to be religiously necessary or appropriate.

However, the matter is considerably more complicated in societies in which there are strong historical ties to a particular Christian faith such as Orthodoxy. This remains the case even if the bulk of the population are not now believers, or are only nominal believers. Many Catholics and Protestants consider this to be precisely the situation in several formerly communist countries, and the sociological surveys that have been done confirm this fact. Often, however, the Orthodox hierarchy considers the area to be geographically "Orthodox." Hence, any work done by other Christian groups is considered by definition "proselytism," a judgment many Catholics and Protestants greatly resent. As the Romanian minister of religious affairs told the author in Bucharest in May 1990, "Any gain for the Protestants is a loss for the Orthodox."

Even American Orthodox converts sometimes adopt this remarkably broad notion of "geographic Orthodoxy" and view other Christian groups as a hostile intrusion into their midst and as "sheep stealers." As Father Alexander Webster has put it:

> The greatest threat to the well-being of the 18-million-member Romanian Orthodox Church is not posed by the defunct communist party or the widely discredited hierarchy . . . The real danger to the Romanian Orthodox community lies with some of the fellow Christian survivors of the old regime and—incredibly—with otherwise well-intentioned American evangelicals.[15]

Surprisingly, Father Webster frankly acknowledges that the Orthodox hierarchy in Romania is "widely discredited," "morally impotent," and guilty of decades of "obsequious collaboration with the communist regime." But somehow, it is nevertheless the Evangelicals who are the "greatest threat" to the Romanian Orthodox Church. Such attitudes reflect a lack of faith either in the positive benefits of pluralism or in the resiliency of the Orthodox faith.

In a published response to Father Webster, this author expressed the belief that there was a "core of agreement" which unites Christians of the three major branches of Christendom, namely, belief in the "existence of God, the sinfulness of human beings, the divinity of Christ and his atoning sacrificial death on our behalf," and asserted that

> In a world that desperately needs this "good news," we ought to rejoice when a lost sheep is found, regardless of whether the shepherd is wearing a Catholic, Orthodox or Protestant robe.[16]

Father Webster's response provides real insight into why many Orthodox are uncomfortable at best with the very notion of pluralism:

> I don't expect any Orthodox—in Romania or this country—to subscribe to his [Hill's] subjective "core of agreement" or his attempt to reduce the distinctions among Catholics, Orthodox and Protestants to a matter of wearing different "robes."[17]

He later identifies the approach he opposes as betraying a "peculiarly Protestant ecclesiology."[18] Figures such as G. K. Chesterton in the Catholic world or Father Alexander Men' of the Orthodox probably would not agree with Father Webster; however, Webster may well represent many Orthodox who consider talk of a "common core" of Christian belief to be shorthand for Protestant heresy or error. If non-Orthodox Christians are wrong even when they preach what they think is a "universal" Christian gospel, let alone when they consciously advance their own understandings, then it is easy to understand why many Orthodox believe pluralism cannot but be a breeding ground for untruth.

Webster, by the way, does believe in complete religious freedom. What he would prefer, however, is that Protestants and others simply decide on their own not to be active in Orthodox areas decimated by decades of communist influence and power. In essence, what this amounts to is an appeal to the non-Orthodox to refrain voluntarily from contributing to the creation of more pluralistic societies. Webster's own commitment to full religious freedom and to legal protection guaranteeing it in fact reflects a Western orientation. The majority of the Orthodox laity or their leaders in non-Western societies, however, may not share Father Webster's firm commitment to religious freedom, including the right either to evangelize or proselytize. In short, I believe there is a deep and fundamental distrust of pluralism in much, if not most, of the Orthodox world.

ORTHODOXY AND PROTESTANTS

This was a time of horrible persecutions. Exiles, arrests, fines, and beatings of believers rained down abundantly upon the audacious followers of the Gospel. Under continual fear of being caught by the police, the brothers nevertheless did not cease their meetings, holding them in basements, across the Dnieper, in the woods, in the cemetery, in ravines, and in the apartments of the more well-to-do brothers.[19]

Many are surprised to discover that this account of persecution has nothing to do with the communists, but relates to what Protestants experienced in the late 19th century in czarist Russia. In 1891, the Holy Synod, the ruling council of the Russian Orthodox Church, decreed that any who left the Orthodox Church to join another denomination should suffer the "loss of all civil and personal rights." To distribute "heretical" (i.e., non-Orthodox) propaganda was punishable by exile to Siberia.[20] However, the last two decades of czarist rule were marked by major improvements in the amount of religious freedom in the Russian empire with respect to Protestants and other religious minorities.

Protestants have experienced discrimination in recent years at the hands of the Orthodox in a variety of places, including Romania and Georgia. In Romania, the Orthodox hierarchy has long been particularly hostile to an ecumenical group called the Lord's Army, which includes many different Protestant groups and several hundred thousand Orthodox. On the one hand, it is a very hopeful sign that diverse Christian groups for many decades have found common theological ground to work together in the wasteland created by communist education. Nevertheless, it must be acknowledged that those who cooperate with the Protestants are viewed with considerable suspicion and anger by the official Orthodox Church leadership. Protestants in Romania in the post-Ceauşescu regime continue to express concerns about their situation at the present time, when Romanian nationalism is closely associated with Orthodoxy. Protestants, however, are not experiencing active persecution and are being allowed to expand their ministry. What problems they face are more of the order of being "second-class citizens."

In Georgia, the tension between Orthodox and Protestants has been quite pronounced. According to a report by Pastor Levan Akhalmosulishvili, pastor of the Gourjaani Baptist Church in eastern Georgia, on August 29, 1990, ᴜᴇ Orthodox are very hostile to evangelicals.[21] He charges that in September 1989 Patriarch Ilia II came to Gourjaani and, in a town meeting, publicly denounced the Baptists and called on Soviet officials to take action against them. This touched off considerable anti-Baptist rhetoric and activity. On August 12, 1990, Father Archil, a prominent member of the Georgian legislature, tried to prevent a Baptist service that was taking place in Gurjaani. He finally agreed to wait until the service was over, at which time he told the Baptists and the Orthodox who had gathered that the Baptists in Georgia were heretics, forerunners of the anti-Christ, sexually immoral, followers of one of the most corrupt men in the world (Martin Luther), and American spies. Local people, now in a frenzy, shouted, "Let us drive them away in order to avoid corruption of our children!"

On Sunday morning, July 28, 1991, Father Georgi took 30 members of his Orthodox congregation in the city of Guaarumi (about 65 miles from Tbilisi) and marched them to the local Baptist church with 300 members. They blocked the entrance to the church and threatened to burn the church down and kill any who sought to return the following week. Fortunately, the threats were not carried out.

This was not an isolated incident. Similar episodes have occurred in Gurgaan (July 1991), Gori (1991), Bolnisi (May 1991), and Akhaltsiche (1990). These problems, and others related to obtaining building sites and permission to publish, were reported to a delegation of Western Christian leaders and lawyers in early August 1991 by Reverend Guram Kumalashvili, President of the Baptist Union of Georgia.

A particularly disturbing sign of anti-Protestant militancy has been visible for millions to see on national television. Father Archil regularly used his weekly television sermon in 1991 to attack the "sectarians" and hold them responsible for everything from moral corruption in the country to earthquakes. Some have even proclaimed evangelicals to be the "Anti-Christ." "Even the communists never attacked us in this way," observed the head of the Georgian Baptist Union.

One of the troubling findings of a joint delegation from Campbell University Law School and the Southern Baptist Convention to Georgia (November 30-December 4, 1991) was the degree to which government decisions related to property and publishing seemed to be dependent on the Orthodox Church. Frequently, in meetings with then-President Zviad Gamsakhurdia or other government officials, the delegation was told that they would need to talk to the patriarch about this or that problem the Baptists were having. His Holiness Ilia II was very cordial to the visiting American delegation, as indeed he often has been to the local Baptists. He insists that it is the government's responsibility to handle such matters, and he rejects the rhetorical excesses of some Orthodox. In contrast, the local Baptists were told by the Georgian Ministry of Justice that the decision whether they would be allowed to print materials rested with the patriarch. It should be noted that the visits by American delegations and the involvement of the European Baptist Federation resulted in some improvement in the situation for the Georgian Baptists. The Georgian Patriarch, in his meeting with Western Evangelicals in December 1991, did make it clear that the Orthodox Church does not accept "proselytism." Here, of course, lies a great debate discussed earlier.

In the Russian Republic, as well, there are examples of problems for Evangelicals. In the Domodedovo region, 30 miles southeast of Moscow, the Baptists came to an agreement in 1990 with the largest state farm in the area to lease a building for religious purposes. The financial transaction was signed and money paid. But at a community meeting before the final occupation of the building, local villagers, incited by the local Orthodox priest, stood up and protested against the Baptists being allowed to use the building. The farm leadership then backed out of the deal.[22]

Another example of Orthodox influence being used to mute the influence of Evangelicals was the decision by Russian television in January 1992 to break a contract that called for the prime-time airing of special evangelical programming. At the last minute, the program times were changed to 1:30 A.M. and 7 A.M. Nevertheless, more than 100,000 viewers responded to the address given for further information, and the TV station did refund their money to the evangelicals for breaking the contract.

Pastor Grigory Kommendant, the president of the Baptists, observed in a remarkably frank comment in late 1991:

> Neither before [the revolution] nor after, nor now do we have the same rights as the Orthodox Church. I predict it will go the same way as in prerevolutionary times; we don't expect repression, but we expect discrimination. We'll be second class.[23]

ORTHODOXY AND CATHOLICS

The Orthodox relationship with the Catholic world has been particularly stormy. In 1946, at Stalin's initiative, the Ukrainian Catholic Church was forcibly absorbed into the Russian Orthodox Church. Many Russian Orthodox were not unhappy about this "union," seeing the original move towards

Rome in 1596 as primarily a result of political, not religious, factors.[24] This absorption by the Russian Orthodox Church created the largest illegal religious group—approximately four million adherents—in the USSR. At one time, there were in the illegal Catholic church between 800 and 1,000 priests, between six and ten bishops, several underground seminaries and monasteries, and (beginning in 1984) the *Chronicle of the Catholic Church in Ukraine,* a secretly published *samizdat* publication. A similar underground Catholic journal existed in Lithuania for some years, starting in 1972.[25]

A number of Russian Orthodox called for the legalization of the Ukrainian Catholic Church—notably, Fathers Georgi Edelshtein, Vladimir Poresh, Gleb Yakunin, and Aleksandr Ogorodnikov. In June 1988, Andrei Sakharov threw his prestige behind the effort. However, the Russian Orthodox hierarchy was not nearly as open to a departure from the status quo as were some of its troublesome priests and activists. Indicative of the problem was the comment in the Soviet press by Metropolitan Filaret of Kiev in June 1989:

> If—God forbid!—the Ukrainian Catholic Church acquires a legal status, its zealots will brew terrible strife and hinder the effort for beneficial change in Soviet life—to live in peace and concord.[26]

Even the more liberal Kirill of Smolensk, chairman of the Department of External Ecclesiastical Relations of the Patriarchate, has made some quite negative statements about the Ukrainian Catholics.

The beginning of the end for the reactionary forces in Ukraine was signalled by the ousting from power of the communist party leader Volodymir Shcherbitsky in September 1989. Two days before the meeting between Pope John Paul II and Mikhail Gorbachev on December 1, 1989, an announcement was made in Ukraine by the Council for Religious Affairs that registration of Ukrainian Catholics was to be allowed.

But problems have continued to exist. Ukrainian Catholics argue that the Russian Orthodox Church is dragging its feet and that there is more *glasnost'* among the communists than among the Orthodox hierarchy. The Orthodox charge that the Catholics have resorted to violence. Much of the dispute involves questions of church property.

Tensions between the Russian Orthodox Church and the Vatican are also indicative of how far the Orthodox have to go before they become comfortable with true pluralism. When an Italian journalist interviewed Patriarch Aleksi II in August 1991, in answer to a question on the condition of Orthodox-Vatican relations, the Patriarch responded:

They are extremely difficult . . . I must tell you that today, the attitude of our believers to the Roman Catholic Church is getting worse each month. I will say more, it is getting worse with each step that the Vatican takes aimed at establishing itself on traditionally Orthodox territories, not only in the Ukraine but in European Russia, in Siberia. How, for example, can you justify the appointment of a Catholic bishop to Novosibirsk. All the Catholics there would make up one, or at most two parishes . . . Our church has retained its apostolic structure with its fundamental rule—one city, one bishop, and now when "parallel" bishops appointed by the Vatican appear in Russian and Ukrainian cities, we consider this to be an open affront to Orthodoxy. In our opinion, the current proselytism of the Catholics and the action of the Uniates in the Eastern Ukraine are erecting an even higher wall between Russia and Western Christianity.[27]

On October 30, 1991, Patriarch Aleksi II asserted on a visit to England (the first by a Russian Patriarch since 1964) that at that time a "papal visit is not a suitable event to take place."[28] He charged that the Vatican had broken the mutual agreement not to proselytize members from each other's churches and that the Catholic Church was seeking to make converts "from the western Ukraine to the easternmost reaches of the former Soviet Union."[29] Aleksi was particularly angry at what the press often incorrectly reported as the papal appointment of a "Catholic Archbishop of Moscow." In fact, as Cardinal Sodano, the secretary of state of the Holy See, has pointed out several times, the Vatican appointed an "apostolic administrator" with headquarters in Moscow for the pastoral care of Catholics in western Russia.

DISPUTES AMONG THE ORTHODOX

So much attention has been paid to the Catholic-Orthodox dispute in Ukraine that many have failed to recognize the divisions that exist between the Russian Orthodox Church and Orthodox in Ukraine. There is, after all, the Ukrainian Autocephalous Orthodox Church (UAOC), which has been particularly active since August 1989.[30] The UAOC charges that the Russian Orthodox Church has been a tool of the communists since the 1920s and that the transformation of the Ukrainian Exarchate of the Moscow Patriarchate into the Ukrainian Orthodox Church in 1990 was simply window dressing that denies real independence.

The Russian Orthodox Church has excommunicated priests of the very rebellious Ukrainian Autocephalous Orthodox Church. One must be very cautious not to draw too many conclusions about the Orthodox Church's attitude towards pluralism simply on the basis of the dispute with the UAOC. There are two reasons for this. First, internal church discipline matters must be dealt with by all churches, and the fact that a group is at odds with the center does not necessarily indicate a lack of commitment by the center to political pluralism outside the church. Second, matters of excommunication touch upon profound ecclesiastical questions of ordination and authority. They cannot be considered within the normal political parameters of a discussion of pluralism.

It is of course true that hierarchical, episcopal models of ecclesiastical governance are not, and do not want to be, pluralistic or democratic. Truth, it is argued, is not determined by majority votes. True as this may be, history is full of examples of the authoritarian keepers of religious or political truths abusing their power and seeking, in the name of fidelity to "truth," to snuff out the voices of those who correctly called for reform. This brings to the threshold such complex and thorny questions of church polity as are beyond the scope of this chapter to discuss.

Judging the Russian Orthodox Church's attitude towards pluralism by its stormy relationship with its dissidents is an extremely dangerous enterprise, especially for non-Orthodox. However, two observations can be made. First, the Orthodox Church is an extremely hierarchal church. Second, of all the organizations of the former Soviet Union, the Russian Orthodox Church has emerged as one of the most stubborn in resisting *glasnost'*—that is, telling the complete truth about the past. In a pluralistic society, opportunities for truth-telling are multiplied. For an organization that is nervous about what has happened in the past and unwilling to face up to it squarely, the advance of pluralism is a rather frightening development.

The most painful issue, of course, is the degree to which the Orthodox hierarchy was manipulated and controlled by the communist organs of power—the party, the KGB, and the Council for Religious Affairs. The evidence is massive that the communist authorities used Orthodox leaders (and the leaders of virtually every other religious confession) to advance their foreign policy agenda abroad.[31] Independent leaders were weeded out, imprisoned, or killed. Many good people managed to maintain some power, but at the price of restricting their activities and remaining silent about their difficulties. Others were coaxed or blackmailed into going much further to advance the communist agenda, and there were outright agents planted within the church's leadership as well. This often successful attempt to co-opt the church is one of the most shameful chapters in the history of communism in power.

The debate for the church today, of course, concerns the issue of facing squarely this painful past. In January 1991, the author met with a high-ranking official of the patriarchate who denied that the Council for Religious

Affairs had significantly interfered in internal church politics. This same official warned against the "exaggerations" of Michael Bourdeaux and his research center, Keston College, which has been recognized for over two decades as one of the most reliable sources of accurate information on religion in communist countries. In contrast, at an October 30, 1991, meeting in the KGB Lubyanka headquarters, Vice Chairman General Nikolai Stolyarov responded with a great deal more candor to a question regarding KGB involvement with the Council on Religious Affairs to control the church. With television cameras rolling, he responded, "I will not deny that in the past that was the situation."[32]

The refusal of the Russian Orthodox Church to face its past squarely at a time of greater pluralism and openness in Russian society is made all the more painful by a whole series of revelations in the Russian press about KGB involvement in the Russian Orthodox Church. These revelations have been based largely on archival materials from the Central Committee of the CPSU and the KGB. Father Vyacheslav Polosin, chairman of the Russian Republic Freedom of Conscience Committee, reported in *Izvestia* in early 1992 that a document had been found in the archives of the *Cheka* spelling out the need to recruit church leaders so as to make each of them an "eternal slave of the *Cheka*."[33]

State security documents identify Metropolitan Filaret of Kiev as KGB agent "Antonov," Metropolitan Yuvenali as "Adamant," and Metropolitan Pitirim, in charge of Orthodox publishing, as "Abbot."[34] There is, of course, considerable question about just what is meant by "agent." The KGB clearly considered the churchmen in question to be reliable in carrying out party instructions in their work, often with foreign religious groups. It is certainly possible that many of the dozens of "agents" identified in KGB documents did not view themselves as agents, but rather as churchmen compelled to go along at least in part with the secular, communist authorities. Metropolitan Pitirim, for example, denies knowingly collaborating with the KGB, although he concedes that he reported on his contacts with foreigners to the government Council for Religious Affairs. However, according to Michael Dobbs, "Parliamentary deputies who have examined KGB archives find his denials unconvincing, noting that none of the accused church leaders has taken legal action to defend his reputation."[35]

Students of church schools even refer to the Holy Synod as the "Metropolitburo."[36] Father Gleb Yakunin, who spent much of the 1980s in prison and is now a member of the Russian Republic Freedom of Conscience Committee, believes that 20 percent of the clergy collaborated with the KGB.[37] Writing in the mass periodical *Argumenty i fakty* (*Arguments and*

Facts) in September 1991, Father Georgi Edelshtein of Kostroma stated that he believed the figure to be 50 percent.[38]

On one occasion in 1991, the author posed the following issue to Father Edelshtein, one of the most outspoken critics of the church hierarchy: "Perhaps it would be better for the Orthodox Church simply to leave unexposed the many skeletons in its closet and get on with the important task of meeting the spiritual needs of the people." His response was direct. "But that is contrary to the New Testament model. There can be no revival without repentance. Peter had to repent before he could be powerfully used by God."

Father Edelshtein has tried to live up to his own words. In the September 1991 issue of *Argumenty i fakty,* he charged that there were still KGB collaborators in the Russian Orthodox Church. As a result, his bishop called a special session of the priests in his diocese at which he was criticized, and for the most part Father Edelshtein was not allowed to respond. No one disagreed with his allegations, but he was told that such realities should not be stated publicly. According to Edelshtein, it is understood that the clergy are never to talk about the reality of "informers" in the church.[39]

Evidence of continued serious problems within the Orthodox Church is substantial. In the early 1990s, a group of students sought to organize a student youth group in a church. The Bishop of Chelyabinsk, however, turned the list over to the local KGB and told it to deal with the "troublemakers." The KGB, however, sent a letter back to the bishop noting that it was no longer involved in such "internal matters." The KGB then sent a copy of the bishop's letter to the local soviet, which in turn had it published.[40]

In addition, there are clear indications that some powerful people or organizations are determined not to lose hold of the reins that have so effectively bridled the church in recent decades. There is evidence that the KGB is still seeking to control the Orthodox Church. As late as February 4, 1992, in hearings in the Russian Republic Supreme Soviet into the August 1991 coup, continued KGB involvement in the churches was charged. This is confirmed by interviews the author conducted on January 29, 1992 at the Russian Supreme Soviet with Father Vyacheslav Polosin and Father Gleb Yakunin. Yakunin reported that, only a few days before, a priest had called him to report that an attempt had just been made to recruit him as an agent. Father Yakunin also reported in the same interview that, a few days earlier, the head of intelligence for the KGB and Patriarch Aleksi II had come separately on the same day to the Supreme Soviet commission investigating the KGB archives on the church and requested that the investigation be cut short. A few hours later, according to Father Polosin, access was indeed denied to the Supreme Soviet deputies charged with working in the archives.

The refusal of the present Russian Orthodox leadership to come to terms with the revelations about the deeply compromised character of its own collaboration with communist rulers during the Soviet period is not healthy for the church—and is not a good omen regarding the church's openness to pluralism and *glasnost'*.

ORTHODOXY AND NATIONALISM

The strong link between Orthodoxy and Slavic nationalism may well play an important role in determining the degree to which full religious freedom and pluralism emerge in the portions of the former Soviet Union where Slavs are in the majority. It must be noted at the outset that there is no one "Orthodox" perspective on such matters. The patriarchate is frequently not in agreement with Russian Republic deputies or with former dissidents such as Father Gleb Yakunin. Other Russian deputies who are priests enjoy the warm support of the church hierarchy. In general, the Christian Democratic groups, which are often at odds with one another, are more supportive of full religious freedom and the formation of a pluralistic society than is the Holy Synod.

It is encouraging that the patriarch himself has publicly affirmed his support of full religious freedom. Even if it turns out that his words are sometimes undermined by actions taken at high church levels to interfere with the activities of other religious groups, it is still highly significant that at least the ideal of religious freedom is advanced by the church leadership. In contrast, in many Islamic circles, for example, there is a direct rejection of democracy, religious freedom, and pluralism as products of the "secular" and "anti-religious" West.

As the postcommunist Slavic societies cast about for some sort of ballast for a new ship of state, it is natural that Orthodoxy is a rallying cry for many who seek something around which to unify the people. However, there are at least three problems with this. First, any development which carries society back to the precommunist days of a state religion undermines progress towards complete religious freedom. Secondly, such a return would be unfortunate for the Orthodox Church because historically state churches have been notoriously weak and anemic. Those who truly care about the spiritual vitality of the Orthodox Church must insist that it steer clear of any romantic return to the alluring but deceptively safe harbors of the past. Thirdly, many who raise the "Orthodox flag" as a unifying symbol care far more for the political advantages they think they can gain from the support that the church can give them than they do for the message, or the well-being, of the church. The Orthodox Church, indeed every Christian church, must remember the old adage that whoever marries the spirit of the time will soon find himself a widower.

Furthermore, given the highly compromised and weakened moral status of the present Orthodox leaders following decades of manipulation by communist authorities, the likelihood that they will truly be independent in any new relationship with the government is very slight. It is far more likely that they will find themselves once again carrying someone else's water.

THE FUTURE OF ORTHODOXY IN SLAVIC SOCIETIES

An unpublished poll, conducted by the All-Union Polling Center for Socio-Economic Issues and the International Center for Human Values,[41] indicated that the most popular social institution in Russian society is the Russian Orthodox Church, followed in descending order by the army, the "Green" ecological movement, the KGB, the communist party, and "Democratic Russia." This ought to be extremely encouraging for the Orthodox, because it means that the population is quite willing to forgive lapses of courage during which the church leadership so often seemed to flounder and lose its way. One of the great strengths of the Orthodox Church during the years of communism was that it never altered its basic theological commitments to the great truths of the faith. The liturgy remained the same, day in and day out—a beautiful, timeless testimony to the historic truths of the faith. In this, the Orthodox have proven to be far more faithful to their callings than many of their counterparts in other Christian traditions in the West.

But the poll data also showed that although 39 percent reported that they believed in God and 32 percent considered themselves Orthodox, only 27 percent believed the Bible to be the Word of God, only 12 percent of those polled prayed at least once a week, only 6 percent attended church at least once a month, only 7 percent managed to take communion several times a year (more than 81 percent said they had never taken communion), and only 4.3 percent read religious literature regularly. In short, although a significant proportion of the population says it believes in God, relatively few regularly participate in the life of the church.

There can be little question that three generations of communist education have played a role in eroding the basic religious knowledge of the people. There is strong reason to believe that the statement "I am a believer" ought to be understood more as a rejection of atheism than as an affirmation of knowledgeable and deep faith. Thus, there is much to be done if the Orthodox Church is to pass on effectively to the population the truths of Christianity to the population. From the perspective of this writer, it would be in the best interests of the Orthodox, and of the Kingdom of God, for the Orthodox to view the Catholics and Protestants as allies in the process of promoting genuine spiritual renewal in the Commonwealth of Independent States. There will be plenty of time later to discuss the "family" differences within the Christian community of faith. But to be fair to one group of Orthodox friends, perhaps this author's perspective is hopelessly "Protestant." On the other hand, other Orthodox friends completely embrace these ideas and find them in agreement with their own basic Orthodox beliefs.

On the issue of whether the Slavic societies are likely to return to a government or state church, the indications are that they will not. It is not just the Russian Orthodox dissidents and the secular intelligentsia who oppose this, but prominent churchmen as well, including the patriarch. In the summer of 1991, Archbishop Pimen of Saratov, who was extremely gracious and warm in his reception of a visiting delegation of American Protestants, rejected the idea of a return to a state religion in Russia. One of the leading ecumenical liaison figures in the Orthodox Church of America, Father Leonid Kishkovsky, also frequently argues against any suggestion of returning to a state religion in Russia.

On the question of tolerance in the Orthodox Church, John Dunlop, a senior fellow at Harvard and himself a practicing Orthodox, argues that genuinely religious Orthodox Christians are the least authoritarian, least nationalistic, most supportive (for example, of the right of the Uniates to exist), and the most tolerant overall. In his opinion, Father Alexander Men' was such a person. According to Dunlop, "Intolerance is highest at the top levels of the patriarchate."[42] And yet, as seen earlier, the present patriarch has been willing to affirm publicly the importance of religious freedom.

Also encouraging is the fact that, in the poll discussed earlier, 47.8 percent answered "fully disagree" to the question, "Do you or do you not agree with the opinion that members of the Orthodox Church should have advantages compared to atheists and people of other religious beliefs?" An additional 18 percent "mainly disagreed." Of concern, however, was that 9.6 percent "strongly agreed" that the Orthodox should have advantages over others, and another 5.3 percent "mainly agreed" with the proposition.[43] It is not clear that the majority of either Ukrainian Catholics or the Russian and Ukrainian Orthodox are willing to grant one another full religious freedom. This, of course, represents a profound threat to the emergence of a mature pluralism.

THE CHALLENGE AHEAD

In the years ahead, in the quest of Russians, Romanians, Ukrainians, Belorussians, Georgians, and other predominantly Orthodox peoples to recover from the communist assault on their culture, and particularly their faith, they will certainly maintain considerable interest in religion.

This interest will represent a curious mixture of genuine religious searching—a natural reaction to the obvious limitations of atheist materialism—and a more politically motivated nationalism, which sees religion as an important defining ingredient in Russian culture. For example, the Russians face the challenge of recovering their culture and the best of their religion and moving forward to full religious freedom and tolerance, something which the Russian Empire was evolving toward, but had not yet fully achieved, in 1917.

One thing is certain: Orthodoxy will continue to play a major role in the future of many regions, particularly the Slavic areas, in the CIS. Christians and others would do well to remember this fact. Orthodoxy could be a key catalyst in a spiritual and cultural renewal that will revive the peoples of these troubled lands.

However, for the sake of the continued development of a democratic and pluralistic society, with full religious freedom for all and full freedom of conscience for all, including atheists, agnostics, and non-Christians, one has to hope that those forces open to pluralism in the Orthodox Church come to the fore and lead the way into an historical period for which there is little precedent in the Orthodox past.

NOTES

1. Quoted by Pedro Ramet, ed., *Eastern Christianity and Politics in the Twentieth Century* (Durham, NC: Duke University Press, 1988), p. 7.
2. *Ibid.,* p. 8.
3. Aristeides Papadakis, "Church-State Relations Under Orthodoxy," in Ramet, ed., *Eastern Christianity and Politics,* p. 41.
4. *Ibid.,* pp. 41-42.
5. Quoted in Matt Murphy, "Sowing Confusion Among the Flock: Church Leaders and Anti-Gulf War Reasoning," Institute on Religion and Democracy Briefing Paper, Washington, D.C., 1991, pp. 27-28.
6. Quoted in Father Georgi Edelshtein, "The Russian Orthodox Church Today in the Eyes of Foreign Historians and Eyewitnesses," unpublished article, 1991. Father Edelshtein is a Russian Orthodox Priest from Kostroma; he gave the manuscript to the author in the fall of 1991 in Washington, D.C.

7. Anthony Ugolnik, "The Orthodox Church and Contemporary Politics in the USSR," October 1991, report for the National Council for Soviet and East European Research, p. 64.

8. Ramet, *Eastern Christianity and Politics*, p. 13.

9. Quoted in Kent R. Hill, *The Soviet Union on the Brink* (Portland, OR: Multnomah Press, 1992), p. 92.

10. Quoted in Serge Schmemann, "St. Petersburg Journal: Patriarch's Church Revives, but Will Spirituality?" *The New York Times*, November 9, 1991.

11. Statement given to the author by the Association of Concerned Christians of America, Arlington, Virginia.

12. Quoted in Elisabeth Rubinfien, "Orthodox Revival," *The Wall Street Journal*, December 20, 1991.

13. The theme of the World Council of Churches' General Assembly held in the spring of 1991 in Canberra was "Come Holy Spirit, Renew the Whole Creation." The materials prepared by the organizers in advance of the meeting and the program content represent a curious mixture of traditional theology and eclectic non-Christian spirituality. The emphasis on environmental concerns often reflected pantheist, more than theist, understandings of God. See Larry Adams, "The WCC at Canberra: Which Spirit?" *First Things*, June/July 1991; Adams, "The Greening of the Spirit: WCC Assembly Convenes in Australia," *Religion and Democracy*, Institute on Religion and Democracy, January 1991.

14. See Hill, *The Soviet Union on the Brink*, pp. 129-49, for further information on the ecumenical organizations' political beliefs and the way in which they failed to respond with either wisdom or courage to the persecution of believers in communist countries.

15. Father Alexander F. C. Webster, "Evangelicals vs. Orthodox in Romania," *Christian Century*, May 30-June 6, 1990, p. 560.

16. Kent R. Hill, "One 'Fold' for Romania?" *Christian Century*, August 8-15, 1990, p. 748.

17. Webster's response, *ibid.*

18. *Ibid.*, p. 749.

19. Quoted in Walter Sawatsky, *Soviet Evangelicals Since World War II* (Scottdale, PA: Herald Press, 1981), p. 35.

20. Walter J. Hollenwerger, *The Pentecostals* (Minneapolis: Augsburg Press, 1972), p. 269.

21. Unless otherwise indicated, the description of Protestant difficulties in Georgia is taken from Kent Hill, "Evangelicals Face Orthodox Pressure in Soviet Georgia," *Religion and Democracy*, September 1991, p. 7; and "Report of Baptist Delegation to Tbilisi, Republic of Georgia," December 1991, produced by Norman Adrian Wiggins School of Law at Campbell University, Buies Creek, North Carolina and the Christian Life Commission of the Southern Baptist Convention.

22. Rubinfien, *The Wall Street Journal*, December 20, 1991.

23. Quoted in *ibid.*

24. For information on the Ukrainian Catholics, see Hill, *The Soviet Union on the Brink*, pp. 119, 352-358.

25. *Ibid.*, p. 320.

26. *Ibid.*, p. 335.

27. Joint Publications Research Service (JPRS), UPA-91-042, October 7, 1991, p. 66. Trans. from *Golos*, no. 33 (August 26-September 1, 1991), p. 11, quoting from an interview with the patriarch published in the Italian weekly *Sabato*.

28. Quoted in Damian Thompson, "Pope Not Welcome in Russia, Says Orthodox Leader," *Daily Telegraph*, October 31, 1991.

29. *Ibid.*

30. On the Ukrainian Autocephalous Orthodox Church, see Hill, *The Soviet Union on the Brink*, pp. 358-360.

31. These problems are covered in Hill, *The Soviet Union on the Brink*.

32. Perhaps Stolyarov was sincere in saying that KGB involvement in the life of the church was a thing of the past, but there is evidence that the interference continues. A high-ranking official during the Gorbachev years told the author in February 1992 that Stolyarov resigned as a KGB vice chairman because he was discouraged about the prospects for reforming the massive and powerful bureaucracy.

33. Vyacheslav Polosin, "The Eternal Slave of the Chekha," *Izvestia*, January 22, 1992.

34. Michael Frankov, "Mysteries of the Holy Synod," *Moscow News* (Russian edition), no. 6 (February 9, 1992), p. 24; P. Vasil'ev, "'Abbat' Makes His Contact," interview with Father Gleb Yakunin, *Argumenty i fakty*, no. 1 (January 1992).

35. Michael Dobbs, "In Hard Times, No Time to Hunt Down KGB Agents," *International Herald Tribune*, February 12, 1992.

36. Frankov, *Moscow Times*, February 9, 1992.

37. Vasil'ev, *Argumenty i fakty*, no. 1 (January 1992).

38. Father Georgi Edelshtein, "Chekists in Cassocks," *Argumenty i fakty*, no. 36 (September 1991).

39. Edelshtein, "The Russian Orthodox Church Today in the Eyes of Foreign Historians and Eyewitnesses," p. 22. The author is also very upset with prominent historians abroad who argue that all is different now in the Orthodox Church, that revival has come, and that independence is a reality (see pp. 19, 27).

40. Ugolnik, "The Orthodox Church and Contemporary Politics," pp. 12-13.

41. Both these centers are located in Moscow. The poll, conducted in the Russian Federation in May 1991, focused on the "Attitudes of the Population to Religion, Politics, Law, etc."

42. Conversation with John Dunlop in Washington, D.C., October 1991.

43. See footnote 41.

Growing Protestant Diversity in the Former Soviet Union

Mark Elliott and Robert Richardson

Protestantism, almost by definition, means diversity. As a rule, for Christians in the Reformation tradition, personal investigation of Scripture is preferred over denominational or clerical prescriptions of biblical truth. Of course, many Protestants do listen carefully to the interpretation of Scripture provided by their churches and pastors. Nevertheless, they just as often draw theological conclusions based on their own personal study of the Bible, which is the simplest and most satisfactory explanation for the proliferation of Protestant denominations since 1517.

Not so under Stalin. Apparently for administrative convenience, he and his successors from 1944 to 1985 favored centralization and amalgamation for Protestants, the better to control these worrisome nonconformists. Thus, the 1944 merger of two denominations, the more Calvinistic Baptists and the more Armenian Evangelical Christians, took place ultimately because the state preferred to place its heavy hand on one nationwide (in Soviet terminology, "all-union") Protestant denomination.[1]

From 1929 to 1985, other Protestants were made to join this union, or disappear, or take up residence in the Gulag, or, at best, manage a precarious and illegal existence. Under state pressure, some communities merged with Evangelical Christians-Baptists, such as sizable numbers of Pentecostals in 1945 and Mennonite Brethren in 1963. A number of denominations had to content themselves with an organized existence only in peripheral areas: Lutherans only in the Baltic republics, Methodists only in Estonia, and

Hungarian Reformed only in Transcarpathia. Other churches simply ceased to exist by state fiat, with individual members fleeing abroad or, more usually, joining Evangelical Christian-Baptist or Lutheran congregations. This fate befell Molokane, Moravians, Plymouth Brethren, and members of Churches of Christ and the Salvation Army.

Conscious state policy, therefore, explains the unprecedented level of Protestant uniformity from Stalin until Gorbachev. After 1985, however, and especially after 1988, the Kremlin tended to let Protestant relationships be decided by Protestants. The reduction in state interference in church affairs means that, for the moment, believers living in the former Soviet Union enjoy a fragile but nearly full-blown religious liberty unique not only in the Soviet era but, arguably, in all of Russian history.[2] Under Gorbachev, Christians were pleasantly surprised to witness:

- the release of virtually all prisoners of conscience
- a significant increase in emigration
- an end to restrictions on the importation of Christian literature and the elimination of most bureaucratic impediments to religious publishing
- an end to all jamming of Western radio broadcasting
- the opening of ever-increasing numbers of churches, seminaries, and monasteries
- the revival of organized forms of Christian charity
- all-union, Baltic, and Russian Republic laws on freedom of conscience that answer the vast majority of concerns of human rights advocates
- the dismantling of the atheist establishment in Soviet education, cultural life, and the media
- government authorities no longer thwarting, but now rather pleading for, church assistance in filling the moral vacuum left in the wake of Marxism's collapse[3]

These examples of a stunning array of changes, such as recently occurred in East Central Europe as well as in the former Soviet Union, confirm the truth of Czech prisoner-turned-president Vaclav Havel's recent lament, "We have no time to be astonished."[4]

For Protestants, the end of all but sporadic and localized state harassment of churches has meant the beginning of a return to their normal state of existence, which naturally tends toward ever more confusing diversity, interpreted by some as democracy, by others as anarchy. There is not yet a critical need for a Soviet equivalent of Mead's *Handbook of Denominations in the United States*.[5] But if history is any guide at all, such a manual shortly will be in order.

In the former Soviet Union, increasing diversity and pluralism in Protestant ranks are expressed in a variety of ways, the most obvious being institutional. Proliferation of denominations already is underway and almost certainly will continue for the foreseeable future.

The only Protestant church permitted a nationwide organization without interruption from World War II to the present has been the Union of Evangelical Christians-Baptists (UECB). In 1961, this church suffered a split over the issue of state interference in its internal affairs. Those who refused to accept the increased restrictions of the Khrushchev antireligious campaign were called *initsiativniki,* i.e., reform, dissident, unregistered, or underground Baptists. This community, whose membership at one point may have been more than 100,000, appears reduced today to about 15,000 members; if we include adherents, the total may possibly amount to 45,000.[6] In contrast, UECB-registered church adherents number approximately 625,000. (See Appendix II.) However, reported membership of baptized adults dropped sharply in the late 1980s from some 550,000 to 204,156, due to large-scale German emigration, the 1989 departure of Pentecostals from the union, and presumably more accurate reporting.[7] In the near future, evangelistic efforts, new converts, and new churches most likely will compensate for these losses, if they have not already done so.

Finally, under the Baptist rubric, congregations independently registered with the state without UECB affiliation include perhaps 75,000 members and adherents.[8] By all accounts, these autonomously registered Evangelical Christian-Baptist churches are growing more rapidly than UECB congregations for several reasons:

- they do not suffer the onus of having bowed to state pressure in the early 1960s to curtail evangelism, as the UECB was forced to do;
- increasing numbers of reform Baptist congregations seeking legal status have been amenable to autonomous registration, but could not be persuaded to affiliate with the UECB, which they deemed compromised;
- finally, autonomously registered churches have been the most active, daring, and creative in their evangelistic outreach.[9] Viktor Hamm, a Soviet émigré evangelist who has close ties to all three groups, which is no mean feat in itself, estimated in the fall of 1991 that autonomously registered Evangelical Christian-Baptist churches were being established at a rate of 20 to 50 per month.[10]

At the same time, the UECB also is rapidly expanding, though its growth is counterbalanced, as noted, by recent losses to emigration and Pentecostal departures. One conclusion to be drawn from this overview of Evangelical Christians-Baptists is that the situation is extremely fluid, requiring numerical estimates to be attempted only with generous margins for error. That said, a combined UECB, autonomous, and unregistered membership of 248,705 would mean a total Evangelical Christian-Baptist community of approximately 746,000. (See Appendix II.)

While the purges of the 1930s all but extinguished Evangelical Christian and Baptist life, Stalin's repression did eliminate all Lutheran churches by 1938.[11] But in the course of World War II, with the annexation of the Baltic states, he came into possession of Lutheran communities too large to dispense with outright. Nevertheless, as a result of wartime deaths and flight, Central Asian and Siberian deportations, and a concerted antireligious campaign, Lutheran membership plummeted drastically.

It could be safely stated that, throughout most of the postwar period, the Estonian and Latvian Lutheran Churches were among the most quiescent and thoroughly tamed religious communities in the Soviet Union. "The Latvian Lutheran Church in particular," Marite Sapiets has noted, "has always remained quiet, subdued and willing to cooperate with Soviet laws on religion."[12] However, dissatisfaction with a pliable hierarchy slowly developed around 1983, bursting into public view in a surprisingly strong manner in 1987 with the emergence of the reform-minded Rebirth and Renewal Movement. Its unexpectedly rapid challenge to the church-state status quo dramatically altered the situation, with the result that on April 11-12, 1989, the Latvian Lutheran General Synod actually replaced the standing Archbishop Eriks Mesters and the entire eight-member Consistory with Rebirth and Renewal supporters.[13] Substantive changes occurred as well in the Estonian Lutheran Church at its June 12-13, 1990 Synod. Finally, it should be noted that the U.S. Lutheran Church, Missouri Synod (separate from the Evangelical Lutheran Church of America), has now begun work in the former Soviet Union.[14]

On the eve of *glasnost'*, Lutheran adherents in the Soviet Union were thought to number approximately 1.1 million: 250,000 in Estonia, 350,000 in Latvia, 20,000 in Lithuania, and 500,000 mostly German Lutherans in Central Asia and Siberia.[15] Due to emigration to the West, and possibly more precise accounting, current estimates are well below these figures. Approximate current membership is as follows:

Estonia	175,000
Latvia	120,000
Lithuania	25,000
Central Asia and Siberia	250,000 [16]

Including adherents, a possible total for the Lutheran community in the former Soviet Union would be 1,140,000.

Pentecostals who secured status in 1945 by joining the Evangelical Christian-Baptist Union were required to abstain from tongues-speaking in corporate worship, roughly the equivalent of requiring Catholics to disavow the pope. Indeed, an undisputed majority preferred unrelieved state persecution to merger on Baptist terms. Of those Pentecostals who did unite with the Evangelical Christians-Baptists, approximately one-half left between 1949 and 1979 in a series of running battles, primarily over glossolalia. A formal departure of most remaining Pentecostals occurred in June 1989. At that time, the State Council for Religious Affairs officially recognized the denomination for the first time since the 1920s.[17] The Pentecostal Union numbers some 100,000 adult members, including believers, in: a) churches which left the Baptist Union; b) formerly autonomous churches (a phenomenon dating from 1967); and c) a portion of formerly unregistered churches.[18] Since the vast majority of Pentecostals live outside the Russian Republic, the future of this Moscow-based union would appear to be precarious.

Unregistered Pentecostals number approximately 80,000 under the loose leadership of Bishop Ivan Fedotov of Moscow. Pentecostals who baptize in the name of "Jesus only" number no more than 4,000, but could experience considerable growth given the likelihood of substantial assistance from the "Jesus only" United Pentecostal Church in the West. A Ukrainian Free Union has roughly 3,000 members while charismatic Word of Life churches in the Baltic states, heavily influenced by Scandinavian and U.S. health and wealth prosperity theology, as yet claim the allegiance of no more than 3,000 members.[19] Finally, approximately 1,000 Pentecostals remain in the UECB fold.[20] If Mission Possible president, attorney Ralph Mann, is correct that there are "at least 400,000 children in the Soviet Pentecostal churches," then the total community, including 191,000 members, 100,000 or more unbaptized adherents, plus children, could approach 700,000 for all of the former Soviet Union.[21]

Disputes over what to render unto Cæsar and what to render unto God have spawned a protracted division in Seventh-day Adventist as well as Baptist and Pentecostal ranks. Distinguished by their pacifism, Saturday worship, and adherence to strict dietary laws, Adventists frequently have run afoul of the Soviet state since the early 1920s. Unregistered congregations have naturally, though not exclusively, borne the brunt of the regime's ill will. Dissident True and Free Adventists, under the courageous leadership of the Gulag veteran Vladimir Shelkov, would appear to hold the distinction of having produced the greatest volume of religious *samizdat* per capita of any Christian community.[22] Registered and unregistered Adventist churches each claim the allegiance of about 40,000 members, with a combined community of adherents in the neighborhood of 160,000.[23]

As with Baltic Lutherans, Hungarian Reformed believers found themselves in the USSR after World War II due to the westward advance of the Red Army and shift of the Soviet frontier. Today, approximately 100,000 members and a total community of perhaps 200,000 reside in Western Ukraine (85 percent) and Lithuania (15 percent).[24]

Unlike Moscow's World War II acquisition of Hungarian Reformed believers, German Mennonites first entered the Russian empire in the 18th century as immigrants, invited by Catherine the Great to settle her newly conquered Ukrainian and south Russian steppe lands. State toleration of their pacifist faith, coupled with pronounced material success, could hardly have prepared them for the multiple shocks of the late 19th and 20th centuries. Under the last Romanov czars, growing intolerance for non-Russian, non-Orthodox, and unpatriotic (read pacifist) elements of the population precipitated waves of Mennonite immigration to the Western Hemisphere.[25]

After 1917, Mennonites suffered not only under their traditional disabilities, but also because of their prosperity. Their diligence, industry, and sobriety contributed to their material advancement, which in turn made them special targets in Stalin's collectivization campaign. This brought with it wholesale property confiscations and mass deportations. The Nazi invasion dealt another blow as Soviet citizens of German extraction, including Mennonites, had to endure decades of draconian administrative restrictions and state-fueled popular prejudice. It is little wonder that, with the relaxation of emigration barriers, the Mennonite community in the former Soviet Union fell from about 100,000 in 1982 to 23,500 in 1991.[26]

The Soviet authorities expelled American Methodist missionary George Simons from Petrograd in 1918, and by 1923 they had put an end to the remaining Methodist presence in the Soviet Far East and the former capital. The denomination, however, enjoyed modest growth in the interwar years in the independent Baltic states that had been lost by the czars, but then reacquired by the Kremlin commissars as a result of World War II. Because Methodists lacked strength in numbers, which had helped the Lutherans, Soviet occupation forces had little difficulty in closing all the denomination's churches in Latvia and Lithuania. That Estonian Methodism survived a German and two Soviet occupations and started afresh after the war with a handful of members and pastors was an exceptional feat, particularly when it is noted that a much larger Moravian church did not survive Soviet rule. Dedicated leadership, a number of innervating revivals, and Western

Christian assistance and encouragement, especially beginning in the 1960s, all helped ensure appreciable postwar Methodist growth, although from a very low base. Pathbreaking contemporary Christian music and a wave of youth conversions led to a peak membership of some 2,363 in the late 1970s.[27] Substantial emigration and losses to health and wealth charismatics, however, reduced current Estonian Methodism by 1991 to under 1,800 members.[28]

On a brighter note, new life for Methodism in the former Soviet Union is emerging from surprisingly diverse quarters: Polish Methodists actively working in Western Ukraine and American Korean and South Korean Methodists resurrecting the denomination among the 420,000 Soviet citizens of Korean descent. Already two registered Korean Methodist churches meet in Moscow, with other registered congregations existing in the Crimea, Tashkent, and Alma-Ata, in addition to an unknown number of unregistered Korean Methodist churches in Central Asia.

Texas United Methodist attorney Joe Holland has been instrumental in recent years in helping a small Methodist congregation in Syktyvkar, Komi Autonomous Republic, while a Louisiana United Methodist church has spearheaded an evangelistic outreach to Ekaterinburg (formerly Sverdlovsk). A single Sunday in September 1991 saw 199 baptisms from a congregation of 1,000. And if that is not improbable enough, Liberian Methodist Christine Hena is now serving as the denomination's first missionary to Russia since 1923. Serious discrimination notwithstanding, Miss Hena leads Russian seekers in Bible studies, works in a Moscow hospital for children with leukemia, and ministers to families with handicapped children.[29]

Orthodox detractors labeled one indigenous sect Molokane, or Milk Drinkers, because they did not observe the Lenten fast prescribed by the established church. Dating from 1765, these "Spiritual Christians," as they called themselves, numbered 1.2 million before the end of the 19th century.[30] Large-scale emigration in the late 19th and early 20th centuries, conversion to Baptist faith, plus severe Soviet repression from the 1930s meant an apparent total eclipse of the Molokane—until the year 1952, when two of their representatives joined other religious leaders in orchestrated public endorsements for Stalin's peace policies at an interconfessional gathering at Sergiev Posad (then called Zagorsk). At that meeting, tens of thousands of Molokane were said to live in remote villages in the Caucasus and Central Asia.[31] Recent evidence indicates the presence of "Spiritual Christians," strikingly similar to Baptists except for the absence of adult baptism, in all 11 Soviet time zones. Georgia and Central Asia continue as strongholds, with identified communities also in the Moscow, Stavropol, Krasnodar, and Rostov districts of the Russian Republic, as well as in Moldova, Ukraine, Armenia, and Azerbaijan.[32]

A Californian Molokan with close ties to his Soviet counterparts notes that the greatest concentrations of Molokane live in the Tbilisi area while several new churches recently opened in Moscow.[33] Since 1990, Moscow also has served as headquarters for a USSR Union of Spiritual Christians (Molokane) that was formally recognized in August 1991, and for a new journal, *Spiritual Christian*.[34] According to three separate sources, Molokane are in the midst of a significant widespread resurgence, with reports of revival in the Caucasus being singled out in particular.[35]

It is not absolutely clear whether or not it is accurate to speak of the reemerging Molokane as having been completely repressed in the past. However, four other small Protestant churches definitely did disappear and now are attempting a comeback: the Churches of Christ, the Salvation Army, the Brethren, and the Armenian Evangelicals. Churches of Christ are fundamentalist in their theology, separatist in their ecclesiology, and congregational in their polity. They lack a high profile in the West but are highly energetic for their size. For quite some time, their East European Mission and Bible Foundation, headquartered in Houston, has owned a large printing plant in Vienna, which for years has published large quantities of Christian literature in Eastern European languages. The Soviet authorities forced the closure of all Churches of Christ in the 1930s in Ukraine, and after World War II eliminated them in the newly annexed Western Ukraine as well. In the late 1980s, Churches of Christ reemerged in the Soviet Union, especially in Ukraine. Sixteen congregations now exist, ranging in size, a U.S. spokesman says, from two to 100 members. Cities outside Ukraine with congregations include Kaliningrad, Minsk, St. Petersburg, Moscow, Yaroslav, Rostov, Novosibirsk, and Tbilisi.[36]

At least one Moscow Church of Christ, which appears to have no ties with U.S. Midwest denominational centers, draws 200 persons each Sunday to its rented meeting hall off New Arbat Street (formerly Kalinin Prospekt). The singing of new translations of Western hymns, which have been available in the Russian language for decades, is one illustration of the separatist, independent approach characteristic of Churches of Christ.[37]

Salvation Army founder William Booth visited St. Petersburg in 1909. Efforts to establish Army work in Russia finally succeeded in 1913, to be followed, however, by banishment ten years later. This church, better known as a charity, carried on in the Baltic states, only to see World War II and Soviet occupation eliminate these Salvationist posts as well. Now the Salvation Army is quite literally on the march again in Russia. In its issue of August 31, 1991, the Army's periodical *The War Cry* carried a summer 1991 photo of its Oslo Temple Band parading and playing its way across Winter Palace Square in St. Petersburg, a very striking and improbable visual representation of a degree of religious *glasnost'* that no one could have imagined a few short years ago.[38] Also marching with the band in the ceremonies marking the denomination's formal return to work in Russia were the international head of the Salvation Army, General Eva Burrows, and Captain Sven-Erik Ljungholm, carrying the Army's flag across Palace Square just as his own grandfather had 75 years before.[39]

A small number of churches out of the Plymouth Brethren tradition of British origin, like the Salvation Army, did not survive Stalinist repression. The handful of congregations that have revived of late probably will grow, at least in part because a number of Western parachurch ministries founded by Plymouth Brethren—for example, U.S.-based International Teams and British-based Radstock Ministries—can be expected to champion their cause.[40]

Evangelical Christians who joined with Baptists in 1944 to form the All-Union Council of Evangelical Christians-Baptists have reestablished a separate identity, at least in a few cases. (Keston News Service reported one instance in March 1991.[41]) In February 1991, the author of this chapter worshipped in an autonomously registered Evangelical Christian congregation of about 80 people crowded into a 21st floor apartment in Kon'kovo, a far southwest Moscow district. Only time will tell if sizable numbers of Evangelical Christians leave the UECB over dissatisfaction with the loss of doctrinal distinctions.

The Armenian Evangelical Church is older by several decades than the Evangelical Christian-Baptist Church. Growing out of Congregational mission activity in the Ottoman Empire, this church spread eventually from Anatolia back to the Armenian homeland. At present, it is difficult to distinguish between Armenian Evangelical and Armenian Evangelical Christian-Baptist congregations. Today, the Armenian Evangelical Union of North America reports that there are 11 churches, mostly in Armenia and Georgia. The congregations in Erevan and Koumairi are identified as Armenian Baptist, and the rest as Armenian Evangelical.[42]

In recent years, at least five new churches have emerged on former Soviet territory. Word of Life charismatics, mentioned earlier, are spreading rapidly in the Baltic States, as are U.S. Assemblies of God–affiliated Estonian Christian Churches, which in a few short years have established ten congregations.[43]

The New Apostolic Church, the third largest denomination in what was East Germany, now has a following of unknown size in the former Soviet Union. A separatist body originating in 19th-century England, Holland, and Germany, this strongly hierarchical and exclusivist communion stresses discipline, gifts of the spirit, obedience to secular authorities, and person-to-person evangelism.[44] A recent article by Walter Sawatsky notes the New Apostolic Church's arrival in the USSR, but hazards no guess at its present size.[45]

A fourth denomination new to the former Soviet Union is the Presbyterian Church. Moscow alone now has four Korean Presbyterian congregations, all registered since 1989. Undoubtedly, other churches of this persuasion have opened in Central Asia, where most Soviet Koreans were deported by Stalin, but the number is unknown. Some Russians reportedly worship with Presbyterians in Moscow, which conceivably could be the beginning of the denomination's outreach beyond the Korean community.[46]

A number of congregations known as Christian Life Centers have emerged. The exact number of these churches, which feature a free form of worship drawing both charismatic and noncharismatic adherents, remains uncertain. But such centers are known to have opened in Moscow (reportedly with 1,800 full members), Kiev, and Riga.[47] Finally, two U.S.-based denominations have begun church-planting efforts in the former USSR: the Church of the Nazarene and the Evangelical Free Church.[48]

In addition to growing denominational diversity, parachurch organizations likely will play an increasing role in Evangelical Protestant life in the emerging Commonwealth of Independent States (CIS). For decades, Western Christians were involved in the Soviet Union in a parachurch capacity, especially in Christian broadcasting and clandestine deliveries of Bibles.[49] What has emerged in the last four to five years, and took many knowledgeable observers by surprise, is the phenomenon of spontaneously generated, indigenous Protestant missions within the former Soviet Union, currently 100-200 in number and growing.[50]

Most have been spawned by Baptist, Lutheran, and Pentecostal initiatives at the grassroots level. For example, three groups founded in 1988-89 are *Svet Yevangeliya* (Light of the Gospel) in Rovno, the Latvian Christian Mission in Riga, and the *Vozmozhnost'* (Possibility) Mission in Donetsk.[51] These three organizations alone support 540 full- and part-time workers in evangelism, publishing, and charitable concerns.[52]

With regard to the issue of denominational diversity, it should be noted that indigenous missions in the CIS presently are, and probably will continue, giving birth to new Evangelical Protestant churches not necessarily beholden to any traditional church allegiance. One thousand supporters of Light of the

Gospel, gathered in a mission conference in Kiev in March 1991, heard reports of the mission's role in the founding of 10 new churches with 20-120 members each.[53] In this case the mission board members are all UECB or autonomous Baptists. Such churches spawned by Light of the Gospel may or may not identify with the UECB or autonomous Baptist movement. It is even less likely that new churches growing out of the work of less homogeneous groups such as the Latvian Christian Mission (part Baptist, part Lutheran, and part Pentecostal) will see the possibility or even the value of identifying with a particular established denomination. The conclusion that may be drawn is that, because of Protestantism's natural tendency to multiply by division and the potential significance of indigenous non-denominational missions, new Protestant churches are likely to emerge which will, initially at least, have few if any ties to existing denominations.

The well-known pastor and evangelist Joseph Bondarenko, an autonomous Baptist leader from Riga, thinks that a new church is desperately needed as a home for new converts who are put off on the one hand by Orthodox hierarchs and priests whose democratic credentials many do not trust, and on the other hand by Baptist legalism and lack of cultural sophistication.[54] His own parachurch Mission of the Cross is involved heavily in evangelism and the formation of new churches, from the Baltic region to Siberia. But for this preacher, often referred to as the "Billy Graham of Russia," past models will not do. "We must organize a new structure for new believers," he argues. "Not Baptist, Pentecostal, not Methodist, not Orthodox. It may become a new denomination. I don't know. We have no experience with this. . . . We want to find the right way to plant new churches."[55] In a September 1991 interview, Bonderenko referred to a successful preaching campaign in Moldova in order to illustrate his point. "This year, 15 people have been baptized, very intelligent people: musicians, teachers, students—a new generation of Christians. I think if these people go to the established [Protestant] churches they cannot stay long. They may [only] last for a while out of curiosity."[56]

U.S. Episcopalian evangelist John Guest, Lausanne Committee for World Evangelization director Tom Houston, and Mennonite scholar Walter Sawatsky all wonder whether existing Evangelical churches are prepared to accept into their fellowship many of the *glasnost'*-era converts. John Guest's meetings in Kiev in 1990 and 1991 spawned some 40 Bible study groups that in time could develop into congregations.[57] Three other Christian organizations, Campus Crusade for Christ, Walk Thru the Bible, and the Association of Christian Schools International, have launched substantial efforts to nurture new converts coming from Crusade's thousands of showings of the "Jesus" film and from the latter two organizations' widespread introduction of graded Christian resources in public schools.[58] Again, Christian fellowships that are likely to emerge from these and similar outreaches may form unaffiliated congregations that over time coalesce into new Protestant denominations. Precedents in Asia and Africa include the several-hundred-thousand-member Korea Holiness Church, founded by the Indiana-based Overseas Missionary Service, and Nigeria's three-million-strong Evangelical Churches of West Africa, founded by the Sudan Interior Mission.

Thus, institutional diversity among Protestants almost certainly will continue to increase as Baptists, Lutherans, and Pentecostals share the field with many other Evangelical Christian churches, quite a few of which are reemerging from past Soviet repression, while others are appearing for the first time. Likewise, Western and indigenous missions very probably will contribute to the growing number of denominations in the former Soviet Union.

Beyond institutional pluralism, Protestants in the future likely will reflect greater demographic diversity. In addition to their present pronounced geographic dispersion and ethnic heterogeneity, one may expect a more decentralized, ethnically varied, younger leadership and a membership reflecting a more representative cross-section of the population in terms of education, employment, and income.

The significant ethnic heterogeneity already present in Protestant ranks is beginning to be reflected in church leadership. Evangelical Christians-Baptists, for example, in their February 1990 Congress—the most democratic ever—changed their name from All-Union Council of Evangelical Christian-Baptists to Union of Evangelical Christians-Baptists, abolished the post of general secretary, and decentralized organizational authority, giving greater influence to regional and local leadership. Prior to 1990, many members distrusted the leadership and chafed under its authoritarian discipline. The administrative structure, topped by a presidium with full and candidate members, reminded many Baptists of the Communist Party Central Committee and Politburo.[59]

In addition, the ECB Congress for the first time elected a Ukrainian president, the 44-year-old Grigori Komendant, the youngest president ever. Komendant is committed to making the UECB headquarters more responsive to the church's ethnically diverse, grassroots membership.[60] On the eve of the February 1990 Congress, 50 percent of Baptist strength was Ukrainian versus 33 percent Russian.[61] Ukraine is a stronghold not only of Evangelical Christians-Baptists, but of Orthodox, Eastern-Rite Catholics, Pentecostals, and Seventh-day Adventists as well.[62] In addition to the well-known Orthodox and Catholic concentrations in Ukraine, 67 percent of Pentecostals live in Ukraine versus under 3 percent in the Russian Federation.[63] As for Adventists, nearly 50 percent reside in Ukraine compared to 21 percent in Russia.[64] No wonder that U.S. scholar William Fletcher has described Ukraine as the former Soviet Union's "Bible Belt."[65]

Paralleling the breakup of the USSR's political union, the ECB union has suffered an avalanche of defections: Pentecostals, Mennonites, the membership in the Baltic republics, an unknown number of Evangelical Christians dissatisfied with the 1944 merger, and many younger believers channelling their energies into a host of new missions and Christian publications.[66] The end of the denomination's pronounced centralization and the emergence of strong republican and multi-ethnic leadership clearly parallel the centrifugal forces in the former USSR, aptly described by the author Os Guiness as a shift "from totalitarianism to tribalism."[67]

If Protestants' new freedom to engage in evangelism is not curtailed by Orthodox pressure on civil authorities, and if state authorities do in fact put an end to longstanding discrimination in higher education against believers, there is a prospect that Evangelical Christians will come to represent a broader cross-section of the population. Presently, Protestants rarely possess a full secondary education, much less higher education, and hold a disproportionate number of low-paying, unskilled, and menial jobs.[68] Dr. Aleksandr Zaichenko, a respected and frequently published economist who was baptized secretly in 1986 as an adult, is a rare find in evangelical circles because of longstanding government discrimination in higher education against believers.[69]

Thus, diversity among Protestants in the former Soviet Union may be seen in the growing proliferation of denominations and parachurch groups; in their multi-ethnic composition; and in the growing likelihood of a membership more varied in educational attainment, employment, and income. However, greater diversity in church life through more public and responsible roles for women would not appear to be likely, at least in the short term. If Christian women have perspectives other than those held by men, who are universally in positions of leadership, they traditionally have difficulties finding channels to express their particular concerns. Should this change under *glasnost'*, most church leaders could find themselves challenged by discomforting discussions on such issues as the role of women in the church, the concept of mutual submission in Christian marriage, family size and birth control, and the need for Christian fathers as well as mothers to take an active part in childrearing.[70]

However pronounced Protestant pluralism in the USSR may be or may become in terms of denominational and parachurch proliferation and ethnic and social composition, it definitely does not relate to theology. All Protestant churches, with some possible Baltic Lutheran exceptions, tenaciously hold to doctrinal positions best described as either fundamentalist or evangelical. For the most part, Christians in the Soviet Union were not exposed to the tradition of German higher criticism of the Bible, to theological modernism in general, or to liberation theology in particular. The last, if they have heard of it, they find scandalous. Church leaders now dispensing with state-imposed restrictions are not unhappy to have been spared this type of Western influence. Some of the handful of seminarians allowed to study in the West, for example, have returned to the Soviet Union unfit for service in the eyes of their superiors. That unwelcome Western theological influences could be an incidental byproduct of *glasnost'* has not been lost on theologically conservative Christian leaders in the new eastern Commonwealth.[71] By all reports, Grigori Komendant and the other ECB leaders are as wary of unorthodox Western theological currents as their predecessors were in the 1960s when they vowed that "not a milligram of this modern poison" would be tolerated in the training of their pastors.[72] For church leaders in the former Soviet Union, in this regard including Orthodox and Catholics as well as Protestants, a vital concern is whether or not it will be possible to stem the tide of Western-style theological pluralism.

Evangelical Christians are likely to see the growing institutional and social pluralism of Protestantism in the former USSR as, in the main, a healthy development. At the same time, responsible Evangelicals, East and West, regret the flowering of various self-promoting, publicity-hungry, culturally insensitive, West-knows-best, "save Russia" campaigns. Take, for example, the ugly-American evangelist in Kiev in the summer of 1991 who publicly advised a very large audience that one thing needed by his accompanying translator and many others like him was deodorant. And to show his good intentions, this preacher promised to bring cases of body freshener on his next trip.[73]

Most Evangelicals would see such abysmal behavior as atypical, whereas Orthodox in traditionally Orthodox territories and Catholics in traditionally Catholic territories would view this episode as symptomatic of the flood of Protestant interlopers who have no business bringing Christianity to lands that are viewed as having been Christian for many centuries.[74] The difficulty here would seem to center on one's definition of what constitutes a "Christian land," and whether or not 20th-century atheist inroads provide a legitimate opportunity for a Christian witness that is neither Orthodox nor Catholic.

Interconfessional strife apart, several forms of the massive ongoing Western invasion of the East are distressing to members of all Christian confessions: crass materialism, pornography, and new religious movements. Sometimes, Russian Orthodox—and, sometimes, Russian atheists—have defined all non-Orthodox churches and faiths as sects or cults. Since both terms have highly charged, pejorative connotations, this chapter will dispense with their use altogether, referring instead to the emergence of new or newly tolerated religious movements in the former Soviet Union. Non-Christian religions of long standing on the territory of the former Soviet Union include Islam, Judaism, Buddhism, and animism. In contrast, modern religious professions now active in the Commonwealth that have Christian genealogies, but have departed from historic trinitarian Christianity, are Jehovah's Witnesses (since the 1940s), Mormons (since the 1980s), and the Unification Church/Moonies (since the 1980s).[75] Finally, Eastern religions, including Hare Krishna, Baha'i, and the quasi-Eastern New Age Movement, not to mention a wide array of homegrown spiritualists, levitators, astrologers, and clairvoyants, are increasingly making their presence felt.[76] Regardless of what Christians or nonbelievers would regard as the errors of these religions and pseudo-religions, from the perspective of universally recognized tenets of religious liberty, they all merit protection under the newly codified republic laws on freedom of conscience.

Religious *glasnost'* holds forth promise and peril for the former USSR's Protestant as well as Orthodox and Catholic believers. A society free of oppressive state controls will be free to choose faith, but it also increasingly will face the flood of self-destructive temptations with which the West has long been plagued. The possibility of many more openly plied, harmful choices, however, can in no way serve as a justification for past or future state interference in church life, any more than European colonialism could be justified on the basis of "mistakes" that were to be expected on the part of inexperienced independent nations. One of the heroes of the African independence movement, Kwame Nkrumah, wrote of the necessity of freedom in words that ring true for Protestants in the former Soviet Union and all advocates of religious liberty as well as for African nationalists: "We prefer self-government with danger to servitude in tranquility."[77] If there is no freedom to make what someone or another would deem a mistake, there is no freedom.

APPENDIX I

PROTESTANT DENOMINATIONS IN THE FORMER SOVIET UNION

Churches Present Since 1917 (regardless of official status)
Evangelical Christian-Baptist
Lutheran
Mennonite
Pentecostal
Seventh-day Adventist

Churches in Lands Annexed in World War II
Hungarian Reformed
Methodist (now active outside Estonia)

Reemerging Churches
Armenian Evangelical and Baptist
Brethren
Church of Christ
Evangelical Christian
Molokane
The Salvation Army

Churches New to the Former Soviet Union
Christian Life Centers
Estonian Christian Church
Lutheran Church, Missouri Synod
New Apostolic
Presbyterian
Word of Life

Churches Anticipating Work in the Former Soviet Union
Church of the Nazarene
Evangelical Free

Unaffiliated Churches (founded by Western and Indigenous Parachurch Missions)

APPENDIX II

PROTESTANTS IN THE FORMER SOVIET UNION	MEMBERSHIP		TOTAL COMMUNITY INCLUDING CHILDREN AND ADHERENTS	
	SUBTOTAL	TOTAL	SUBTOTAL	TOTAL
EVANGELICAL CHRISTIANS-BAPTISTS		248,705		746,115 [4]
Registered	208,705 [1]		626,115	
Autonomous	25,000 [2]			75,000
Unregistered	15,000 [3]			45,000
LUTHERANS		570,000		1,140,000 [9]
Estonia	175,000 [5]		350,000	
Latvia	120,000 [6]		240,000	
Lithuania	25,000 [7]		50,000	
German, mostly in Central Asia and Siberia	250,000 [8]		500,000	
PENTECOSTALS		191,000		700,000 [11]
Pentecostal Union	100,000 [10]		370,000	
Unregistered Pentecostals (Fedotov)	80,000 [10]		290,000	
Other Pentecostals	11,000 [10]		40,000	
HUNGARIAN REFORMED		100,000 [12]		200,000
SEVENTH-DAY ADVENTISTS		80,000		160,000
Registered	40,000 [13]		80,000	
Unregistered (True and Free)	40,000 [14]		80,000	
MENNONITES		3,300 [15]		7,050 [16]
METHODISTS		1,743 [17]		2,500
TOTALS		1,204,748		2,955,665
TOTALS IN ROUND FIGURES		1,205,000		2,960,000

SOURCES FOR APPENDIX II

1. Marilyn Chapman (Evangelism Department of Baptist World Alliance), interview, November 5, 1991. Outgoing Union Secretary Aleksei Bychkov gave a total membership of 204,156 at the Evangelical Christian-Baptist Congress of February 21-24, 1991. "Soviet Baptist Union Shake-Up," Keston News Service 345, March 8, 1990, p. 7.

2. Walter Sawatsky, "Protestantism in the USSR" in *Religious Policy in the Soviet Union,* ed. Sabrina Ramet (Cambridge: Cambridge University Press, 1991), p. 41. Open Doors (*The Soviet Union State and Religion; 1990 Update* [Ermelo, Netherlands: Open Doors, 1990], p. 4) puts autonomous membership at 10,000 while Andrew Semenchuk of USSR Ministries (interview, November 6, 1991) estimates 40,000.

3. Interview with Semenchuk, November 6, 1991. Eugene Grosman of Slavic Gospel Association (interview, November 5, 1991) sets current unregistered membership at 3,000 to 10,000 while Walter Sawatsky ("Protestantism in the USSR," p. 41) estimates 18,000.

4. The Estonian Methodist Heigo Ritsbek, one of the few pastors of the former Soviet Union with training as a historian, suggests the total Evangelical Christian-Baptist total community may be three to four times the membership (interview November 14, 1991).

5. E. Theodore Bachmann and Mercia Brenne Bachmann, *Lutheran Churches in the World: A Handbook* (Minneapolis, MN: Augsburg-Fortress Press, 1989), p. 324. Sawatsky ("Protestantism in the Soviet Union," p. 41) and Ritsbek (interview, November 14, 1991) respectively suggest an Estonian Lutheran membership of 50,000 and 62,000, while *The Lutheran* magazine recently estimated 200,000 members (David A. Miller, "Profile: Lutheran Churches in the Baltic," reprinted in *Mirror,* Fall 1991, p. 6).

6. Bachmann and Bachmann, *Lutheran Churches in the World,* p. 324. Sawatsky ("Protestantism in the Soviet Union," p. 41) figures Latvian Lutheran membership at 50,000 while *The Lutheran* used a figure of 350,000 in October 1991 (reprinted in *Mirror,* Fall 1991, p. 6).

7. Bachmann and Bachmann, *Lutheran Churches in the World,* p. 325.

8. Sawatsky, "Protestantism in the Soviet Union," p. 28.

9. The total Lutheran community is estimated at double the membership, smaller in proportion to membership than Evangelical Christians-Baptists, based on their smaller average family size.

10. Ralph Mann, "Soviet Pentecostal Demographics," unpublished paper, October 1991, p.1.

11. Very large families are the rule with Pentecostals. *Ibid.*

12. Aladar Komjathy, Hungarian Reformed minister, interview, November 11, 1991.

13. Marite Sapiets, *True Witness, The Story of Seventh Day Adventists in the Soviet Union* (Keston, Kent: Keston College, 1990), p. 14; Richard Wilcox, director of the Office of Soviet Affairs, Seventh-day Adventists (interview, October 29, 1991), sets the figure for registered Adventists at 43,000.

14. Sapiets, *True Witness*, p. 274.

15. Sawatsky, "Protestantism in the Soviet Union," p. 41. Adding 7,700 Mennonites who are members of Evangelical Christian-Baptist congregations gives a total registered membership of 11,000 Mennonites. Sawatsky, interview, December 7, 1991.

16. Sawatsky, "Protestantism in the Soviet Union," p. 41. Adding 16,450 in ECB congregations gives a total Mennonite community of 23,500. Sawatsky, interview, December 7, 1991.

17. Ritsbek, interview, November 14, 1991.

INTERVIEWS

Avakian, Karl (Armenian Evangelical). November 6, 1991.
Chapman, Marilyn (Baptist World Alliance). November 5, 1991.
Chesneau, Claudia (Salvation Army). November 14, 1991.
Cho, Susan (Methodist). October 6, 1991.
Choe, Samuel (Korean World Mission). November 15, 1991.
Cook, Franklin (Nazarene). October 25, 1991.
Deyneka, Anita (USSR Ministries). November 15, 1991.
Edwards, Debbie (Nazarene). November 15, 1991.
Grosman, Eugene (Slavic Gospel Association). November 5, 1991.
Hamm, Viktor (Baptist/Mennonite). October 6, 1991.
Hena, Christine (Methodist). October 6, 1991.
Komjathy, Aladar (Hungarian Reformed). November 11, 1991.
Mann, Ralph (Pentecostal). October 6, 1991.
Ritsbek, Heigo (Methodist). November 14, 1991.
Samarian, Ed (Molokan). November 14, 1991.
Sawatsky, Ben (Evangelical Free Church). November 6, 1991.
Sawatsky, Walter (Mennonite). October 28, 1991; December 7, 1991.
Schuibert, Joe (Churches of Christ). October 7, 1991.
Scott, Robert (Nazarene). December 6, 1991.
Semenchuk, Andrew (USSR Ministries). November 6, 1991.
Slevecove, Jim (Molokan). October 29, 1991.
Wilcox, Richard M. (Seventh-day Adventist). October 29, 1991.
Yoder, William (The Lutheran). December 17, 1991.

NOTES

1. Seventh-day Adventists originally had an all-union administration but lost that advantage in 1960 in the Khrushchev antireligious campaign. See Marite Sapiets, *True Witness, The Story of Seventh Day Adventists in the Soviet Union* (Keston, Kent: Keston College, 1990), p. 63. For a helpful discussion of Evangelical Christian versus Baptist distinctions see Greg Nichols, *Pashkovism: Nineteenth Century Russian Piety*, M.A. thesis, Wheaton College Graduate School, 1991, pp. 73-81.

2. This freedom of conscience very well may be short-lived as republican nationalists favor former state churches over so-called foreign confessions.

3. Walter Sawatsky, "Protestantism in the USSR," in Sabrina Ramet, ed., *Religious Policy on the Soviet Union* (Cambridge: Cambridge University Press, 1991).

4. Quoted in letter from Brian O'Connell to author, October 24, 1991.

5. Frank Spencer Mead, *Handbook of Denominations in the United States*, 9th ed. (Nashville: Abingdon Press, 1990).

6. Interview with Andrew Semenchuk, November 6, 1991; Sawatsky, "Protestantism," p. 36. The first major Western account of the Baptist schism was Michael Bourdeaux, *Religious Ferment in Russia* (New York: St. Martin's Press, 1968). The category of "adherents" includes children, plus adults who regularly participate but have not officially become members.

7. Sawatsky, "Protestantism," pp. 33-34; Michael Bourdeaux, *Gorbachev, Glasnost and the Gospel* (London: Hodder and Stoughton, 1990), p. 128; Interview with Anita Deyneka, November 15, 1991.

8. This figure assumes a total community perhaps three times the size of the estimated membership of 25,000. Sawatsky, "Protestantism," p. 41. Estonian Methodist pastor Heigo Ritsbek, a trained historian, suggests that ECB communities total three to four times this estimated membership (interview, November 14, 1991).

9. Interview with Semenchuk, November 6, 1991; interview with Eugene Grosman, November 5, 1991; Sawatsky, "Protestantism," pp. 23, 37; Bourdeaux, *Gorbachev*, p. 118.

10. Interview with Viktor Hamm, October 29, 1991.

11. Sawatsky, "Protestantism," p. 6.

12. Sapiets, "'Rebirth and Renewal' in the Latvian Lutheran Church," *Religion in Communist Lands* 16 (Autumn 1988), p. 236.

13. "Latvian Lutheran Synod Replaces Entire Church Leadership," Keston News Service 324, April 27, 1989, pp. 2-3.

14. Sawatsky, "Protestantism," p. 27; interview with William Yoder, December 17, 1991.

15. Philip Walters, *World Christianity: Eastern Europe* (Monrovia, CA: MARC, 1988), p. 86.

16. See source note 5 of Appendix II for statistical documentation.

17. Sawatsky, "Protestantism," pp. 7-8, 34.

18. Ralph Mann, "Soviet Pentecostal Demographics," unpublished paper (Denton, TX: Mission Possible, October 1991), pp. 1-2.

19. *Ibid.* On the Word of Life movement see Antonia Barbosa da Silva, "The 'Theology of Success' Movement: A Comment," *Themelios: An International Journal for Theological Students* 11 (April 1986), pp. 91-92; Mark Elliott, "Methodism in the Soviet Union Since World War II," *The Asbury Theological Journal* 46 (Spring 1991), p. 16.

20. Mann, "Demographics," pp. 1-2. Andrew Semenchuk of the USSR Ministries suspects that more than 1,000 Pentecostals remain in UECB churches; interview, November 6, 1991.

21. Mann, "Demographics," p. 1.

22. Sapiets, "V.A. Shelkov and the True and Free Seventh-day Adventists of the USSR," *Religion in Communist Lands* 8 (Autumn 1980), pp. 201-17; Sapiets, *True Witness,* pp. 78-79; Mark Elliott, "Seventh-day Adventists in Russia and the Soviet Union," *Modern Encyclopedia of Russian and Soviet History* 34 (1983), pp. 109-15.

23. Walters, *World,* 83; Sapiets, *True Witness,* pp. 14, 274. Western Adventists admit to only 3,000 unregistered who, in fact, they contend, are not Adventists because they are not registered; Sapiets, *True Witness,* p. 274. Sawatsky ("Protestantism," p. 41) uses somewhat lower estimates of 32,000 each for registered and unregistered Adventists, while an official Western Adventist spokesman sets membership in the state-sanctioned denomination at 43,000; interview with Richard M. Wilcox, October 29, 1991.

24. Interview with Aladar Komjathy, November 11, 1991; *Soviet Union . . . Update,* p. 4; Trevor Beeson, *Discretion and Valour: Religious Conditions in Russia and Eastern Europe* (London: Fount Paperbacks, 1982), p. 119.

25. Mennonite flight continued in the Soviet period up to 1929. Sawatsky, "Protestantism," p. 5. See also John B. Toews, *Czars, Soviets and Mennonites* (Newton, KS: Faith and Life Press, 1982), pp. 107-50.

26. *World Christian Encyclopedia,* ed. David B. Barrett (New York: Oxford University Press, 1982), p. 696; interview with Walter Sawatsky, October 28, 1991; Art Moore, "The Challenge of Evangelism in Central and Eastern Europe, and the Former Soviet Union" *News Network International,* October 11, 1991, p. 40; Toews, *Czars,* pp. 151-76. In a 1991 study Sawatsky ("Protestantism," p. 41) gave membership figures of 1,100 Church Mennonites and 2,200 independent Mennonite Brethren. Adding some 7,700 Mennonite Brethren still remaining in UECB congregations gives a total registered membership of 11,000. Including adherents gives a figure of 23,500. (See Appendix II.)

27. Elliott, "Methodism," pp. 10, 22. On Methodism in Siberia see L. Dana Roberts, "The Methodist Episcopal Church, South, Mission to Russians in Manchuria, 1920-1927," *Methodist History* 26 (January 1988), pp. 72-73.

28. Interview with Heigo Ritsbek, November 14, 1991. At present this Estonian Methodist pastor puts the Estonian membership at 1,743 and a total community of 2,500 in 16 churches.

29. Mark Elliott, "Methodism After Marx," *Good News* 25 (September/October 1991), pp. 15-18; Mark Elliott, "Korean Methodists in the Soviet Union," *Challenge to Evangelism Today* 24 (Summer 1991), p. 10; interview with Christine Hena, October 6, 1991; numerous articles in *United Methodist Record*, July 1991, pp. 3-4, 10; October 1991, pp. 6-7; November 1991, pp. 5-7.

30. Walter Kolarz, *Religion in the Soviet Union* (New York: St. Martin's Press, 1961), p. 349.

31. *Ibid.*; Moscow Patriarchate, *Conference in Defense of Peace of All Churches and Religious Associations in the USSR* (Zagorsk: Moscow Patriarchate, 1952), p. 16; Oxana Antic, "Conditions Improve for Old Believers, Dukhobors, Molokans, and Mennonites," *Report on the USSR* 2 (June 21, 1991), p. 10; interview with Jim Slevecove, October 29, 1991; Beeson, *Discretion*, p. 95.

32. Antic, "Conditions Improve," p. 10; interview with Ed Samarian, November 14, 1991.

33. Interview with Slevecove, October 29, 1991.

34. Antic, "Conditions Improve," p. 10; Keston News Service 370, March 7, 1991, p. 12.

35. Interview with Semenchuk, November 6, 1991; interview with Samarian, November 14, 1991; interview with Deyneka, November 15, 1991, reporting on recent conversation with Yuri Pishchik, Director of the Religious Studies Institute of the USSR Academy of Social Sciences.

36. Interview with Joe Schuibert, October 7, 1991; interview with Semenchuk, November 11, 1991; "Directory of Known Churches of Christ in Eastern Europe and the Soviet Union, October 1991," *Eastern European Mission and Bible Foundation Quarterly Report,* 3rd quarter, 1991, p. 6.

37. Interview with Grossman, November 5, 1991.

38. *The War Cry* 111 (August 31, 1991), p. 3.

39. The corps (church) in St. Petersburg is led by Lt. and Mrs. Geoffrey Ryan. Captain and Mrs. Sven-Erik Ljungholm have been assigned to work in Moscow. *Salvationist,* July 20, 1991, p. 4; Keston News Service 370, March 7, 1991, p. 12. As of November 1991 12 people belonged to the new St. Petersburg Corps; interview with Claudia Chesnau, November 14, 1991.

40. Interview with Semenchuk, November 6, 1991.

41. Keston News Service 370, March 7, 1991, p.11.

42. Interview with Karl Avakian, November 6, 1991. In contrast, the Armenian Missionary Association of America provided a list of six Armenian Evangelical and Evangelical Baptist churches (Dikran Youmashakian, Manager, to Robert Richardson, November 18, 1991).

43. Interview with Ritsbek, November 14, 1991. According to Ritsbek the E.C.C. draws heavily from Baptist and Methodist youth.

44. Arvan Gordon, "The New Apostolic Church: The GDR's Third Largest Religious Community," *Religion in Communist Lands* 16 (Spring 1988), pp. 26-35.

45. Sawatsky, "Protestantism," pp. 3, 41.

46. Interview with Susan Cho, October 6, 1991; Elliott, "Korean Methodists," *Challenge to Evangelicalism Today* 24 (Summer 1991), p. 10: another report documents Korean congregations, either Presbyterian or Methodist, in St. Petersburg and in Armenia; interview with Samuel Choe, November 15, 1991.
47. Interview with Ritsbek, November 14, 1991.
48. Interview with Franklin Cook, October 25, 1991; interview with Debbie Edwards, November 15, 1991; interview with Robert Scott, December 6, 1991; interview with Ben Sawatsky, November 6, 1991.
49. Mark Elliott, "Responding to Crisis in the Household of Faith," *Eternity* (July/August 1986), pp. 28-29; Elliott, "New Openness in USSR Prompts Massive Bible Shipments to Soviet Christians in 1987-88, A Statistical Overview," *News Network International*, March 20, 1989, pp. 24-29; Elliott, *East European Missions Directory* (Wheaton, IL: Institute for the Study of Christianity and Marxism, 1989), pp. 11-20; Walter Sawatsky, "Another Look at Mission in Eastern Europe," *International Bulletin of Missionary Research* 11 (January 1987), pp. 12-18; Anita Deyneka, "Good Things Come to Those That Network," *Evangelical Missions Quarterly* 28 (January 1992), pp. 42-45.
50. Susan Isaacs, "An Introduction to the Soviet Union's Emerging Indigenous Missions," *News Network International Special Report*, February 12, 1991, p. 1; Sawatsky, "Protestantism," p. 30; Steve Weber, "USSR Questionnaire; Interim Report," August 26, 1991, p. 7, unpublished paper appended to "Strategic Framework Study on Eastern Europe and the Soviet Union," prepared by Issachar Frontier Mission Strategies and the Lausanne Committee for World Evangelization, September 1991. See also Will Triggs, "The Soviet Union: A Different Kind of Mission Field," *Evangelical Missions Quarterly* 26 (October 1990), pp. 437-38.
51. Isaacs, "Indigenous Missions," pp. 2-4; Joe and Sarah Smith, *Handbook for Christian Travellers to the USSR* (Wheaton, IL: Institute of Soviet and East European Studies, Slavic Gospel Association, 1991), p. 54; Sawatsky, "Protestantism," p. 39.
52. The full-time/part-time total per mission is 50/100 for Light of the Gospel, 30/300 for Latvian Christian Mission, and 13/47 for Vozmozhnost'; Isaacs, "Indigenous Missions," pp. 2-4.
53. "Reaching the Unreached in Siberia," *Bridging Peoples* 10 (October 1991), p. 2.
54. Interview with Grosman, November 5, 1991; Sawatsky, "Protestantism," p. 21. On the lack of perestroika within the Russian Orthodox hierarchy, see the excellent study by Fr. Anthony Ugolnik, "The Orthodox Church and Contemporary Politics in the USSR," National Council for Soviet and East European Research, October 16, 1991.
55. Moore, "Challenge," p. 40.
56. *Ibid.*, p. 39. Bondarenko calls the independent congregations he has helped found Christian Missionary Churches; *ibid.*, p. 40.
57. Interview with Grosman, November 5, 1991; Tom Houston, "A Strategic Response," unpublished paper appended to "Strategic Framework Study," pp. 4-10; Sawatsky, "Protestantism," p. 2.

58. Interview with Deyneka, November 15, 1991. Information provided to the author by Bruce H. Wilkinson, President, Walk Thru the Bible, December 19, 1991.

59. "New Baptist Union President in Moscow," Keston News Service 343, February 8, 1990, p. 4. See also "Soviet Baptist Union Shake-Up," Keston News Service 345, March 8, 1990, pp. 6-8; Michael Rowe, "Soviet Baptists Engage in Perestroika," *Religion In Communist Lands* 18 (Summer 1990), pp. 184-87.

60. "Soviet Baptist Union," pp. 6-8; interview with Semenchuk, November 6, 1991; Sawatsky, "Protestantism," p. 33.

61. Walters, *World Christianity,* p. 72; Sawatsky, "Protestantism," pp. 18-19. Sawatsky also notes that the churches are concentrated in western Ukraine, much of which had been under Kremlin control only since World War II.

62. Mark Elliott, "Glasnost: A Mixed Blessing," *News Network International,* June 12, 1989, p. 20.

63. Mann, "Demographics," p. 2.

64. Kent Hill, *The Soviet Union on the Brink: An Inside Look at Christianity and Glasnost* (Portland, OR: Multnomah Press, 1991), p. 373; Sapiets, *True Witness,* pp. 274-78.

65. William Fletcher, "The Soviet Bible Belt: World War II's Impact on Religion," in Susan J. Linz, ed., *The Impact of World War II on the Soviet Union* (New York: Rowan and Allanheld, 1985), p. 91.

66. The new independent evangelical newspaper *Protestant* is a good example of the latter. Smith, *Handbook,* p. 54; Sawatsky, "Protestantism," pp. 39-40; Elliott, "Mixed Blessing," p. 20.

67. Ted Okada, "Institute on Religion and Democracy Celebrates 10th Anniversary," *News Network International,* October 11, 1991, p. 10.

68. For data on the social composition of Evangelical Christians-Baptists, see Christel Lane, *Christian Religion in the Soviet Union, A Sociological Study* (London: Allen and Unwin, 1978), pp. 149-51; William Fletcher, *Soviet Believers: The Religious Sector of the Population* (Lawrence, KS: Regents Press of Kansas, 1981), pp. 91-92.

69. Bob Chuvala, "A Russian Atheist Finds Jesus," *Christian Herald* 114 (November/December 1991), p. 27.

70. Elliott, "Mixed Blessing," pp. 20-21; Ralph Mann, "Soviet Pentecostal Doctrines and Customs," unpublished paper, October 1991, p. 10. Baltic Lutherans and Methodists allow for somewhat larger roles for women in their churches. See also the account of Baptist Maria Ananewna, ordained in Siberia in 1956 because of a "severe shortage of pastors" in Carol Ann Paul, "Report of the Meeting With Eastern European Women Leaders," Berlin, Germany, September 23-26, 1991, Commission on Women's Concerns, World Evangelical Fellowship, p. 7.

71. Elliott, "Mixed Blessing," p. 21.

72. Lane, *Christian Religion,* p. 144, quoting *Bratski vestnik* 6 (1966), p. 17, and 3 (1969), p. 63. Andrew Semenchuk (interview, November 6, 1991), has noted the extreme caution exercised by UECB leadership in choosing conservative Western settings for a select few seminary students: Moody Bible Institute,

The Master's College, Western Conservative Baptist Seminary, Trinity Evangelical Divinity School, and Eastern Baptist Seminary.

73. Mark Elliott, "New Opportunities, New Demands in the Old Red Empire," *Evangelical Missions Quarterly* 28 (January 1992), pp. 36-37.

74. For an example of divergent Evangelical and Orthodox perspectives, see the exchange between Kent Hill and Fr. Alexander Webster: Alexander Webster, "Evangelicals vs. Orthodox in Romania," *Christian Century* 107 (May 30-June 6, 1990), pp. 560-61; Kent Hill, "One 'Fold' for Romania," *Christian Century* 107 (August 8-15, 1990), pp. 745-48; Alexander Webster, "Alexander Webster Replies," *Christian Century* 107 (August 8-15, 1990), pp. 748-49.

75. See also William E. Schmidt, "U.S. Evangelicals Winning Soviet Converts," *The New York Times*, October 17, 1991, pp. A1-2; Oxana Antic, "Smaller Religious Denominations Flourish in New Conditions," *Report on the USSR* 3 (February 15, 1991), pp. 10-12.

76. Jane Mayer, "Moscow Goes Gaga Over Sex, Phantoms and 'Bio-Energetics,'" *The Wall Street Journal*, December 3, 1991, p. 1; Sergei Kapitza, "Antiscience Trends in the USSR," *Scientific American* 265 (August 1991), pp. 32-38.

77. Kwame Nkrumah, *Ghana: The Autobiography of Kwame Nkrumah* (New York: Nelson, 1957), p. 94. See also Elliott, "Mixed Blessing," p. 21.

ABOUT THE EDITORS AND CONTRIBUTORS

KEITH ARMES joined the Institute for the Study of Conflict, Ideology & Policy of Boston University in January 1990 as associate director and editor of the Institute's publications after serving as managing editor of the Atlantic Community Quarterly in Washington, D.C. Earlier he was on the faculty of the University of Minnesota, Minneapolis, where for several years he was chairman of the Department of Slavic Languages. He holds an M.A. in modern languages and economics and a Ph.D. in Soviet studies from the University of Cambridge and an M.A. in security policy studies from George Washington University. He has edited and translated extensively from Russian, including the authorized translation of work by Solzhenitsyn. His publications focus on Soviet politics and literature, U.S. and NATO Alliance security policy, and French defense policy. He recently served as co-editor of the book *State and Nation in Multi-Ethnic Societies: The Breakup of Multinational States*, published by Manchester University Press.

NINA BELYAEVA founded and is president of the Interlegal Research Center, an independent think tank monitoring development of the independent sector in the Russian Federation. She is also a research fellow in the Institute of State and Law, specializing in the study of independent groups and popular movements and their influence in decision-making processes in local and national government agencies. Previously, she served as a political observer covering legal and political reforms for the weekly newspaper *Moscow News*. Dr. Belyaeva also participated in the drafting of laws on the political rights of individuals and associations.

YELENA BONNER is cofounder and president of the Sakharov Foundation of Moscow, dedicated to the furtherance of freedom and civil rights in Russia. Together with her late husband, Andrei Sakharov, she achieved world fame combating the Soviet system and striving to bring about democracy and human liberty in the Soviet Union. On his behalf, she accepted the Nobel Prize for Peace and delivered the Nobel lecture. She has published extensively in the Russian and Western press on political developments in Russia. Her book, *Alone Together,* about her seven years of exile with Sakharov in

Gorky (Nizhni Novgorod) came out in 1987, and her latest book, *Mothers and Daughters,* was published in 1992.

NICHOLAS DANILOFF is director of the School of Journalism at Northeastern University. A foreign correspondent since 1961, Daniloff reported from Moscow in the early 1960s for United Press International and again in the early 1980s for *U.S. News and World Report.* In 1986, Mr. Daniloff was arrested in Moscow on false charges of espionage (in retaliation for the arrest in New York by the FBI of a Soviet physicist employed by the UN Secretariat) and was eventually exchanged for Gennadi Zakharov. He revisited Moscow in August-September 1991 in the aftermath of the "putsch" against Mikhail Gorbachev.

MARK ELLIOTT is professor of history and director of the Institute for East-West Christian Studies at Wheaton College in Wheaton, Illinois. He is the author of *Pawns of Yalta: Soviet Refugees and America's Role in Their Repatriation* (University of Illinois Press), editor of *Christianity and Marxism Worldwide: An Annotated Bibliography* and the *East European Missions Directory,* and co-editor of *Christian/Marxist Studies in U.S. Higher Education: A Handbook of Syllabi.* He has taken six trips to the Soviet Union and East Central Europe in the last three years to negotiate and lead a student exchange program with Moscow State University and to host a Moscow conference on business ethics.

KENT R. HILL is the executive director of the Institute on Religion and Democracy in Washington, D.C. He is a national authority on *glasnost'* and on religion in communist countries. Dr. Hill is a former associate professor of history at Seattle Pacific University and Russian translator for the U.S. Army. He has taught at Moscow State University. He has written on such topics as the Soviet Union, Christian apologetics, Christians and foreign policy, and Marxism. His writings have appeared in numerous publications, including *New Oxford Review, Christianity Today, Religion in Communist Dominated Areas, This World,* and *Slavic Review.* He is a member of the board of directors of Keston, USA.

ROBERT T. HUBER is currently director of the Soviet Studies Program of the Social Science Research Council in New York. He was a staff consultant for the Committee on Foreign Affairs of the U.S. House of Representatives. His publications include *Soviet Perceptions of the U.S. Congress: Impact on Superpower Relations,* and (co-editor with Donald R. Kelley) *Perestroika-*

Era Politics: The New Soviet Legislature and Gorbachev's Political Reforms. He has also helped prepare numerous government-sponsored studies on Soviet negotiating behavior, Soviet policy toward developing countries, and the conduct of U.S.-Soviet arms control negotiations.

VITALY KOROTICH is currently a visiting professor of international relations and journalism at Boston University. From 1986 to 1991 he served as editor-in-chief of *Ogonyok,* a ground-breaking Soviet weekly magazine. Under his tenure the publication's circulation jumped dramatically, and the journal became famous for its bold editorial policies. In 1989, Mr. Korotich was elected as people's deputy when, after an abortive communist party effort to keep him off the ballot, he ran as an independent candidate from Ukraine and won with 84 percent of the vote. He is the author of 42 books, including *Golden Hands* (1961), *Smell of Heaven* (1962) and *Poetry* (1967). Mr. Korotich is the winner of many Soviet and international awards, among them two Soviet State prizes and an award from Poland for his work in Polish culture. In 1988 he was honored as Editor of the Year by *World Press Review* and in 1989 received the Weintal Prize from Washington.

KATE MARTIN edited textbooks, magazines, and newspapers before assuming a senior executive position at the Institute for the Study of Conflict, Ideology & Policy in 1989. Her most recent publication was *State and Nation in Multi-Ethnic Societies.* In addition to her current work with the Institute's publications, she is the organizational force behind the Institute's conferences, lecture series, and special events. She received her degree in journalism from Northeastern University.

URI RA'ANAN is University Professor and Director of the Institute for the Study of Conflict, Ideology & Policy at Boston University. He is Fellow of the Russian Research Center at Harvard University. Author, co-author, editor, or co-editor of 22 books and contributor to 19 others, as well as 21 monographs and congressional publications, his latest publications include *State and Nation in Multi-Ethnic Societies, Inside the Apparat,* and *The Soviet Empire: The Challenge of National and Democratic Movements.* Prior to his current appointments, he was Professor of International Politics and Director of the International Security Studies Program at the Fletcher School of Law and Diplomacy, where he taught for two decades. Before joining the Fletcher School, he taught at Columbia University and the City University of New York. He obtained his undergraduate and graduate education and degrees at Oxford University (Wadham College, 1945-50).

RICHARD SCHIFTER was U.S. Assistant Secretary of State for Human Rights and Humanitarian Affairs from 1985 to 1992. Previously, he served as Deputy United States Representative in the Security Council of the United Nations, with the rank of Ambassador. He also has held the position of the United States member of the United Nations Human Rights Commission. A lawyer by profession, Mr. Schifter practiced law in Washington, D.C. from 1951 until his entry into full-time government service. He has since returned to law practice.

SAVIK SHUSTER is managing editor and anchor of the Radio Liberty nightly Russian news program, a position he has held since 1987. Previously he spent several years as a special correspondent in war zones and has worked for *Newsweek International, Liberation, La Nazione, La Repubblica* and *Panorama.* Mr. Shuster also has written a book on the Soviet Union and another on Afghanistan.

VERA TOLZ is a senior research analyst in the RFE/RL Research Institute (Munich). She is also a Ph.D. candidate at the Center for Russian and East European Studies at the University of Birmingham (United Kingdom). A regular contributor to the *Report on the USSR* of RFE/RL and other journals of Russian studies, Ms. Tolz is the author of *The USSR's Emerging Multiparty System* (Praeger: 1990), and editor of *The USSR in 1989: A Record of Events* (Westview Press: 1990).

J. MICHAEL WALLER is an Earhart Fellow at the Institute for the Study of Conflict, Ideology & Policy at Boston University, where he is completing a doctoral dissertation on Russia's absorption of the Soviet security and intelligence services. He is working with Russian reformers to build a system of civil control over the former KGB. His has written and contributed to articles in *Commentary, National Review, The New Republic, The New York Times, Readers Digest, Strategic Review,* and *The Wall Street Journal Europe,* as well as in the Institute's periodical, *Perspective.* His book, *Third Current of Revolution: Inside the North American Front of El Salvador's Guerrilla War,* was published by University Press of America in 1991.

INDEX

Abalkin project 30, 88
ABC News 131
accountability 39
Afghanistan 49, 95, 149, 159-60
Agamirov, Karen 152
Air Defense Forces 158
Akhalmosulishvili, Levan 175-6
Aleksi II 62, 159, 170, 178-9, 182-3
Aleksi I 170
Algeria 1
Alksnis, Viktor 155
All-Russian Bolshevik Communist
    Party 22
All-Union Polling Center for Socio-
    Economic Issues 184
All-Union Television and Radio
    Company 78-9
All-Union Council of Servicemen's
    Parents 157
all-volunteer armed forces 31
allocation of economic powers 30
Alpha Group 51, 103, 135
anarchism 22
Anarcho-Syndicalists 15-16, 19
Andreyeva, Nina 19, 95, 111
Andropov, Yuri 11-12, 120
anti-communism 17, 22
anti-Semitism 140, 144
APN 131
apparatchiki 58, 61-3, 73
Archil, Father 176
archives 45, 58-9, 63
Argumenty i fakty 58, 129, 135, 181-2
Armenia 94-7, 101, 107-12, 196, 198

Armenian Evangelical Union of
    North America 197
Armenian Evangelicals 189, 196-7
arms procurement reform 31
arms control negotiations 30, 33
Army, Soviet 17, 49, 57, 103-4, 116,
    120, 155, 157, 184
Artyom, Father 171
Assemblies of God 197
Association of Christian Schools In-
    ternational 199
Association of Concerned Christians
    of America
atheism 113, 184-6, 203
August 1991 coup attempt 3, 9-10,
    20-1, 28-9, 35-42, 45-7, 49, 51,
    57-8, 76-81, 85, 96, 103, 106,
    116, 122, 128-32, 141, 147-61,
    166, 182
autocephalous churches 169
autonomous republics 23
Azerbaijan 94-5, 97, 151, 196

Babich, Isabella 130
Babitsky, Andrei 130, 152
Baha'i 203
Bakatin, Vadim 47, 49, 52-4, 56,
    58-9, 100, 120-2
Baker, James A. 54, 101
Baltic states, the 1, 10, 14-15, 17-18,
    50, 74, 98, 128, 135, 145, 155,
    161, 189-90, 194, 196-7, 199, 202
Bank for Foreign Economic Activity
    (Vneshekonombank) 82

Baptists 176-7, 189-202
Barannikov, Victor 55-6, 62
Baturin, Yu. M. 133
Belgium 60
Belorussia 18, 50, 186
Beria, Lavrenti 103, 120
Bessmertnykh, Aleksandr 30
"Black Berets" 50
Black Sea Fleet 96
Bol'shakov, Boris 62
Bolsheviks 12, 63, 103-4, 119, 166
Bombin, Mikhail 152
Bondarenko, Joseph 199
Bonner, Yelena 129, 155
Borovik, Artyom 131
Borovik, Genrikh 131
Bourdeaux, Michael 181
Bourgeois-Democratic Party 21
Brezhnev, Leonid 29, 57, 106, 110
Britain 60, 117, 161, 179, 197
British Broadcasting Corporation
    (BBC) 147-9, 160-1
Buddhism 203
budgetary approval 28, 38, 40-1
Bukovsky, Vladimir 58
Bulgaria 105, 169
Burbulis, Gennadi 90
bureaucratic institutions 2-4, 27, 30
Burlatsky, Fedor 11-12
Burrows, Eva 197
Bush, George 50-1, 135-6
Byzantium 168

Cabinet of Ministers 82
Cable Network News (CNN) 131,
    153, 161
Cæesaropapism 168, 193
Calvin, John 167, 189
Campbell University Law School 176
Campus Crusade for Christ 199

Catherine the Great 194
Catholicism 167-8, 171-4, 177, 179,
    185, 193, 202-3
Caucasus, the 47, 78, 159-60, 195-6
CBS News 131
Ceauescu, Nicolae 169-70, 175
censorship 29, 117, 133
Central Asia 22, 109, 192, 195
Central Committee, the 9, 18-19, 47,
    83, 115, 200
Central Europe 3
Central Intelligence Agency (CIA)
    53-4, 119, 130
Central Intelligence Service (TsSR) 52
Central Television 128, 152
chauvinism 16
Chechen-Ingushetia 90
Cheka 119
Chekists 46, 55, 64
Chernenko, Yuri 12
Chesterton, G.K. 174
Chile 105
Christian Life Centers 198
*Chronicle of the Catholic Church in
    Ukraine* 178
Church of the Nazarene 198
Churches of Christ 190, 196
civil liberties 73
"civilism" 76, 115-6
civil society 1-2, 11
collective bargaining 107
collective farms 117
Comintern, the 100
command system 118
Commission to Investigate the
    Causes and Circumstances of the
    Coup d'Etat of August 1991 62
Committee for Protection of the
    USSR State Borders 52
Committee for State Security, *see*
    KGB

Committee for the Salvation of the Volga River 19
Committee on Defense and Security 61-2
Committee on Publishing Houses and the Press 140
Committee on Questions of Defense and State Security 46-7
Commonwealth of Independent States (CIS) 59-60, 83, 85, 95, 97, 101, 135-6, 161, 165-6, 185-6, 198, 202
Commonwealth of Independent States intelligence treaty 59-60
communist parties (successor) 37-9
Communist Party of the Soviet Union (CPSU) 9-10, 14-20, 23, 36, 72, 82-3, 140-1, 181, 184
Conference on Security and Cooperation in Europe (CSCE) 95, 98-9, 105, 109
Congregationalists 197
Congress of People's Deputies 15, 29, 31-2, 35-7, 46-7, 52, 60, 78, 94, 113, 115, 149-51
conscription 31
Constantine 169
constituency work 34
Constituent Assembly (1917) 113
Constitution (Soviet) 9-10, 16, 20, 73, 95
Constitutional Commission 85
Constitutional Control Committee 46, 48
Constitutional Court 55-6, 86, 96
Constutional Democratic Party 19
consumer rights 30
cooperatives 88
corruption 11, 63, 111, 121-2
Council for Religious Affairs 178, 180-1, 193

Council of the Union 36
Council of Workers' Committees of Kuzbass 155-6
counterintelligence 49
credit control and management 30
Crimean Tatars 97-8, 109
culture, freedom of 2-3, 12, 14, 16
customs 82
Czechoslovakia 61, 142, 190

Dagestan 154
de-Stalinization 13
debate, political 2
Defense and State Security Committee 31, 33
defense spending 31
Deich, Mark 152
demobilization 30-1
Democratic Club of the Moscow Intelligensia 75
Democratic Party of Russia 19, 37
Democratic Platform of the CPSU 16
Democratic Reform movement 37
Democratic Russian Movement 19-20, 36-7, 39
demonstrations 73, 90
Department of External Ecclesiastical Relations of the Patriarchate 178
Directorate for the Defense of the Constitutional System 59
Directorate Z 59
dissidents 4
"Dniestr Republic" 97, 100
Dobbs, Michael 181
Draft Law on State Security Organs 47, 49
Duma, the 1
Dunlop, John 185
Dzerzhinsky, Felix 57, 119, 165

East European Mission and Bible Foundation 196
Eastern Europe, Soviet troop demobilization in 34-5
ecology 13-14, 99, 184
economic growth rate, decline of 10
ecumenism 171-2, 175
Edelshtein, Georgi 178, 182
education 2, 13
Ekho Moskvy 130, 154
El Salvador 105
elections (1989) 15, 113
emigration 33, 108-15, 190, 192, 194
Entin, V.L. 133
entrepreneurs 21, 71, 75, 87, 89
Episcopalians 199
Esenin, Sergei 13
Estonia 74, 159, 189, 194-5
Estonian Christian Churches 197
Estonian Lutheran Church 192
ethnic diversity 1-2
European Baptist Federation 177
European Economy Community (EEC) 95, 101
Evangelical Churches of West Africa 200
Evangelical Lutheran Church of America 192
Evangelical-Free Church 198
Evangelicals, the 173-4, 177, 200, 202
evangelization 173-5, 191
Evdokimov, Sergei 157
exchange rate 89

factionalism 2-3
fascist-communist opposition 144
Federal Bureau of Investigation (FBI) 54, 60, 118
Federal Security Agency (AFB) 53, 55-6

Fedotov, Ivan 193
Fedotov, M.A. 133
Fifth Wheel 135
Filaret, Metropolitan 178
filibustering 34
Finland 60
Fitzwater, Marlin 51
Fletcher, William 201
Foreign Economic Commission 29
foreign policy 28, 30, 38
France 98, 117
Franco, Francisco 117-8
Franklin, Benjamin 115
Free Labor Party 21
free peasantry 2
freedom of speech 73, 90
fundamentalism 1

Gamsakhurdia, Zviad 3, 10, 94, 176-7
Gannett Freedom Forum 131
Gates, Robert 53-4
genocide 96
Georgia 3, 10, 17, 54, 94, 97, 135, 143, 145, 151, 155, 171, 173, 175-6, 186, 195-6
Georgian Baptist Union 176
Georgian Ministry of Justice 177
German Democratic Republic 30, 198
German reunification 30-1
Germans, Volga 97-8, 107-12, 191-2, 194
Germany 4, 64, 144, 160, 168, 198, 202
glasnost' 11, 90, 93, 110, 114, 128, 130, 139, 143, 149, 154, 178, 180, 183, 192, 197, 199, 201
Glasnost' (publication) 79
glossolalia 193
Golikov, Vyacheslav 156
Gonchar, Nikolai 21

Gooding, John 10
Gorbachev, Mikhail 10-15, 18, 29-35, 40-1, 45-53, 57, 71-2, 74, 78, 93-6, 103-4, 106-15, 120-1, 128, 135, 147-9, 153-5, 158, 161, 178, 190
Gourjaani Baptist Church 175-6
GPU 119
Grachev, Pavel 157
grass-root activism 11
Greens, the 19, 184
Gromov, Boris 49
Group of Seven (G-7) 50, 60, 99
group rights 1
Grushko, Viktor 46
Guest, John 199
Guiness, Os 201
Hamm, Viktor 191
Handbook of Denominations in the United States 190
Hare Krishna 203
Havel, Vaclav 190
health and wealth prosperity theology 193, 195
health care 86
Helsinki Final Act 108
Hena, Christine 195
historical monuments, preservation of 13
Hitler, Adolf 99, 117, 160
Hobbes, Thomas 2
Holland, Joe 195
Holmes, Oliver Wendell 133
Holy Synod, the 175, 181, 183
housing 86
Houston, Tom 199
human rights 56, 74, 94-5, 98-101, 103-23, 135, 144, 166, 171, 190
Hungarian Reformed 190, 194
Hurst, Steve 131
Hussein, Saddam 99, 153

Ilia II, Patriarch 176-7
"In the Country and the World" 150-61
independence, demands for 15-16
Industrial Union 99
information revolution 117
Initiative Congress of the CPR 22
initsiativniki 191
Innocent III 167
institutionalization of reforms 27, 29-42
insurance companies 83
intellectual property rights 30
intellectuals 12, 106-7
intelligence services 31
inter-republic conflict 86
Inter-Republican Security Service (MSB) 52
Interfax 129
"internal migration" 4
internal state security 49
International Affairs Committee 31, 33
International Center for Human Values 184
international law 95
International Teams (Brethren) 197
Interregional Group of Deputies 18, 35, 57-8
Interrepublic Economic Committee 36
Iran-Contra Affair 54
Iraq 95
Isaev, Andrei 22
Islam 1, 183
Israel 105, 110
Ivanenko, V.V. 100
Izvestia 13, 55, 128

Jefferson, Thomas 136
Jehovah's Witnesses 203
Jews 107-12, 203
John Paul II 178

joint stock companies 83
joint ventures 83
"just war theory" 169
Justin, Patriarch 169-70

Kadets 37
Kadyrov, Zakir 159
Kagarlitsky, Boris 21
Kalugin, Oleg 48, 57
Kartashev, A.V. 169
Kazakhstan 120-1
Kerensky, Aleksandr 167
Kesey, Ken 142
Keston College 181
KGB, the 17, 33, 45-64, 77, 86, 100,
    103-4, 107, 118-22, 127-8, 135,
    140, 144, 150, 153-4, 157, 165,
    180-2, 184
KGB Border Troops 47, 52
KGB Eighth Directorate 51
KGB Fifth Directorate 59
KGB First Chief Directorate 52, 60
KGB Ninth Directorate 51
KGB Second Chief Directorate 52-3,
    55-6, 61
KGB Special Troops 51
Khasbulatov, Ruslan 37-8, 54, 62,
    85, 158
Khrushchev, Nikita 105-6, 111, 120,
    128
Kishkovsky, Leonid 185
Kobets, Konstantin 157
Komi Autonomous Republic 195
Kommendant, Grigory 177, 200, 202
Kommersant 129, 143
Komsomol' skaya pravda 22, 128-9
Komsomol 15
Kondratenko, Nikolai 129
Kopysev, Valentin 156
Korea Holiness Church 200
Korean Methodist Church 195

Korean Presbyterian Church 198
Koreans 198
Korgun, Alex 128
Korotich, Vitali 16
Kosygin, Alexei 93
Kravchuk, Leonid 90
Kryuchkov, Vladimir 46-50, 56-7,
    59, 63, 103, 151-2
Kumalashvili, Guram 176
Kuranty 129
Kurashvili, Boris 14
Kurds 95
Kuznetsov, Nikolai 62
Kyrgyzstan 117, 121

labor management 30
Landsbergis, Vytautas 155
Latvia 49-50, 115, 152, 155, 199
Latvian Christian Mission 198-9
Latvian Lutheran Church 192, 194
Lausanne Committee for World
    Evangelization 199
law on property 89
law, respect for 1
law on cooperation 88
law on privatization 87
law on public associations (October
    1990) 9, 16
law on state enterprises 30
law on the mass media 14, 29, 32-3,
    72, 80, 127, 132-5, 141
law-based state (*Rechtsstaat*) 4, 46-7,
    71-91, 153
lawyers 72, 75
Lazutkin, Valentin 131
leasing 89
Lebed', Aleksandr 157
Lednyova, Zinaida 157
"legal lawlessness" 83
legislative institutionalization 27-42,
    116-7

legislative committees 28
Lenin, Vladimir 57, 71-2, 104-6, 111-4, 119, 141, 143-4
Leningrad Popular Front 16
Leninskoe Znamya 79
Leonov, Yuri 129
Liberal Democratic Party of the USSR (LDPSS) 19, 37
Liberal Union 21
liberalism 21
liberation theology 202
Liberian Methodist Church 195
Ligachev, Yegor 111
Light of the Gospel 198-99
Literaturnaya gazeta 13
Lithuania 10, 15, 50-1, 98, 115, 133, 151, 154-5, 158, 194
living standards, decline in 34
Ljungholm, Sven-Erik 197
local government 40
Locke, John 105
Lopatin, Vladimir 31, 33
Lord's Army, the 175
Louisiana United Methodist Church 195
"Loyal Opposition" 54
Luk'yanov, Anatoli 19, 32-5, 47-8, 158
Lutheranism 167-8, 198-9, 202
Luxembourg 98

Madison, James 136
Mal'tsev, General 158
Mamut, Leonid 75
Mandrygin, Vladimir 156
Mann, Ralph 193
market economy 20, 86
Marxist Platform of the CPSU 19, 22
"mass organizations" 2
mass participation 11

media (electronic and print) 2, 4, 10, 13-14, 15, 17-19, 21, 29, 38, 60, 62, 73, 78-9, 81, 98, 107, 111-2, 117, 127-36, 139-61, 190
Medvedev, Roy 14
Megapolis ekspress 129
"Memorial" society 12-13, 18
Men', Alexander 174, 185
Mennonite Brethren 189, 194, 199
Mesters, Eriks 192
Methodists 189, 194-5
Mezey, Michael 40-1
Middle East 1
Mikhailov, Rasul 154
military reform 31
military versus security leadership 103
Milosevic, Slobodan 160
Milwaukee Journal 129
miners 74, 155-6
Ministry of Communications 130-1, 134
Ministry of Defense 31, 33, 77
Ministry of Finance 46, 82
Ministry of Internal Affairs (MVD) 45, 47, 49-51, 53, 55-7, 64, 77, 86, 114
Ministry of Justice 50, 114
Ministry of Press and Mass Media 132
Ministry of Roads 29
Ministry of Security (MB) 56-7
Ministry of Security and Internal Affairs (MBVD) 55
Ministry of the Timber Industry 29
Mir (Peace) 13
Mission of the Cross 199
Mission Possible 193
Moldova 97, 155, 196, 199
Molokane, the 190, 195-6
monarchy, restoration of the 97

monetary projection 30
morality, private 12
Moravians, the 190, 194-5
Mormons 203
Moscow city government 10, 17, 21, 130
Moscow News 14, 47-8, 61, 129, 132
Moscow University 130; School of Journalism 131
Moskovskaya Pravda 79
Moskovsky komsomolets 129
Moskva 158
Movement for Democratic Reform 21, 99
"municipal property" 89
Murashev, Arkadi 57-8
Mussolini, Benito 117

Nagorno-Karabakh 94, 100
nationalism 10, 13, 17, 21-3, 101, 145
Nazarbaev, Nursultan 90
neformal' nye gruppy (informal organizations) 13
Nersisiantz, Vladik 76
Netherlands, the 60, 198
Nevzorov, Aleksandr 132-3
New Age Movement 203
New Apostolic Church 198
New York Post 129, 143
Nezavisimaya gazeta 129, 132-3, 136, 153
Nicholas II 104, 119
Nigeria 200
Nkrumah, Kwame 203
NKVD 55, 119
Nobel Peace Prize 50
nomenklatura 9, 49, 94
North-West Information Agency 130
Northeastern University 131
Norway 50

Novikov, Yevgeni 56
Novosti 79
nuclear deterrence 99-100

Obshchaya gazeta 129
October Revolution 12, 144
Ogonek 14, 16, 75, 140-2
Ogorodnikov, Aleksandr 178
OGPU 119
Okhrana 119
Oleinik, Boris 19, 56
OMON 50, 56
opinion polls 19, 22
organized crime 60, 121
Orthodox Church (American) 173, 185
Orthodox Church (Eastern) 168
Orthodox Church (Romanian) 1773-4
Orthodox Church (Russian) 62, 165-86, 199, 202-3
Orthodox Church (Ukrainian) 179
Ossetia 94, 97, 100
Ottoman Empire 197
Overseas Missionary Service 200

Pakistan 98
Pamyat' 16, 19, 160
Papadakis, Aristeides 168
"parade of sovereignties" 74
penal colonies 86
Pentecostal Union 193
Pentecostals 112, 189, 191-2, 198-9, 200
perestroika 10-11, 13, 15, 17, 39, 45, 71-4, 90, 93-4, 132, 148-9, 154
periodicals and magazines 139-42, 146
Persian Gulf crisis 30-2, 95, 153, 169
Peter the Great 118-19, 168
Pico, Giandomenico 160
Pimen, Archbishop 185

Pitirim, Metropolitan 181
Plymouth Brethren, the 190, 196-7
Poland 149, 195
Polish Methodist Church 195
Politburo, the 9, 11, 51, 54, 200
political debate 2
Polosin, Vyacheslav 181-2
Poltoranin, Mikhail 132, 146
Ponomarev, Lev 57, 61-2
Popov, Gavriil 21, 58
popular fronts 14-15
Poresh, Vladimir 178
pornography 134, 203
Portugal 129
Possibility Mission 198
post-coup leadership 4
post-totalitarian society 2
Postfactum 60, 129
Prague Spring 142
Pravda 111, 128, 132-3, 140
Presidential Council 48
Presidium of the Supreme Soviet 32-3,
35, 38, 77-8
price deregulation 30, 38, 90
Primakov, Yevgeni 56, 62
Prince, The 106
prisoners of conscience 109
privatization 39, 86-90
Procuracy, the 46, 50, 73, 75, 80
proizvol 29, 33
property rights 75-6, 82-9
"proselytism" 173-5, 177
Protestantism 167, 172, 175, 185,
189-203
Provisional Government (1917), the 1
psychiatric abuse 107-12, 121
Pugo, Boris 49, 63, 103, 131, 156

Rabochaya Tribuna 79
racism 144

Radio Free Europe/Radio Liberty
(RFE/RL) 148, 150
Radio Liberty 128, 130-1, 147-61
Radstock Brethren 197
Ratushinskaya, Irina 121
Reagan, Ronald 107
Rebirth and Renewal Movement 192
"refuseniks" 110
religious freedom 1-2, 4, 100, 107-8,
140, 165-203
revolutions of 1848 3
Romania 169-71, 173-5, 186
Romodanovsky, Fedor 119
Rossiiskaya gazeta 129
Rossiiskie vesti 129
RSFSR Bank for Foreign Economic
Activity 82
RSFSR Central Bank 82
RSFSR Congress of People's Depu-
ties 38, 75
RSFSR Council of Ministers 81, 83,
88
RSFSR Declaration of Sovereignty
76
RSFSR elections (1990) 16-17, 19
RSFSR Law on Land 89
RSFSR Ministry of Justice 21
RSFSR Ministry of Information and
Mass Media 79-80
RSFSR State Committee on Adminis-
tering State Property 82
RSFSR Supreme Soviet 81
Rubanov, Vladimir 45
ruble convertibility 30
Russian Constitution and the Law on
the President of the Russian Fed-
eration 81
Russian Federation Supreme Soviet
10, 38
Russian Federation Law on Enterprises
and Entrepreneurial Activity 87

Russian Government White House 77, 104, 130-1, 135, 152-4, 156-7, 159
Russian Guard 79
Russian Orthodox Monarchists 19
Russian People's Front 19
Russian Popular Front 16
Russian Republic Freedom of Conscience Committee 181
Russian Television Company 130
Rutskoi, Aleksandr 79, 157
Ryzhkov, Nikolai 19, 30
Ryzhov, Yuri 151-2

Sajudis 15
Sakharov, Andrei 94, 97, 99-100, 108, 129, 149
Salvation Army, the 190, 196-7
samizdat 13-14, 117, 193-4
Samsonov, Viktor 158
Sapiets, Marite 192
Savost'yanov, Yevgeni 57-8
Sawatsky, Walter 198-9
Sawyer, Diane 131
Scharansky, Nathan 170
scientific/technological revolution 3
Secret Office, the 119, 121
secret police 4, 45-64, 109, 111-2, 118-23
security forces 2-4, 45-64
self-censorship 127
self-determination 3, 99-100
separation of church and state 167
separatism 23
Seventh-day Adventists 193, 200-1
Shakhrai, Sergei 55
Shatalin project 30
Shcherbitsky, Volodymir 178
Shchit (Shield) 51
Shelkov, Vladimir 193
Shevardnadze, Eduard 21, 30-1, 49, 99-100, 106-7, 114, 123

Shmelev project 30
Sholokhov, Sergei 135
Shuster, Savik 151
Simons, George 194
Sitoryan-Abalkin recommendations 88
Slavic nationalism 183-4
Slipyi, Josef 170
Sobchak, Anatoli 21, 128, 131-3, 135, 158, 167
social democracy 21
social justice 21
Socialist Party 21
Socialist Party of Working People 22
socialist democracy 11
Sodano, Cardinal 179
Sokolov, Mikhail 130, 153
Solovki bishops, the 171
Solzhenitsyn, Alexander 171
South Africa 105
Southern Baptist Convention 176-7
Sovershenno sekretno 131
Sovet ekologii kul' tury (Council of Cultural Ecology) 13
Sovetskaya Rossiya 111
Soviet Central Television 131
Soviet Studies 10
Soyuz faction 30, 35
Spain 117-8
Spasnie (Salvation) 13
Spiritual Christian 196
St. Petersburg/Leningrad city government 10, 13, 17
Stalin, Josef 11-13, 18, 22, 55, 95, 98, 105, 109, 111, 119-20, 135-6, 160, 170, 177, 189-90, 192, 194-5, 198
Stankevich, Sergei 158
State Committee for Special Communications 51
State Bank (*Gosbank*) 82
State and Nation in Multi-Ethnic Societies 2

State Commission to Investigate the
Activities of the Security Organs
49, 53
State Committee on Prices 29
State Council 36
State Emergency Committee 76-8,
148, 152, 154-5, 156
Stepashin, Sergei 53, 62
Stolitsa 129
Stolyarov, Nikolai 181
strikes 73-4
succession 2
Sudan Interior Mission 200
Supreme Soviet Council of Nationalities 19
Supreme Court 85
Supreme Soviet 19, 29-33, 35-41,
46-7, 51-3, 58, 74, 113, 158
Supreme Soviet Science Committee
151
Sweden 50
Synod of Bishops of the Orthodox
Church of America 169

TASS 22, 79
taxation 30, 89
technology theft 60
terrorism 56, 60, 121
Texas United Methodist Church 195
*The Socialist Legal State: Problems
and Opinions* 72
*The Soviet Empire and the Challenge
of National and Democratic
Movements* 2
Thisen, Henning 60
Tolmachev, Vladimir 156
totalitarianism 1-2, 4
trade unions 107
Transcarpathia 190
"transmission belts" 2-3
Tret'yakov, Vitali 129, 133, 136

Trud 146
True and Free Adventists 193
Tsypkin, Mikhail 47
TVK television station 130

Ukhtomsky, Bishop 167
Ukraine 50-1, 116, 132, 156, 167,
177-9, 186, 194-5, 196, 200-1
Ukrainian Autocephalous Orthodox
Church (UAOC) 179, 185
Ukrainian Catholic Church 113, 172,
177-9, 185
Ukrainian Exarchate of the Moscow
Patriarchate 179
Ukrainian Free Union 193
Uniates (Eastern-Rite Catholics)
185, 200
Unification Church (Moonies) 203
Union of Evangelical Christians-Baptists 190-203
Union Treaty 19, 83, 96
United States Congress 54, 63
United Nations 95, 98-9, 112, 149, 160
United Nations Human Rights Commission 105
United Pentecostal Church ("Jesus
Only") 193
United States of America 30, 53-4,
59-60, 63, 104-5, 108, 118, 121,
141, 168, 170-1, 197-8, 202
United States Lutheran Church, Missouri Synod 192
United States State Department 107-15
United States Supreme Court 133
Unity for Leninism and Communist
Ideals 19
Universal Declaration of Human
Rights 95, 98
USSR Council of Ministers 19, 46
USSR Academy of Sciences 87
Uzbekistan 74

Vatican II 172
Vesinsky, Vladimir 129
Vneshekonombank 82
Voice of America (VOA) 147, 160
Vol'sky, Arkadi 21, 99
Volchek, Dmitri 130, 152
Voltaire 105
Vox Populi 147
Vremya 131, 159

wage indexation 38
Walk Thru the Bible 199
Wall Street Journal 143
"war of laws" 36, 39, 72-4, 84
War Cry, The 197
Warsaw Pact 59
Watson, Patrick 60
Webster, Alexander 173-5
Western democracy 17
wiretapping 49
Word of Life 193, 197
workers' rights 22, 30
"workers' collectives" 87
World War II 96, 99, 191-2, 194,
    196-7
World Council of Churches 172

Yakovlev, Aleksandr 11, 75, 99-100,
    106
Yakunin, Gleb 171, 178, 182-3
Yanaev, Gennadi 29, 128, 135, 153,
    256
Yazov, Dmitri 49, 103
Yel'tsin, Boris 10, 20, 37-9, 50-3,
    55, 58, 60, 77-8, 83-4, 89-90, 96,
    98, 104, 114-5, 127-8, 130-2, 135,
    141, 147-54, 156-7, 159-61, 167
Yevtushenko, Yevgeni 16
Yugin, Viktor 132-3
Yugoslavia 95
Yuvenali, Metropolitan 181

Zaichenko, Aleksandr 201
Zamoshkin, Sergei 61
Zaslavskaya, Tat'yana 14
Zasurky, Yasen N. 131-2
Zelinskaya, Yelena 130
Zhirinovsky, Vladimir 95-6, 155, 160
Zhivkov, Todor 105
Zor'kin, Valeri 86
Zorin, Valerian 105